Assemblages of cancer

Manchester University Press

INSCRIPTIONS

Series editors
Des Fitzgerald and Amy Hinterberger

Editorial advisory board
Vivette García Deister, National Autonomous University of Mexico
John Gardner, Monash University, Australia
Maja Horst, Technical University of Denmark
Robert Kirk, Manchester, UK
Stéphanie Loyd, Laval University, Canada
Alice Mah, Warwick University, UK
Deboleena Roy, Emory University, USA
Hallam Stevens, Nanyang Technological University, Singapore
Niki Vermeulen, Edinburgh, UK
Megan Warin, Adelaide University, Australia
Malte Ziewitz, Cornell University, USA

Since the very earliest studies of scientific communities, we have known that texts and worlds are bound together. One of the most important ways to stabilise, organise and grow a laboratory, a group of scholars, even an entire intellectual community, is to write things down. As for science, so for the social studies of science: Inscriptions is a space for writing, recording and inscribing the most exciting current work in sociological and anthropological – and any related – studies of science.

The series foregrounds theoretically innovative and empirically rich interdisciplinary work that is emerging in the UK and internationally. It is self-consciously hospitable in terms of its approach to discipline (all areas of social sciences are considered), topic (we are interested in all scientific objects, including biomedical objects) and scale (books will include both fine-grained case studies and broad accounts of scientific cultures).

For readers, the series signals a new generation of scholarship captured in monograph form – tracking and analysing how science moves through our societies, cultures and lives. Employing innovative methodologies for investigating changing worlds, it is home to compelling new accounts of how science, technology, biomedicine and the environment translate and transform our social lives.

To buy or to find out more about the books currently available in this series, please go to: https://manchesteruniversitypress.co.uk/series/inscriptions-writing-the-social-studies-of-science/

Assemblages of cancer

Experiences and contexts of breast cancer in the UK, France and Italy

Cinzia Greco

MANCHESTER UNIVERSITY PRESS

Copyright © Cinzia Greco 2025

The right of Cinzia Greco to be identified as the author of this work has been asserted in accordance with the Copyright, Designs and Patents Act 1988.

An electronic version of this book has been made freely available under a Creative Commons (CC BY-NC-ND) licence, thanks to the support of the Wellcome Trust, which permits non-commercial use, distribution and reproduction provided the author(s) and Manchester University Press are fully cited and no modifications or adaptations are made. Details of the licence can be viewed at https://creativecommons.org/licenses/by-nc-nd/4.0/

Published by Manchester University Press
Oxford Road, Manchester, M13 9PL

www.manchesteruniversitypress.co.uk

British Library Cataloguing-in-Publication Data
A catalogue record for this book is available from the British Library

ISBN   978 1 5261 7144 3   hardback

First published 2025

The publisher has no responsibility for the persistence or accuracy of URLs for any external or third-party internet websites referred to in this book, and does not guarantee that any content on such websites is, or will remain, accurate or appropriate.

EU authorised representative for GPSR:
Easy Access System Europe – Mustamäe tee 50, 10621 Tallinn, Estonia
gpsr.requests@easproject.com

Typeset
by New Best-set Typesetters Ltd

Contents

Acknowledgements	page vi
Introduction	1
1 The political context of breast cancer in Europe	27
2 The cultural landscape of breast cancer	51
3 Biomedical innovations and the redefinition of breast cancer	72
4 Assembling bodies: breast cancer and post-diagnosis metamorphoses	97
5 Breast cancer: an exercise in uncertainty	125
6 Between disruptions and recompositions: the post-diagnosis life	148
Conclusion: the meaning of assemblages and assemblages of meanings in breast cancer	171
References	183
Index	207

Acknowledgements

Even if academic work can be a solitary endeavour, there is often a network of people who sustain and support us. First of all, I would like to thank the interviewees who generously agreed to discuss with me their different experiences with breast cancer as patients, medical professionals and researchers. Their help has been invaluable.

I have had the opportunity to follow my interest in breast cancer through a research project conducted at the CERMES3 laboratory and the École des Hautes Etudes en Sciences Sociales, with funding from the Cancéropôle Île-de-France. During this project I learned much from Ilana Löwy. I am grateful for her thoughtfulness, encouragement and understanding. My colleagues at CERMES3 also provided me with a space for stimulating discussions and a friendly community, and I thank them for that. I have also had the opportunity to conduct research at the Centre for the History of Science, Technology and Medicine (CHSTM) of the University of Manchester, with funding from the British Academy (grant number NF161448) and the Wellcome Trust (grant number 212736/Z/18/Z). Carsten Timmermann has been a great support in both projects. My colleagues at CHSTM, with whom I have discussed and laughed, have significantly improved my life in the UK.

The *Remaking Cancer* project, which Carsten Timmermann, Elizabeth Toon and I co-founded, has also been an important resource for discussions within humanities and social sciences applied to cancer.

I would further like to thank Des Fitzgerald and Amy Hinterberger as series editors of *Inscriptions*, Shannon Kneis and Laura Swift for their editorial work at Manchester University Press and the anonymous reviewers of the book proposal and the manuscript. Their advice and guidance have been essential.

During this time, I have been very fortunate to meet several colleagues with whom I have shared insights, discussions, ideas and, in many cases, drafts of articles and chapters. A non-exhaustive list includes: Ignacia Arteaga, Grazia De Michele, Fatima Elfitouri, Corinne Fortier, Sarah Gibbon, Nils Graber, Maica Gugolati, Natasia Hamarat, Robert Kirk, Cynthia Kraus, Anne Lovell, Lenore Manderson, Anastasia Meidani, Pascale Molinier, Neil Pemberton, Ana Porroche Escudero, Linda Sifer-Rivière, Gayle Sulik, Julia Swallow, Stephanie Snow, Elizabeth Toon, Bernadette Wegenstein and Duncan Wilson.

During this time my colleagues on the editorial team of *Anthopologie & Santé* have provided me with several occasions for scholarly and friendly discussions and have taught me about the great deal of editorial work behind every academic publication.

My parents, my mother in particular, my grandmothers and my aunts have always helped and supported me. I would not be here without the sacrifices and efforts of the older members of my family, who fought for the rights of working-class children to receive an education.

Last but not least, this book is for Djordje. Thank you for everything.

Introduction

When I was a child of six or seven living in southern Italy, I overheard my mother and aunt having a serious and tense conversation about a friend, a young woman with '*un brutto male*'. An Italian euphemism for cancer, this phrase is difficult to translate but means something like 'a nasty disease'.

I cannot recall the word 'cancer' ever being used explicitly in my family. Even now, I carefully avoid saying it when talking to my mother because I know how much the mere mention of cancer would upset her. Despite the silence, *il brutto male* has been present in our lives. The young family friend about whom my mother and aunt were talking had breast cancer, as did several other female relatives and friends. My personal encounter with breast cancer came when I was 23 and a suspect lump led me to undergo a breast ultrasound. The test results were unclear and opened a space of doubt. The following weeks were characterised by an uncertainty that was finally resolved through surgery and histology that showed the lump was benign. When I asked the radiologist whether I was 'at risk' the answer was that 'every woman is at risk'.[1] I have not (at the time of writing) received a breast cancer diagnosis, but the risk of the disease has been with me ever since, accompanying me as a young adult and an adult migrant woman.

Unlike the older women in my family, I used the word cancer. I also looked for information online and asked explicit questions of medical professionals. When I was younger, I thought that the word's rejection represented the residue of past beliefs dominated by magical thinking.[2] This might be accurate, but I know now that this is only a portion of the truth.[3] The refusal to mention cancer was one of the many strategies that women, including the women in my family, used to deal with it, to accept, negotiate and reduce its role in their lives. However, so was my reaction to the risk of breast cancer. These different behaviours are part of the processes of assemblage that I explore in this book.

Years later, when I started to research breast cancer, I returned to the small towns where I grew up, as well as meeting women in France and the UK and interviewing medical professionals from a long list of hospitals. *Assemblages of cancer* is the result of my long-standing interest in breast cancer, and it illustrates the tensions and contradictions extant in the experiences and representations of breast cancer in Western Europe, with a focus on the UK, France and Italy. In the European Union (EU), breast cancer is the most common cancer, with over 355,000 cases diagnosed in 2020 in the EU-27, and the third most common cause of death by cancer, after lung and colorectal.[4] These numbers give an immediate idea of the magnitude of the phenomenon and can explain why, nowadays, the euphemistic language of the past has become much less common and breast cancer has been pushed to the forefront of public discourse. To fully comprehend its impact, it is crucial to examine the challenges it poses to individuals and how social and political views of the disease shape individual responses. As I discuss below, the social attention on breast cancer needs to be understood as a combination of factors, including its high incidence and gendered nature, its importance to medical innovation, and advocacy initiatives that have been very successful in attracting funds.

Breast cancer is a multiform presence in our lives. For some of us, it is a risk; for others, a diagnosis, whether ours or that of someone close to us; for others still, it is a reminder to book a screening appointment. However, despite its ubiquity, breast cancer is far from experienced in the same way by all those directly or indirectly touched by it. As Zillah Eisenstein reminds us, our bodies, and breast tissue in particular, 'absorb their environs in unique ways' (2001: 61). In *Assemblages of cancer*, I consider the different responses and reactions resulting from the fact that inequalities and cultural, social and political differences are absorbed by our bodies and model our experiences. In the following pages, I discuss how this book uses the concept of assemblage and how the organisation of breast cancer treatments has developed historically around specific scripts and regimes. I then turn to the strongly gendered nature of breast cancer and the discourses built around the disease and elaborate the specificities of the Western European context for breast cancer. I conclude this Introduction with a presentation of the methodology of the different research projects on which this book is based and an overview of the chapters that follow.

Cancer experiences

In this book, I explore how inequalities and different social and cultural landscapes shape experiences of breast cancer and responses from patients, medical professionals and institutions. My use and understanding of experiences as an empirical tool are informed by reflections and explorations in the social sciences, including anthropology and science and technology studies (STS). Moreover, the dynamism and fluidity of experiences of cancer are strongly linked with another central concept in this book, that of assemblages (see below).

How to understand the experiences that individuals have of the societies and cultures in which they are located, and the methods by which such experiences can be accessed, are key questions in different social sciences, including anthropology. As Willen and Seeman have discussed, starting with the late 1980s and 1990s, ethnography has shown a strong interest in experiences. However, ethnographers have taken a 'pluralistic […] stance' (Willen and Seeman, 2012: 5) in approaching the topic. Phenomenological and psychoanalytical perspectives have been central in informing theories and positions in the ethnographic study of experience. This interest in experiences has not diluted the attention on how social and cultural forces shape human events. It has instead 'provided a conceptual bridge between individual lifeworlds and the much broader political-economic trends and cultural-symbolic systems that constrain and inform them' (Willen and Seeman, 2012: 6). The greater attention to individual experiences has also influenced how we look at diseases and how individual suffering and pain are interwoven into the broader social and cultural ideas surrounding health and illness.

Medical anthropologist and physician Arthur Kleinman is among those who gave a central role to individual experience, starting from the introduction of the central distinction between disease and illness. Disease is presented as a 'natural process' and is opposed to 'the experience of illness', which 'is a cultural or symbolic reality' and 'involves feelings, ideas, values, language and non-verbal communication, symbolic behaviour, and the like' (Kleinman, 1973: 209). For Kleinman (1997), the centrality of individual experience is a barrier to reductionism – that is, to the limitation of the multiplicity of values and meanings of disease to a reduced set of categories and terms – present above all in biomedicine, but from which anthropology is not exempt. If we focus on illness experiences, there is a gap between individual experiences and how healthcare systems and cultural constructions of illness plan the unfolding of these events and inform the meanings that individuals attribute to them. However, experience is not simply individual and intimate, as approaches coming from STS have underlined, focusing on the relationships between different entities and how they 'become what they are in relation *to* other entities' (Skeide, 2021: 454). Skeide (2021) analyses the experience of labour pain, considering it a 'shared relations-in-practice' and showing how labour pain is not just a central element in the experience of women giving birth, but also a catalyst capable of modifying the actions and behaviours of medical staff and family members. More generally, we can understand experiences as the meanings and emotions that people attach to specific events, and such meanings involve the combination not only of individual sensations and memories but also different interactions with external actors and objects. Individual experiences, although partially ineffable, allow us to glimpse a reality that oscillates between the intimacy of individual and embodied knowledge while structuring relationships between the people and cultural and social contexts in which they move.

Another central aspect is how ethnography can access individual experiences. Geertz (1986: 373) affirms that '[w]hatever sense we have of how things stand with someone else's inner life, we gain it through their expressions'. A way of accessing the expressions of experience is therefore by understanding the culture in which experiences develop. In this sense, detailed ethnographic accounts are a good proxy for understanding individuality. For Turner (1986), the experience can be revealed clearly in ritual and aesthetic presentations of social norms and conflicts. Both the latter two approaches presuppose the subsumption of experience into culture and its cultural manifestations. According to Willen and Seeman (2012), Kleinman's reflections emphasising that individual experiences are only partially linked to their cultural and social context are a 'vital corrective' (Willen and Seeman 2012: 9) of understanding of individual suffering as completely filtered through cultural rituals and interpretations (in this regard, see also Seeman 2004). The reconstruction of the cultural context and meaning of an individual's narrative therefore can give us an essential, but still incomplete, access to their experiences, especially those of illness. In this book, the illness narratives represent the main tool for accessing the experiences of illness. However, I further consider how these experiences structure and reorganise the relationships between patients, the medical system and the various social and personal spheres in which the women I met move. In this sense, my approach is a strong interpenetration of the analysis of individual experience and the context – cultural, social and economic – in which they are located. This further means not only reconstructing the individual specificity and the wider context, but identifying the deep links between these two dimensions. To do this, I use the concept of assemblage, which, as Chenhall and Senior highlight, 'provide[s] a variety of ways of capturing social phenomena in relation to individuals' (Chenhall and Senior, 2018: 182).

Assemblage as an analytical framework for cancer

I adapt the concept of assemblage with reference to Deleuze and Guattari's formulation (1980). The two philosophers discussed assemblage in an effort to decentre the notions of subjectivity, power, territory, language and signification. My use of assemblage is linked to how Deleuze and Guattari apply the concept in their theory of the body (Deleuze and Guattari, 1980; see also Grosz, 1994; Currier, 2003). This theory was formulated in opposition to psychoanalysis and the idea that bodily and psychical unity is the norm, and that any violation of bodily unity is in itself pathologic.[5] For Deleuze and Guattari, bodies are normally connected with various elements outside the limits of the skin.[6] Their work has been applied to medicine to underline how ideas of health and illness exist as a combination of individual bodies, diagnostic and medical tools and procedures, and larger social contexts (Fox, 2011; Duff, 2014). Deleuze's work has also been used to advance an approach to health that focuses on experiences in becoming rather than on factors of risk projected onto the future. In this sense, Deleuze's focus on positive and negative 'encounters' has been used as a framework to explore experiences of health as they manifest in a given moment, contrasting the focus on long-term developments that preoccupies much of public health (Duff, 2014). Many of the assemblages I discuss in the book (of pathways, meanings, relationships and uses of the body), especially on the patient side, could be compared with the role of the bricoleur (Marcus and Saka, 2006; Sassen and Ong, 2014). While I incorporate such concept explicitly within the idea of the bricolage-assemblage (see below), I also question some of the optimistic approaches often linked to the concept, which generally assume creative subjects that use limited resources to create spaces of agency (De Certeau, 1980). In discussing assemblages, I instead highlight how women with cancer not only can often reach only provisional re-compositions but also have to do so with bodies and social roles significantly altered by the disease. According to Marcus and Saka, assemblages offer 'a time-limited object for contemplation' (2006: 102) that underscores their contextual and provisional nature. This point is crucial for exploring experiences with breast cancer. Because the different assemblages are temporary, women need to reassemble and renegotiate them when circumstances change. These configurations involve both material and non-material associations, transformations of the self and attempts to redefine one's position in the world. Some of the formulations within the assemblage approach tend to present these as 'states of being', or to argue categorically against the existence of subjectivities. In my analysis I, on the other hand, often explore assemblages as work conducted by different actors – from the cognitive/emotional work of making sense of one's illness, to organising and navigating healthcare systems. In this sense, my use of assemblage as a concept privileges highlighting the uncertainty and incompleteness of different kinds of relations, as well as how activities that are usually understood as purely cognitive or limited to the coordination of individuals have an impact not only *on* the bodies but also *within* the bodies of patients, being ultimately linked to medical interventions.

I consider assemblage as a general-level concept that is on the same level as, for instance, the structure or practice, and that is capable of offering insight into social phenomena located at different scales. My choice of assemblage as a framework for the analysis derives from its capacity to conceptualise fluid and uncertain relations as those that emerged in my fieldwork. Fluidity and uncertainty inform not only the patients' experiences (e.g. Greco, 2022c) but also aspects often presented as specific and stable, including targeted therapies and therapeutic pathways. Further, the concept of assemblage illustrates how apparently remote social constructs, such as epidemiological tools or the regulation of healthcare systems, can affect individual bodies of patients.

As with all general-level concepts, particularly those focused on fluid relations, assemblage poses the risk of encompassing everything and, therefore, losing analytical power if it is not delimited in some way (Duff, 2023). Rather than confining the concept at a specific level, I use different declinations of assemblage – some linked to existing concepts and others taken inductively from my data – to provide a rigorous analysis. Such articulations are the focus of the next section.

The articulation of assemblages

In this book, I consider assemblages at three levels: the body level, the macro-institutional and cultural level, and the socio-relational level. Within these levels, a number of different processes can be understood as different typologies of assemblages. At the body level, the bodies of patients are transformed by different treatments, both materially (e.g. through surgery and drugs) and by establishing links between bodies, cancerous cells, and medical tools such as protocols, survival curves and the promises of personalised medicine. I explore such phenomena through the concepts of medical-bodily assemblage, indicating both biomedical procedures that directly shape patients' bodies – such as surgery – and the more indirect connections between biomedical concepts and tools and the patients' bodies. At the institutional and cultural level, global ideas about breast cancer built within biomedicine, and cultural discourses about the disease, are transformed when introduced into local contexts and further negotiated and redefined by patients. Such phenomena can be understood through the concepts of cultural-political assemblage – that is, how public discourses about breast cancer are negotiated collectively and individually; of organisational assemblage (cf. Tlili, 2008) – which I use to analyse how healthcare organisations set up standardised pathways and protocols to manage the patients; and of bricolage-assemblage – which capture how patients themselves navigate the healthcare system. At the social and relational level, women contend with uncertainties about possible relapse and survival times and with disruptions to their work and to their family, romantic and friendship relations by assembling provisional and tentative biographies and social roles. These aspects can be understood through the idea of the biographical assemblage, that is, how patients make sense of their own experience and try to understand their possible future, and relational assemblage (Lahti and Kolehmainen, 2020), that is, how relations between patients and the people around them change as a consequence of the illness.

Breast surgery represents the most visible process of bodily assemblage through which bodies are reassembled by breast cancer: tissue – and, in some cases, the whole breast – is removed and, for those that choose to undergo reconstruction, the breast is recreated by either a prosthesis or using auto-transplant techniques (with tissue from other parts of the body). Beyond surgery, bodies are further transformed by the side effects of radiotherapy and drug therapies, including chemotherapy and hormonal therapy. The embodied effects are linked in a causal chain with several medical tools (Fox, 2011), in processes of medical-bodily assemblage. In other words, decisions about which therapies to administer, when and for how long, depend on medical tools such as estimation techniques, guidelines and organisational and procedural criteria. Among these tools are survival curves, which plot the percentage of patients with a given kind of cancer who are alive at specified intervals, and estimates of the risk of cancer relapse after treatment (Jain, 2013). The benefits and side effects of treatments are balanced based on these probabilistic estimates. The introduction of new treatments also depends on both clinical trials and local authorisations of new treatments, with the latter based on efficacy and cost considerations. Treatment combinations are increasingly standardised by national guidelines, and the distributions of sequences of treatments across different medical institutions are increasingly standardised by local patient pathways. Thus, the ways that different medical tools define the impact of a disease and its treatments on patients' bodies align with the general concept of assemblage, especially its evocation in the idea of 'human, social and technical machines' (Deleuze and Guattari, 1980: 50). Such medical-bodily assemblages intersect with organisational and cultural-political assemblages. The standardisation of treatments and the standardisation of pathways are both discourses central to contemporary biomedicine, which aims to create optimal approaches that are universally valid. Dominant cultural discourses around breast cancer also have a global reach, defined by the emphasis on early diagnosis, expectations about positive transformations, and the pink ribbon approach of glamorisation and cause-related marketing (King, 2006; Sulik, 2011). The concept of global assemblages (Collier and Ong, 2007; Ong, 2016) describes how these phenomena with claims to universality are adapted to local histories, values, politics and organisations. This entails both the development of local biomedicines (Lock, 2017) and reconfigurations of cultural discourses, advocacy and activism.

Once global biomedicine has been adapted to local healthcare systems, the consequent standardisation still leaves gaps in patient trajectories. Extensive gaps in cancer knowledge, together with the probabilistic nature of much of what is known about the evolution of cancer, leave patients needing to actively assemble the available information to make sense of the disease and plan their lives. Similarly, women with breast cancer confront cultural discourses that promote normative ideas of patienthood, ranging from adherence to screening and treatments, to gendered ideas about the appearance and the attitude one should maintain during treatment and including moral requests to use the cancer experience to improve oneself. Both these processes can be understood as aspects of biographical assemblages through which patients make sense of their experiences. Actual experiences of navigating healthcare systems are often far less linear than the ideal version presented in patient pathways. Patients often have to produce bricolage-assemblages, i.e. to assemble their own pathway, either to fill gaps in the organisation of healthcare systems or to obtain access to specific preferred treatments. Further, as I discuss in the book, some aspects of the pink ribbon discourse, such as the glamorisation of the disease and cause-related marketing, have seemingly become less important in the countries I study, in a process of redefinition of cultural-political assemblages. However, normative ideas of patienthood persist.

Finally, the impact of breast cancer extends beyond the body and involves patients' biographies, life perspectives, social roles and relations. The probabilistic estimates about relapse and survival not only guide transformations of the body but also drive patients to deal with the uncertainty introduced into their future lives. Therefore, patients need not only to make sense of their biography, including the disease, but also to assemble partial and provisional visions of the future that might await them, visions always tainted with uncertainty, all of which constitutes biographical assemblages. Furthermore, the disease and the treatments limit the capacity to work and socialise by changing the body and the status of cancer patients. In a neoliberal context, women often have to assemble a new professional profile that includes the limitations introduced by the disease. New relations emerge, particularly around a shared disease (Rabinow, 1996), while other relations do not hold. This requires women to manage relational assemblages, reassembling existing and new connections while managing the expectations to provide care that continue to fall upon women even after the diagnosis (Sulik, 2007).

These are not only theoretical considerations. Assemblages describe concrete situations, such as having prostheses or one's own tissue inserted, having to learn about new therapies and think of one's survival time, consulting several doctors and pondering the need to stop working because the treatments make it impossible to continue.

Paradigm changes in breast cancer regimes

Breast cancer is presented as a success story in oncology. The development of cancer screening campaigns, among which those for breast cancer are some of the most visible, has promoted the belief that 'early diagnosis saves lives'. The historian of medicine Ilana Löwy explains that the early twentieth century saw the affirmation of a conceptual framework, or 'cancer schemata', according to which the idea that 'small, localized tumours were an early stage in the development of a malignancy was linked with the idea that cancers can be cured at that stage' (Löwy, 2010: 2). Thus, the early stage is considered a window of opportunity during which identifying a tumour can radically change the prognosis. This linear vision of the development of cancer is only partially correct, as it does not account for the specific biology of the tumour, nor for the fact that the smaller dimensions of the tumour at diagnosis do not exclude the possibility that malignant cells that could produce future metastases are already circulating in the blood or the lymphatic system. Still, the model remains dominant both within biomedicine and in the media and social representations of breast cancer. The emphasis on early diagnosis, and the campaigns that both public health organisations and major advocacy organisations promote, are the most visible expressions of such cancer schemata.

A diagnosis of breast cancer is followed by a series of treatments, which have been synthetised in the 'slash/poison/burn' triad, or surgery, chemotherapy and radiotherapy. These approaches, which have the objective of 'curing' the tumour by eliminating it, define a therapeutic 'cancer script' (Löwy, 2010), that is, a sequence of treatments to which a person with breast cancer should submit. There is a strong link between the therapeutic script and the emphasis on early diagnosis, as the idea behind the therapeutic script is that the linear progression of cancer can be interrupted by treatment, especially if the tumour has been 'caught early enough'. Early diagnosis is thus promoted as the best way to obtain optimal results from the treatments, and at the same time every improvement in treatment is presented rhetorically as increasing the need for an early diagnosis. One example can be found in the introduction of conservative breast surgery following clinical trials in the 1980s, which showed that a quadrantectomy (that is, the removal of one quadrant of the breast) followed by radiotherapy resulted in the same survival rates as the previously prevalent treatment, mastectomy (that is, the removal of the whole breast). Conservative surgery for smaller lesions thus introduced the idea that early detection can save not only patients' life, but also their breast.

Early diagnosis further shapes what US sociologist Maren Klawiter has termed 'cancer regimes' (Klawiter, 2008). The first regime, that of medicalisation, was put in place in the first half of the twentieth century, and included women with breast cancer symptoms. The regime of medicalisation depicted the breast cancer as curable, especially through radical surgery. The second regime, which Klawiter defines as biomedicalisation and locates as starting in the 1970s and 1980s, is strongly determined by the availability of effective screening tools. In effect, in the biomedical regime breast cancer is redefined as a risk for all women, and public health policies extend screening to women with no symptoms, who are reframed as being 'at risk'. The development of genetics and the discovery of the BRCA genes mutations has further redefined the definitions of risk for women without symptoms. As the carriers of BRCA mutations have a higher risk of developing breast cancer, 'pre-vivor' identities have developed around BRCA (Gibbon, 2007; Gibbon et al., 2014), and mastectomies of healthy breasts have been introduced as a possible preventive measure (Löwy, 2010).

In *Assemblages of cancer*, I discuss another change of regime. Despite early diagnosis and the availability of effective treatments, the number of cases in which an early diagnosis does not ensure a positive outcome has opened the way for what can be defined a regime of personalisation (Greco, 2024). Some of the patients who successfully complete all treatments still develop metastases at a later date, along with those who are metastatic at first diagnosis. Patients with metastatic breast cancer will almost certainly die from breast cancer; the key question is when it will happen – how long the disease can be kept at bay. Metastatic breast cancer has been a major site of medical innovation with the introduction of new treatments, often defined as 'personalised' or 'stratified', aiming to target the specific biochemical properties of a tumour, such as the presence of receptors sensitive to specific hormones or proteins. The new treatments aim to extend survival times, but the extension of the survival time is dependent upon the availability of and access to a new array of treatments and therapies. At the same time, the results of targeted therapies, even when successful, remain highly uncertain, and patients often live in a precarious situation in which the assemblage work, even in the best-case scenario, has to be repeated several times – for instance, to find new treatments when a line of treatment stops working.

Introduction

Breast cancer as a social paradigm for cancer survivorship

In 2014, a campaign organized by the British charity Pancreatic Cancer Action featured an image of a young woman with a bald head and the quote 'I wish I had breast cancer'. This image is part of larger project in which patients with pancreatic cancer expressed the wish to have a different type of cancer. An explanatory text offered some context to better understand these shocking quotes: pancreatic cancer has some of the lowest survival rates among cancer subtypes, and many patients die within a few months of their diagnosis. In this sense, pancreatic cancer is not a success story within oncology. As expected, the campaign generated vast debate and also drew critique. This episode captures the tensions around the phenomenon that anthropologist Kirsten Bell has described as the 'breast-cancer-ization' of cancer experiences (Bell, 2014). Breast cancer has been turned into a reassuring pink ribbon (chosen as a badge for breast cancer campaigns), and its prominence in the media has turned the disease into a template for the right behaviours and emotions that should accompany also the diagnoses of other kinds of cancer.

Along with the therapeutic cancer script, that is, as mentioned, the sequence of treatments that a patient should undergo, there is a 'social script' for breast cancer (Klawiter, 2008). This script includes a set of prescriptions and expectations defining how patients should behave, their duties and the socially appropriate ways to react. The therapeutic script and the social script mutually reinforce each other, as the promise of cure following an early diagnosis is linked to the injunction to follow the screening recommendations and exercise optimism in the face of a diagnosis. Both are located in cultural and biomedical landscapes that define practices and behaviours linked to the treatment of cancer and that inform patients' experiences of the disease. Breast cancer has become the paradigm both for medical success and for the optimistic approach required of patients. Awareness campaigns, 'pink' rhetoric and cause-related marketing have turned breast cancer into a linear experience that starts with a timely diagnosis and ends the day the last treatments are administered. One of the main shortcomings of this simplified and marketised presentation of breast cancer is that it leaves out the complexities of the disease. Women who, without or despite an early diagnosis, develop metastatic breast cancer are usually not part of this optimistic narrative. However, this representation of the disease is gradually changing: the lengthening of survival times for metastatic breast cancer and the expansion of the regime of personalisation are fostering new experiences of breast cancer and new forms of activism.

Through breast cancer awareness raising, women have been offered constricting social scripts (Klawiter, 2008) marked by gendered definitions of courage and resilience. These scripts are gradually incorporating the experiences of women living with metastatic breast cancer, with the latter defined as an 'incurable but treatable condition'. The individualistic and consumeristic ideas of breast cancer until recently emphasised the possibility of curing breast cancer; now these ideas are changing to include the possibility of living with a treatable form of cancer. In this way expectations of optimism and resilience are extended to patients with terminal cancer. However, the recent nature of these changes creates a fluid and unstable situation in which new and old tendencies coexist. Both women living with early stage and women living with metastatic breast cancer are presented with contradictory advice and information. Patients are invited to trust and follow traditional biomedical patterns – such as taking part in screening programmes – while seeing that this is not enough and that many women who develop metastases need to find a way to access the newest drugs or even a clinical trial. At the same time metastatic breast cancer is increasingly being presented as 'chronic', a reassuring medical term, as it is traditionally used to describe long-term, manageable conditions such as diabetes (Greco, 2022a). One of the aims of *Assemblage of cancer* is to offer an analysis of how new and old tendencies are changing the cultural landscape of breast cancer, and to explore the impact of these changes on women's lives.

One of the reasons why multiple actors – such as charities and corporations – have been so successful in creating a neoliberal model of survivorship is because breast cancer can be constructed as a female disease, with women pushed to abide by gendered norms and roles. Exploring the gendered nature of the disease is necessary in order to understand how such a dominant model of survivorship has been built.

Breast cancer as a prism for gender

Breast cancer is presented as a female condition and, although it is recognised that malignant cells can also develop in 'male' breast tissue, male breast cancer is usually considered a rare and unusual occurrence. However, we do not know how many of those diagnosed with breast cancer perceive themselves as women (or men). Queer theorist Eve Kosofsky Sedgwick, discussing her own breast cancer diagnosis, writes: 'One of the first things I felt when I was facing the diagnosis of breast cancer was, "Shit, now I guess I really must be a woman"' (Kosofsky Sedgwick, 1993: 262). Kosofsky Sedgwick perfectly summarises the gendered restrictions of breast cancer: the insistence that the disease is a threat to femininity is in itself a skilful act of construction of femininity as a vague but powerful entity that deeply influences women's lives. Breast cancer, even more so than other typically female cancers, such as endometrial or ovarian cancer,[7] is considered an attack on femininity, and this stems from the centrality of the breast in women's lives. Female breasts are among the most visible body traits used to differentiate between men and women. The term 'mammalian' – which derives from the Latin *mamma/mammae*: breast – was chosen by Linnaeus to redefine the zoologic taxonomy. 'Mammalian' creates a link between human beings and 'all other organisms with hair, three ear bones and a four-chambered heart' (Schiebinger, 1993: 40). While reason – a human feature that through categories such as *Homo sapiens* is defined as eminently male – differentiates human beings from the other animal species, female breasts link humans to other living creatures (Schiebinger, 1993: 55). Through their breasts, women are anchored to the natural world, and therefore it is considered natural for women to have breasts. Prevention campaigns often rely on erotic images, contributing to the sexualisation of the disease, and they have become just another opportunity to disseminate a standardised and normative image of the female body: young, slim and toned (Saywell et al., 2000). During treatments, women can be offered to participate in programmes teaching them how to skilfully apply make-up to hide the signs of treatments (Kendrick, 2008), and many women I met during fieldwork were offered a small tissue prosthesis immediately after a mastectomy.

These examples remind us that the changes brought by breast cancer appear on multiple levels. On the first level, different embodied transformations derive from the condition. Different forms of surgery involving the removal of the breast have been, since the end of the nineteenth century, one of the treatments for breast cancer. Since the 1980s, biomedicine has paid increasing attention to surgical treatments that conserve most of the breast, and to breast reconstruction. Recently, this has developed further with the aestheticisation of oncologic surgery, which now aims to recreate the breast with a better appearance than it had pre-diagnosis.

The aestheticisation of oncologic surgery is another example of how breast cancer can be used to reinforce traditional ideas of femininity. In this case, the breast becomes an object to be saved, lost, rebuilt and rediscovered, but it can also be considered a prism through which patients are invited to refract the different aspects of their experience. However, the femininity built through breast cancer goes beyond the body to become a prescriptive norm regarding behaviours, attitudes and ideas. If the symbol of bodily femininity is compromised, women are invited to redefine femininity in behavioural and moral terms, and to implement a series of strategies that preserve it, to show that they are still women and still feminine.

The intersection between the effects of the disease and gendered norms about the body brought the women I met to develop different kinds of answers, including both critiques of and negotiations with biomedical and social expectations. The reactions to these prescriptions are different, rich and imaginative. Far from a sweetened and positive view of disease as an opportunity for improvement, many of the women I encountered offer a political reading of their experience. If we look at breast cancer through the prism of gender, we can see that there are two different processes of assemblage located in and through women's bodies and their experiences with illness. On one hand, social, cultural and biomedical expectations invite women to assemble the pieces of their experience in a way that reconstructs their body and their role in society according to the traditional gender norms. And while this is in fact the experience of some of the women I met in my research, for many others cancer was an opportunity to reshuffle and reassemble their bodies and their lives in a different order. These stories do not see severe illness as a source of inspiration, but as a political catalyst, capable of providing a critical perception of the world. *Assemblages of cancer* is also a story of the numerous acts of resistance that start from the body and branch out into the different aspects of women's lives, from professional to social to intimate.

Breast cancer in Western Europe

The Western European focus of this book is linked to general considerations about the local variability of both illness and medicine. As mentioned, while biomedicine insists on a standardised nature of international medical science, cancer acquires different meanings and is treated differently according to the place, as a consequence of the variation between local biomedicines and between local biologies (Mathews et al., 2015, following Lock, 2001). This also means that 'global' biomedicine goes through global assemblages (Collier and Ong, 2007; Ong, 2016) when introduced in a specific local context. In this sense, the local assemblages of medicine do not only involve medical institutions and regulations, but extend to therapies themselves. Further, when compared to the extensive literature on breast cancer in North America (e.g. King, 2006; Klawiter, 2008; Sulik, 2011; Jain, 2013), my study of Italy, France and the UK shows distinct patterns in terms of the organisation of healthcare, public images of breast cancer, and forms of advocacy and activism, that it is important to analyse. My study illustrates the relevance of ethnographic engagement with the functioning of healthcare systems. Ethnographic attention to healthcare systems has been mostly limited to two kinds of contexts. The first comprises countries in the Global South with limited healthcare resources, where access to cancer treatments is often delayed and partial (see, e.g. Livingston, 2012, on Botswana; Nédélec, 2018, on Ivory Coast). The second is the United States (US), in which a significant part of the uninsured or under-insured population is excluded from some treatments (see Dao and Mulligan, 2016).

My overall research has allowed me to compare three Western European countries with advanced universal healthcare systems, in which the entire range of treatments for breast cancer is usually publicly covered. Such contexts have attracted less ethnographic attention, apparently based on the assumption that universal coverage avoids inequalities that would need to be explored in detail. One book-length exception is the volume edited by Andersen and Tørring

(2023), which shows how cancer in Denmark can be understood through the welfare state. The authors analyse how the welfare state offers an implicit pact to protect citizens and ensure equal life opportunities, but also asks citizens not to burden the healthcare system with avoidable requests (which can contribute to delays in cancer diagnosis). They show how waiting time in healthcare has become a proxy for the more irregular process of tumour growth (Andersen, 2023: 9), motivating an expansion and acceleration of cancer diagnosis and care. Tørring (2023) shows the process through which this expansion and acceleration has been advocated and found a place within the Danish welfare state, while Merrild (2023) shows how, despite this, the Danish healthcare system cannot offer equality to marginalised people who embody multiple health problems deriving from poverty and exclusion.[8] The three countries I analyse have never had welfare systems as strong as those in the Nordic countries, but universal healthcare has held legitimacy (especially in the UK). In this context, I explore how the organisation of healthcare systems and the need to navigate them and negotiate access to treatments influence patients' experiences, even in the context of full healthcare coverage.

In this sense, the study of breast cancer reveals some of the significant transformations of healthcare systems in Western Europe. These include increasing privatisation and, since breast cancer is a branch of oncology characterised by significant medical innovation, the importance of clinical trials, experimental treatments and new therapies that are often costly for public healthcare, as well as ongoing issues of unequal access for patients. The comparative approach further helps to understand the relevance of the different factors that influence patients' experiences, which is in line with the extended case method approach (Burawoy, 2000; 2009 – see also the next section). Comparative work allows us to differentiate between traits that are common to different contexts and traits specific to a context, identifying what can be generalised and what is more local. Further, conducting an analysis that is multi-sited/comparative and that looks at different scales within a given context allows us to see the relative weight of transnational and local factors in the experiences of individual actors. The comparative stance has been a valuable tool to explore how ideologies and cultural constructions around breast cancer have shaped the experiences of the disease, but also how dominant culture paradigms (for instance, the well-known pink ribbon culture) have been refashioned in local contexts. Comparison has also been a helpful tool to approach biomedical constructions of breast cancer, and their impact on the different actors involved – such as patients and medical professionals – can vary in different contexts. In this case, the comparison between different countries offered a deeper understanding of the social and cultural traits that inform individual experiences of breast cancer and the different processes of assemblages that women put into action.

Constructing fieldwork

This book is the result of ten years of study of breast cancer. My overall research has been a multi-sited ethnography (Marcus, 1995) of the experiences of breast cancer in three Western European countries – France, Italy and the UK – conducted between 2011 and 2020. I focused my research on specific regions within the three countries, conducting ethnography in the Paris region (Île-de-France) in France, in Greater Manchester and Cheshire and more generally in northern England in the UK, and in a northern region (Emilia-Romagna) and a southern one (Apulia) in Italy. In each case, however, I also conducted interviews outside these regions, as specific lines of research brought me into contact with patients and medical professionals in other areas. This focus on specific regions has allowed me to reconstruct the formal (e.g., standardised pathways) and informal networking of medical institutions. It has allowed me to become familiar with the different institutions involved in the experiences of many of the patients I interviewed. In the case of Italy, which is marked by a particularly pronounced north–south divide in terms of economic conditions (and stigma against the south – Greco, 2016a; 2019), including both a southern and a northern region allowed me to capture one of the main axes of inequality in the country. Overall, my fieldwork has been constructed in a way that resembles the *Anti-book* created by Chilean artist Francisca Prieto. This artefact is, at a first sight, a booklet containing a poem, which cannot be read as long as the traditional book format is maintained: the text becomes intelligible only when the book format is altered and the pages are assembled in a three-dimensional icosahedron. Similarly, my fieldwork can also be defined as an 'anti-fieldwork'. I did not spend a well-defined amount of time 'away' in the country or region that I was studying, but, because I studied, worked and lived as a migrant in two of the countries I discuss here, my fieldwork and my personal life were strongly intertwined. I lived in the same contexts as the women I interviewed, and I went to the same medical facilities both as a researcher and as a patient for my own periodical screening. Disassembling the established disciplinary boundaries of the fieldwork has given me a unique perspective, which has been substantiated by more traditional methodological perspectives.[9] In my research I have followed the extended case method approach (Burawoy, 2009) to compare the experience of illness in different contexts, to connect the ethnographic data with structural phenomena located at a larger scale than the one I directly observed and to advance theoretical understandings by exploring the deviation of my research results from existing theories. The research has been informed both by a critical medical anthropology approach (Singer and Baer, 1995) and by a feminist approach that gives priority to understanding the experiences of women with breast cancer (Greco, 2016b).

What I present in the next chapters are, first, illness narratives of women with breast cancer. Although they have focused on different aspects – and a few interviewees preferred not to discuss certain details of their experiences – all have presented rich narratives. My interviews with medical professionals were more focused on the main questions of the three different research projects I conducted. In the first, conducted in Italy and France, the focus was mostly on breast surgery and reconstruction; in the second, conducted in the UK, on metastatic breast cancer; and in the third, also conducted in the UK, on how medical innovation and changes in healthcare policy have influenced patients' experiences. However, in each case the interviews with medical professionals extended to other aspects and experiences of the illness.

During fieldwork, I collected more than 150 in-depth interviews with patients with breast cancer, activists and members of advocacy groups, and with medical professionals working on breast cancer (oncologists, surgeons, nurses, radiologists, psycho-oncologists and administrative staff). I used different strategies to contact medical professionals and patients. I contacted some doctors directly, especially those who had published studies on different aspects of breast cancer, and I contacted other medical professionals through a snowball procedure. For the interviews with patients, in the UK, France and northern Italy, I used the mediation of medical professionals and patients' associations in addition to a snowball procedure involving patients whom I had already interviewed. For the interviews conducted in southern Italy, I also used my own family and personal network. The assemblage of different approaches allowed me to come into contact with a diverse group of patients in terms of age, class and formal education. One dimension of diversity that I was not able to include in my research was the ethnic and racial one. Almost all the patients I met were white, although a few had a migratory background. This was a result of breast cancer patient advocacy being predominantly white in all three countries, and also of the fact that, when contacting patients through medical institutions, I almost exclusively met white women. This is certainly a limitation of my research, and more studies with women of colour are needed for the European context. On the other hand, the medical professionals I met were more ethnically and racially diverse, especially in the UK, given the National Health Service's (NHS) history of recruitment from abroad.

In each case, I avoided conducting single-institution ethnographies, and I included medical professionals from, and patients in treatment at, different hospitals. This allowed for a wider horizon when approaching the study of phenomena that go beyond specific institutions, including medical innovation, healthcare policies, medical cultures and the social representations of breast cancer. This approach further allowed me to explore the unequal distribution of medical techniques between institutions. Finally, it was necessary to avoid limiting my ethnographic focus to single institutions because patients' (and in some cases, medical professionals') experiences are not limited to a single institution. In each country, patients' trajectories while in treatment can cover multiple institutions, although I found stronger patient mobility in France, and especially in Italy, while in the UK the system of referrals and pathways restricted the mobility of patients, who were effectively limited to the nearest hospital offering cancer treatment and specialised centres offering treatments not available locally.

I have integrated the interviews with formalised observations of events organised by patients' associations and/or medical professionals, and of medical conferences. In addition, ten years of continuous exchanges with patient-activists inform my understanding of the political and cultural implications of breast cancer.

Finally, I have included in my research several written sources, such as newspaper articles, websites on cancer, informative materials produced by medical institutions, pathographies written by patients and extensive corpora of medical literature. The documentary part of my research allowed me to obtain further insight into the experiences of medical professionals and patients, to reconstruct public discourses about breast cancer and the history of innovation in treatments and to better link my ethnographic data to structural phenomena. These critical analyses of medical literature have allowed me to reconstruct specific discourses, both about breast cancer and about related social issues, such as gender and behavioural norms, as they emerge from scientific production in biomedicine.

In this book

In introducing *A Thousand Plateaus*, Deleuze and Guattari observe how books themselves are assemblages bringing together different materials and points of view and that 'There is no difference between the subject of the book and the way in which it is done' (Deleuze and Guattari, 1980: 10). This book indeed brings together different research projects conducted in three different countries, more than a hundred individual experiences explored through in-depth interviews and several other materials such as policy documents, medical literature, pamphlets, websites and so on.

Assemblages of cancer focuses on the experiences of breast cancer in Western Europe. In line with the levels and types of assemblage introduced above, in Chapters 1 and 2, I focus on organisational and cultural-political assemblages on an institutional and cultural level; in Chapters 3 and 4 on medical-bodily assemblages that involve the bodies of patients; and in Chapters 5 and 6 on biographical and relational assemblages conducted by the women.

In Chapter 1, I show how global assemblages (Collier and Ong, 2007; Ong, 2016) involving biomedicine and organisational assemblage involving local healthcare systems define the configuration of breast cancer therapies in the three countries. I show, in particular, the different ways the universal public healthcare systems of the UK, France and Italy have seen different forms of privatisation. I further discuss how medical innovation is accompanied in some cases by delays in authorising costly new treatments (especially in the UK) and the unequal diffusion of techniques and treatments throughout the territory. Secondly, I present an analysis of how patients produce bricolage-assemblages involving their own therapeutic trajectories to fill the gaps in the organisation of healthcare, navigate the systems and negotiate specific treatment options. In particular, I discuss how this second type of assemblage is enacted through different kinds of health-related mobility, both local and, particularly in Italy, intra-national.

In Chapter 2, I discuss a second area of global assemblages linked to breast cancer: how the dominant international discourse about the disease has been partially reframed in the three countries, through cultural-political assemblages that renegotiate the dominant public discourse linked to the pink ribbon narrative. I show how North American pink ribbon campaigns have partially lost their dominant role in the three countries, but also how this has not put into question the emphasis on early diagnosis and the idea that cancer should bring a positive change in one's life. I further discuss the associative panorama in the three countries and how, for the patients involved in associations, the experience is a way to assemble answers to both the disease and the dominant cultural messages. Finally, in the chapter, I discuss an aspect of the biographical assemblage: how patients not involved in associations try to make sense of the dominant messages about the meaning of breast cancer.

Having introduced the broader policy, political and cultural contexts, in Chapter 3, I move on to discuss how the evolution of biomedicine has influenced breast cancer. I continue to discuss global assemblages between biomedicine and its local implementation in medical-bodily assemblages, shifting from healthcare systems to the activity of medical professionals. I explore the tensions between the ambition to segment breast cancer further, find effective treatments for each patient and transform metastatic breast cancer from terminal to chronic by introducing new treatments. However, I also show how different interviewees recognise the gaps still existing in breast cancer treatment. Both developments further establish medical-bodily assemblages in which patients' bodies, tumour cells and biomarkers are linked with new biomedical apparatuses. I finally discuss how patients react to such evolutions, how they produce bricolage-assemblages to access specific treatments, and biographical assemblages to attempt to understand how treatments could lengthen their lives.

In Chapter 4, I continue the analysis of medical-bodily assemblages, focusing more specifically on the physical modifications of patients' bodies deriving from breast surgery (which in turn includes tumourectomy, mastectomy and reconstruction). First, I focus on the biomedical perspective and how reconstructive surgery aims to re-establish and, in some cases, create *ex novo* breasts that conform to a gendered canon. Next, I show how most women aim to return to a pre-surgical condition; however, in some cases, this can mean just finding a volume that can pass as a breast in social situations or the acceptance of asymmetry or flatness. This involves bricolage-assemblages and navigating and negotiating the healthcare system to access the preferred reconstructive options. It further involves assembling a public presentation of one's body, especially if choosing to remain asymmetric, depending on different contexts. I conclude by discussing how the different aims of patients and surgeons illustrate the role of gender norms in breast cancer experiences and, at the same time, highlight how post-diagnosis bodies are entangled in gender norms.

Shifting from bodily to biographical assemblages, in Chapter 5, I discuss the different forms of uncertainty that breast cancer introduces in patients' lives. A cancer diagnosis represents a shock, and in this chapter I discuss how patients attempt to manage uncertainty by pursuing information and access to institutions and professionals they can trust. I further show how uncertainties remain with the patients for a long time, regardless of the immediate outcome. If they obtain the best result achievable, 'no evidence of disease', the possibility of a relapse and the side effects of treatments continue to represent uncertainties for several years after the diagnosis. Patients with metastatic development enter a more radical uncertainty, as death from cancer is inevitable, and while survival times have improved in the last years, the ability to predict the life expectancies of individual patients is limited. In both cases, the probabilistic and open-ended perspective of breast cancer makes it necessary to attempt to assemble provisional and fragmented visions of one's future.

In Chapter 6, I discuss relational assemblages. I first show how breast cancer can influence women's working lives in different ways, with some women deliberately reducing their involvement in jobs that they were not satisfied with and others with greater job satisfaction finding obstacles to continuing to work as before. Next, I look at the re-assemblages of family relations and of gendered care responsibilities, examining to what degree different interviewees were able to rely on their immediate families, but also cases in which support was limited, or the illness brought an end to marriages and relationships. Finally, I discuss new forms of sociality developing around the illness, including the redefinition of friendships post-diagnosis.

In the Conclusion, I return to how individual illness experiences and the different political, biomedical and cultural contexts interact. In light of the different analyses conducted in the book, I offer a systematic discussion of the various assemblages linked to breast cancer. I also discuss how breast cancer highlights the differences between the UK, French and Italian healthcare systems, and the economic and social meaning of breast cancer in the US. Finally, I return to the social meanings and implications of the assemblages of breast cancer and discuss how many of the uncertainties visible in breast cancer are also relevant to most other disease–society assemblages.

Notes

1 About 1% of breast cancer cases occur in cis men, and trans men are still at risk from breast cancer, so saying that 'every woman' is at risk remains a partial representation. All the patients I interviewed were cis women, and I did not meet cis men or trans men with breast cancer (on such experiences, see Sledge, 2021). However, in this book I show how the gender norms built around breast cancer exclude even most cis women.
2 I grew up in the province of Lecce, an area important for the history of Italian anthropology following De Martino's (1961) study of magical thinking and *tarantismo* rituals.
3 Research conducted in Italy between the late 1980s and early 1990s (Gordon and Paci, 1997) found practices of silence around cancer, as well as the tendency among oncologists not to disclose the cancer diagnosis to the patients, but only to their relatives, considering the patients to have

better reactions and outcomes if they were not aware. This is one aspect that has changed over time, as I have not encountered such practices in the interviews conducted in Italy.
4 See the report of the European Cancer Information System at https://joint-research-centre.ec.europa.eu/jrc-news/2020-cancer-incidence-and-mortality-eu-27-countries-2020-07-22_en (accessed 22 July 2024).
5 While the anglophone literature usually sees the concept translated as assemblage, Deleuze and Guattari's (1980) original French term is *agencement*, which could be translated more closely as arrangement, that is, refers more to putting different elements in an order rather than to linking them together. My use of the concept encompasses both terms, and the reason I use assemblage rather than arrangement is simply in line with the existing anglophone literature.
6 There is a contiguity between the concept of assemblage and Foucault's concept of *dispositif* or device (e.g. Foucault, 1994; cf. Deleuze, 1989). However, while *dispositif* describes the combination of discourses, rules and institutions that influence or discipline bodies, assemblage describes also a material continuity between bodies and external elements.
7 Ovarian cancer, for example, due to the greater difficulty in diagnosis, is less amenable to the optimistic discourse about early diagnosis and survivorship used for breast cancer (see Gubar, 2012). Moreover, the internal nature of ovaries means that, while the removal of the organ has visible effects on women's bodies, there is both less emphasis on the symbolic role of the organ and less of a script in terms of measures to take to restore femininity after treatments (see Bell, 2014; Tetteh, 2018).
8 A further exception is Pop's study of cervical cancer in Romania (Pop, 2022), which shows experiences in a context that is characterised by healthcare resources comparatively scarcer than those in Western Europe and, especially, by an accelerated transition from socialism to capitalism that has impacted significantly on the healthcare system.
9 I hesitated before adding this note, but in the spirit of making visible the invisiblised contributions of disabled people in academia, it is important to underline that this work is an example of what I have defined as 'divergent ethnography' (Greco, 2022b), conducted by a neurodivergent person.

1

The political context of breast cancer in Europe

In 'Medici' (Doctors), the final episode of *Caro Diario*, a 1993 Italian semi-autobiographical comedy film, Nanni Moretti, the director and protagonist actor, presents his personal experience of navigating the medical world to find the cause of the persistent itching and insomnia from which he is suddenly suffering. The spectator follows Moretti in his numerous meetings with specialists, each offering a different explanation and cure for his problem, with none of these remedies proving effective. At a certain point, the protagonist, tired of failures, turns to alternative medicine specialists, but even this path proves unable to alleviate his symptoms. After several months of tribulations, a doctor orders a chest X-ray which leads to the diagnosis of Hodgkin lymphoma, successfully treated with chemotherapy. In the film, Moretti does not hide his privileged situation, since many of the specialists he goes to are well known and have been suggested to the protagonist by his network of friends and acquaintances. However, the tendency to consult more specialists is present in Italy in various socio-demographic groups. It is partly favoured by the organisation of the healthcare system, which allows greater mobility to patients, and by the stronger links between the private and public systems (cf. Bardazzi, 2009). Furthermore, the frustration and sense of hopelessness that the film vividly displays are also common experiences for many patients who find themselves navigating healthcare systems, in which complex pathways can become an additional difficulty. How patients can access available specialist care and treatments is directly related to how healthcare systems are organised, and their internal differences are structural elements that influence which treatments patients can access.

Differently from the low-resource national systems of the Global South and the for-profit, insurance-centric US healthcare system – the main focus of existing ethnographic work (e.g. Livingston, 2012; Dao and Mulligan, 2016; Nédélec, 2018) – the three countries here considered have universal, high-quality public services that cover most cancer treatments free of charge. It is true that the definition of a universal healthcare system does not take into account the forms of privatisation and increased cuts to public expenditure which, even in these three countries, coexist together with measures to guarantee that all residents can have access to care. Furthermore, more or less implicit and surreptitious forms of privatisation coexist, with entire medical specialities, such as dentistry and cosmetic surgery, predominantly operating in the private sector, with the public accepting this situation. The social insurance system in France, differently from the single-payer systems of the UK and Italy, pushes more patients to resort to the private sector, particularly for treatments that are not considered life saving, such as breast reconstruction (Greco, 2015). The fact that cosmetic surgery is a branch of medicine predominately operating in the private sector is relevant in the case of breast cancer and can have an important role in orienting some patients toward private facilities to undergo breast reconstruction. In addition, the rapid development of new treatments for metastatic breast cancer introduces the question of how rapidly costly oncological drugs are authorised for use in the public sector, with small but growing numbers of patients who decide to pay significant sums out-of-pocket for treatments still not authorised in the public sector. In the following sections, I will outline the main characteristics of the UK, Italian and French healthcare systems, particularly those related to oncology. National healthcare systems are an important part of the process of organisational assemblages that mediate global biomedicine with local biomedicines (cf. Lock, 2001; Collier and Ong, 2007; Ong, 2016). The concept of 'organisational assemblage' indicates both the complex relations between individuals (and their bodies), institutions, procedures and other resources needed to pursue specific aims, *and* the discourses that constitute the organisation on paper (cf. Deleuze and Guattari 1980; Tlili 2008). In this sense, organisational assemblages describe the respective places and tasks of patients, medical professionals and others, including the places and tasks that often remain only 'on paper', without being fully enacted.

While an understanding of assemblage can also be applied to emergent and temporary organisations of healthcare, in this book, I limit the concept to relatively established institutions, while highlighting how these act in a variable and relatively fluid way in their day-to-day functioning.

I will also discuss how patients move within these systems and how they try to navigate them. Patients try to circumvent the shortcomings of healthcare systems characterised by a rigid organisation and increasingly limited budgets. In this context, they try to find, rearrange and reassemble resources to maintain control over their situation or to be able to enter into contact with trusted professionals or institutions, while a minority of patients who can afford to do so draw on personal financial resources to compensate for the gaps and rigidities of the system. I use the concept of 'bricolage-assemblage' to describe these practices. The general concept of assemblage has been used to analyse how more specialised figures – informal and recognised facilitators of international medical travel – fill the gaps in the organisation or give access to configurations of healthcare otherwise unavailable (Chee et al., 2017).ced, The concept of bricolage, on the other hand, has been used to describe the navigation of the system on the part of patients by combining different resources to deal with the same challenges (Phillimore et al., 2019), while noting how such bricolage might legitimate further rollbacks of public healthcare provision. My use of bricolage-assemblage combines these insights to describe the activities of patients and identifies this kind of assemblage as the other face of the organisational assemblages enacted by healthcare institutions.

United Kingdom: the NHS and its transformations

The UK's NHS is the prototype of the universal healthcare system outside socialist countries. Created in 1948, it reflected both the extensive welfare policies of the Labour government elected in 1945 and a wider consensus, at the time partly extended to the Conservative Party, on the need to build a welfare state. The role of the consensus means that the NHS-like healthcare systems are often named 'Beveridge' systems, crediting the Liberal economist author of the 1942 Beveridge report on the perspectives of a welfare state, rather than Aneurin Bevan, the Labour Minister of Health who supervised the creation of the NHS. The NHS has been characterised since its creation by being free at the point of use, and by state control of both funding and delivery of services (one of the few exceptions being general practice doctors (GPs), who resisted plans to be transformed into state employees – Webster, 2002). This organisation ensured greater equality in access to healthcare when compared to social insurance 'Bismarck' systems, but was also open to more stringent rationing. Between 1979 and 2000, the centralised organisation of the NHS facilitated significantly lower funding (Webster, 2002) when compared to many other healthcare systems in Western Europe.

Moreover, unlike other systems (including the Italian one, which, as I discuss below, was explicitly modelled on the UK's NHS), the NHS has always been characterised by the central role of the GPs, who control access to most specialist services through the referral system. Moreover, internal mobility is possible but limited, and, generally, treatment can be accessed only in the services closest to one's residence – an approach that helps to standardise patients' pathways and limits healthcare expenditures but also reduces patients' choice. The possibility to move to seek healthcare and to choose a specialist or a facility is not entirely absent; in fact, patients can move in some cases within the areas corresponding to the Clinical Commissioning Groups (CCG).[1] However, this possibility is generally limited (McPherson and Beresford, 2019), and absent in the case of oncological disease.[2]

The NHS has a central role in British society. Stephanie Snow writes that the institution has shaped the 'experiences of birth, life, health, work, communities, sickness, and death [of people in the UK] since 1948' and underlines how '[t]he core purpose of the NHS is grounded in humanitarianism' (Snow, 2018: 22). However, numerous analyses have also highlighted the privatisation processes that have transformed and continue to transform this pillar of British society. The Community Care Act of 1990 set off the beginning of the internal market in the NHS. Starting in the 1990s, a new approach focused on managing services in a way closer to a managerial and business model by creating a division between providers of health services and organisations that would purchase these services using an allocated budget, with different structures, such as hospital trusts and GP practices, competing to sell their services (Allsop and May, 1993; Paton, 2022). The split between purchasers and providers ended in 2017 and, starting from 2022, Integrated Care Systems – that is, a partnership system between different organisations of services in a territory (Dunn et al., 2022) – were introduced (Bayliss, 2022). The model has received some criticism; for example, the British Medical Association has expressed concern about the risk of involvement of private providers, as well as reservations about a single standard model of integration.[3] Several commentators share these reservations: Roderick and Pollock, for example, consider this reform a further step towards the ongoing privatisation of the NHS and say that, with the introduction of the Integrated Care System,

> Parliament has stood back and handed over most decision-making and power to unaccountable entities who will decide what services will be provided. This outsourcing of control over large sums of public money will also increase the opportunities for corruption. Health services in England will come to resemble those in the United States, where the state has also opted out of health care organization and direct provision. (Roderick and Pollock, 2022: 447)

The changes that have characterised the NHS since 1990 are only partially noticeable from the patient's perspective, since one of the central aspects of the system – being free at the point of use – is still largely valid, despite an increasing porosity between public and private, and forms of co-payment that exist in both Italy and France are absent in the UK or are used only in a reduced number of situations. However, there are increasing elements of privatisation, particularly in the case of oncology. Several NHS Trusts now receive a significant portion of their funds from activities such as car parking, clinical trials and, in particular, paying patients receiving treatment in the private units of public facilities (Exworthy and Lafond, 2021). A significant proportion of private patients are cancer patients from overseas, with many arriving from the Middle East, but also from China and the rest of Europe (Burki, 2019; Hanefeld et al., 2013).

Furthermore, in 2008, after the publication of reports by the Secretary of State for Health (see Jackson, 2010), access to unfunded cancer treatments was extended to patients who could afford top-up payments (Kerr et al., 2021; Arteaga Pérez, 2022a; and Chapter 3).

Among the recommendations of the report was the suggestion to keep ordinary free-at-the-point-of-use healthcare separate from services that involve a payment on the patient's part. Instead of acting as a deterrent, this recommendation has encouraged the creation of wards for private patients in some larger hospitals.

Within the NHS, the internal movements of patients are more limited than in the French and Italian contexts, and often organised in pre-established pathways. GPs have a gatekeeping role, and decide whether a patient needs a specialist referral or further medical tests. While a referral system from GPs is also present in Italy and France, the gatekeeping role in those countries is less stringent, leaving more choices as to where to seek a consultation with a specialist, as well as ways to do so without a referral (cf. Forrest, 2003; Garattini et al., 2023). The unequal distribution of services across the UK, combined with less freedom of movement for patients, has often been referred to as a postcode lottery (Bungay, 2005). It is not always easy to map out the inequalities, since in a given area good provision for some services can coexist with underperforming provision for others. However, the poorest areas often have underperforming services; for example, in the most deprived areas, it can be more difficult to see a GP (Torjesen, 2014). To address the unequal distribution of resources, various solutions have been adopted. In 1999, the central government established an independent public body, the National Institute for Health and Care Excellence (NICE), the objective of which is to provide an assessment of new medical technologies, in particular new drugs (Kelly et al., 2010) and of their cost-effectiveness, centralising across England and Wales the decisions on the availability of specific treatments. NICE is considered a good example of cost reduction based on a rigorous assessment of the benefits of new (and often expensive) treatments (Littlejohns et al., 2019). In some cases, however, its decisions are contested, and there is no shortage of newspaper articles presenting the institutional body as a mechanism that prevents patients from accessing new therapies. The tendency to standardise services across the national territory coexists with forms of devolution of decision-making powers and funds to local authorities, including in the field of health and social care, as in the case of Greater Manchester (the so-called Devo Manc – Coleman et al., 2015), where a significant part of my British fieldwork was conducted. Devolution arrangements might offer greater organisational autonomy to a local area, but they do not necessarily increase the amount of funds allocated to it.

The Italian national healthcare system: a geographically limited universalism?

The Italian healthcare system (*Servizio Sanitario Nazionale* – SSN) was created in 1978, when Law 833 abolished the *mutua* model, a Bismarckian system based on compulsory health insurance (Toth, 2016). The 1978 reform established a universal healthcare service based on general guiding principles, including universality (that is to say, the right to assistance for all people and for all forms of illness), comprehensiveness of the services provided (that is, offering all the services necessary for the well-being of the population) and equity (that is, the fact that the costs are distributed among citizens according to their economic circumstances, generally through a system of taxation, and by offering the same health services to everyone – Toth, 2014a).

As several commentators have pointed out, the application of these principles is limited by numerous obstacles (see, e.g., Mapelli, 2012; Toth, 2014b). The co-presence of public and private facilities is one of them. Indeed, since the 1990s, the Italian system has gradually included private structures in the public sector, thanks to the introduction of the *accreditamento* (accreditation system). The *accreditamento* is a process that allows any private healthcare institution meeting minimum standards to be included among the healthcare structures to which patients have access free of charge, with these institutions then being refunded by the state. In addition, in the 1990s, the introduction of the exercise of private professions within public structures, the *intramoenia*, further strengthened the links between private and public systems in Italy. What changes for patients is the quality of services, especially in terms of speed of access to specific examinations, which often involve a long waiting list in the public system. For certain kinds of services, the population can either use public or accredited structures, thus paying only a percentage of the costs, the 'ticket', or can decide to go to a private structure and pay in full, and out of their own pocket, without any reimbursement from the state (Mapelli, 2012). However, there is a significant variation in the costs in the private sector between services accessed with the *intramoenia* modality and those accessed in private facilities. The strong connections between public and private structures mean that a proportion of public healthcare expenditure, around 35% of the total, is used to fund providers outside the SSN, such as private clinics, medical professionals working in the private sector and private laboratories (Toth, 2016). The situation of the SSN has been made more precarious since the 2008 global financial crisis and the government's responses to tackle it. The Italian government made numerous cuts in various sectors of public spending, including the SSN, while also increasing the co-payments of individual patients (de Belvis et al., 2012; Frisina Doetter and Neri, 2018). These measures, coupled with a difficult financial situation for many, have decreased household expenditure on health in Italy (Sarti et al., 2017). Furthermore, starting around the end of the 1990s, a system of tax breaks has made it more convenient for workers and employers to subscribe to voluntary health insurance, with 21% of the population covered by health insurance in 2017, as compared with just the 2% in 1999 (Marenzi et al., 2021). Many commentators have highlighted how the strong integration between public and private healthcare, accentuated in recent years, can endanger the stability of the public healthcare system and risks accelerating even more extensive forms of privatisation (Domenighetti et al., 2010; Maietti et al., 2023). Furthermore, the organisation of the Italian healthcare system influences the behaviour and expectations of the population. The presence of the 'ticket' means that many patients do not perceive healthcare services as 'free at the point of use', and this makes the use of private services more frequent, not only because they are faster but also because sometimes they have very similar costs to what patients would pay with the ticket (C.R.E.A. Sanità, 2017). In the case of breast cancer, for example, it is not uncommon for Italian women to pay for a mammogram or a consultation with an oncologist (Valent et al., 2020).

A salient aspect of Italian society is the divide between the south and the north of the country, with the north historically considered economically advanced and culturally progressive, while the south is considered backward and marked by a more difficult economic situation (Greco, 2019). Moreover, the cuts to services and containment measures mentioned above have complicated the picture because, if the financial condition of the southern regions continues to be difficult (Gabriele, 2015), more recently the economic situation in the north of the country has also declined (SVIMEZ, 2014). The north–south gap characterises many aspects of the Italian economy and society, including healthcare, and while the Italian healthcare system is universal, there are significant differences in the quality of services between the regions. With the constitutional reform of the *Titolo Quinto* (the section five of the Constitution) of 1999, the competencies of health policies have been attributed to the regions, which have to ensure that regional healthcare meets the minimum levels of quality – *Livelli essenziali di assistenza* (LEA), which are established by the Ministry of Health and periodically revised. While we have seen that in the UK several NHS Trusts earn large sums from private overseas patients, other types of mobility characterise other healthcare systems, and in Italy we see intra-national mobilities of patients, a kind of mobility that has been less explored in the literature (for some exceptions, see Vindrola-Padros, 2012; Edmiston, 2018; Greco, 2019; 2021; Hunleth and Steinmetz, 2022). In Italy, it is often assumed that healthcare in the southern regions is of lesser quality than that of the northern regions, in terms both of the quality of treatments and of the waiting time to access these services. Levels of patient satisfaction in the north and south reflect these differences (cf. Toth, 2014b). In 2007, 800,000 hospitalisations (including day procedures) took place outside the patients' region of residence (Pica and Villani, 2010). Of these, one third were people from southern Italy who had travelled to northern Italy for treatment. Journeys from the south to the north are defined as *viaggi della speranza* – journeys of hope (Viesti, 2001) – and are common experiences for a large part of the population (Greco, 2019). In 2006 Italian citizens were asked to vote in a referendum proposing several changes to the Italian Constitution, allowing, among other things, greater autonomy to the regions in matters of health. This aspect, in particular, was considered problematic, since the opponents of the referendum presented it as a limit to the possibility of residents moving freely within the national territory to receive treatment. The changes were rejected, but the topic periodically resurfaces in the Italian political debate, showing the importance of internal movement for health reasons. In 2020, due to the interregional movements of patients, €3.33 billion passed between regions, with most regions in the north having a positive balance, that is, having treated more out-of-region patients (especially from the south) than the number of local residents who were treated elsewhere (Cartabellotta et al., 2022). However, as we will see later in the chapter, the decision to travel or to remain closer to home to receive treatment can be influenced by a plurality of elements. In Italy, every patient has the right to move to receive treatment in any part of the national territory. Some patients decide to move by paying for private services. Medical referrals for the public sector, such as those made by a family doctor, do not limit the area or region in which patients can request treatment. While doing fieldwork in Italy, I tried to capture this complex healthcare landscape. I conducted fieldwork in Apulia and Emilia-Romagna. Apulia is a southern region with a healthcare system considered less well performing, while Emilia-Romagna, located in the centre-north of the country, is one of the destinations of the 'journeys of hope' carried out by several of my southern-resident interviewees. The experiences of the disease of the women encountered during my fieldwork and inserted into the institutional landscape that I have described here are part of my analysis.

In Italy, cancer is recognised as a major health problem, with the population in some areas considered more at risk (Greco, 2016a). In January 2023, the Italian government allocated €50 million for a five-year cancer plan from 2023 to 2027, with part of the investment aiming to reduce the health inequalities present in the country. General hospitals are the main providers of oncological treatments; however, cancer treatments are also provided in some IRCCSs – *Istituti di ricovero e cura a carattere scientifico* (Institutes of hospitalisation and care of a scientific nature). IRCCSs are institutions distributed throughout the national territory in which clinical activities are coupled with research. These institutions can have different specialisations, with some specifically focused on the research and treatment of cancer. The IRCSS *Istituto Nazionale Tumori* (National Tumours Institute) of Milan and the European Institute of Oncology, created in 1994 by the oncologist Umberto Veronesi and also located in Milan, have significant roles in oncology.

In analysing the experiences of the women whom I encountered in Italy, it is essential to consider two elements: on the one hand, the material difference in health resources available across Italy, and on the other hand, how this difference intersects with broader social inequalities, particularly between the north and the south of the country, and with how the population understands such inequalities, as I discuss later in this chapter.

The French system: between universalism and liberalism

The classifications of the French health system in comparative studies of healthcare systems diverge. Böhm et al. (2013) consider France as an example of a statist social health insurance system, taking into account the organisation of the French healthcare system where two levels of financial support coexist. The first is national medical insurance (*Sécurité sociale*), which covers a significant portion of health expenditures. However, the percentage funded varies according to the type of service, and a relevant portion remains to be paid by the patients. The second level of coverage is provided by *les mutuelle*s, that is, insurance companies, often linked to employment, that cover part or the entirety of the remaining costs and sometimes also cover healthcare services not included in the national medical insurance (cf. Jusot, 2014). Other authors (cf. Hecketsweiler et al., 2001) consider that the French system is situated between a system based on social insurance, whose ideal type is the German model, and a universal system, the ideal type of which is the UK. Steffen (2010) defines the French system as a liberal universal system because it is, indeed, characterised by an important role of private non-profit organisations, as in Germany, but the co-presence of a system of reimbursement and the strong development of complementary insurance makes the French system different from universal systems (such as the Italian system, as we have seen above). In France, the 'mutual benefit societies, which dominate the market for complementary health insurance, are a gray area between the public and private sectors' (Steffen, 2010: 361). Medical professionals working in what is known as 'sector II' play an important role. In the 1980s, a reform of the convention between the doctors and the healthcare system was the basis for the creation of a dual sector:

> Alongside the doctors in the so-called 'approved' ['*conventionné*'] sector (or sector I) – who remain committed to the rules and obligations of the system developed in 1960 – others, at the cost of the loss of some social and tax benefits, decide to opt for a 'non fixed fee' contract

(or sector II) in the hope of maintaining or improving their socio-economic position despite the difficulties of the moment.[4] (Arliaud and Robelet, 2000: 95)

Physicians choosing to be part of this group could, and still can today, freely increase their fees, with social security refunding the patients only up to the sum set by public authorities.

As we will see later in this chapter, the patients I met moved through the system using different strategies and combining in different ways the options available. The majority of them had treatment in public hospitals and facilities. A very limited number of patients choose to receive their treatments in the private sector paying out of their own pocket, although the total or a portion of those fees could be covered by a private health insurance, if the patient had one. Different French health insurances (*mutuelles*) can cover different types of health expenses and, as the type of the insurance is often linked to the patient's place of work, this stratifies further the capacity to pay. Several patients who decided to undergo a breast reconstruction did so in a private facility, as the waiting lists for this kind of operation are usually quite long and the availability of some specific techniques might be patchy (see Chapter 4). Some patients were covered by a good health insurance, but others were not, and in order to fund their breast reconstruction they had to for it themselves; some asked for a loan to do so.

If we look more closely at the cancer services available in France, an important distinction exists between the *Centres de lutte contre le cancer* (CLCC – Centres for the fight against cancer) and the *Centres Hospitaliers Universitaires* (CHU – University Hospital Centres). The former are organised around so-called 'transversal' oncology, the latter around 'organ oncology'. In the CLCCs, the disease approach is transversal and transdisciplinary; linked to the idea of cancer as a condition that 'transcends the organ' (Tursz, 2004: 30), this vision extends to taking into account the global well-being of the patient, including post-disease follow-up, psychological well-being and palliative care. A form of holistic support is also offered in university hospitals. The CLCCs had a central role in the management of cancer until the 1960s. Then, between the 1970s and 1980s, the CHUs took on major importance. From the 1990s, thanks to several factors, including the development of research and the partnership with the League against Cancer, the CLCCs regained a predominant role in the treatment of cancer (Castel and Friedberg, 2010; Sifer-Rivière, 2012). The interviews which I conducted in France showed that the first medical professional whom women contact when they find a suspicious lump, or seek information about breast screening, is often the GP or the gynaecologist. If further tests are needed, these types of doctors can refer patients to a specialised centre, and this might be a CLCC or a CHU. The patients whom I met in France were treated in both types of facilities, and their opinion of the quality of care received did not seem to be related to the nature of the facility (CLCC or CHU) but, rather, to the approach of the medical staff.

In the different institutions, patients can have a first contact either with a surgeon or with an oncologist. In the French part of my research, I focused on the Île-de-France region, where almost all of the patients interviewed lived. Île-de-France is one of the wealthiest areas in France, and the population can generally have access to high-quality establishments and services. However, in France, like in the UK and Italy, geographical disparities in healthcare provision exist, and they seem to develop along the centre–periphery axis.

Authorisations and cost of oncological drugs

The panorama of oncological therapies since the 1980s has seen the inclusion of numerous new treatments (see Chapter 3 for more details), and a considerable part of them are intended for the treatment of breast cancer. One of the salient features of the new drugs is their high cost. Historically, the UK has been among the countries where pharmaceutical companies had relative freedom in establishing the price of new drugs, while in France and Italy the prices have been negotiated. In the UK, the Pharmaceutical Price Regulation Scheme defines the limits to the price of drugs in relation to capital investment; the NICE evaluation then decides whether the price/effects relation justifies the coverage of the cost of the new drug. The result is a higher incidence, when compared to France and Italy, of non-coverage of new drugs (see Jommi, 2015). To limit the negative impact that this situation can have on cancer patients, in 2010, the UK government introduced additional funds dedicated to the purchase of oncological drugs, the Cancer Drugs Fund (CDF), which is managed on a local level. In 2014 the nature of the CDF was modified, the use of these funds was aligned with the NICE guidelines and the role of the fund is now mainly to offer access to treatments for which the NICE assessment has given uncertain results. According to some commentators, although the CDF has been the result of strong public and political pressure to align the UK with other countries of the Global North in terms of access to treatments, the results it has produced in terms of improved survival are minimal because '[t]he majority of CDF-approved indications have been based on studies that reported minimal to no benefit in survival' (Aggarwal et al., 2017: 1746). Another essential element that characterises the UK is that from 2020 onwards the country is no longer a member of the EU. One consequence of Brexit is that the British regulatory agency, the Medicines and Healthcare products Regulatory Agency (MHRA), is no longer under the remit of the European Medicines Agency (EMA). In 2022, the MHRA approved eleven cancer drugs, a number very close to the twelve approved by EMA and US Food and Drug Administration in the same period, so the approach to new drugs in the UK seems to be still aligned with that of other countries. However, it is difficult to predict how this new situation will affect future decisions regarding the approval of new drugs in the UK (Lancet Oncology, 2023).

In France and Italy, new drug prices are negotiated with the regulatory institutions and the drugs are classified according to their innovativeness (the improved results in trials when compared to the drugs currently used). However, in France, innovativeness is established separately from the negotiation itself and influences both the market price (in a logic of higher return on invested capital for highly innovative drugs) and the part of the cost not covered by health insurance. The French system is generally considered generous and has rarely attracted public criticism as NICE has (Drummond et al., 2014); however, the constant increase in the prices of oncological drugs is considered a problem for the stability of the reimbursement system (Guillot, 2017). Despite different evaluation mechanisms between the UK and France, there are indications that a more stringent evaluation of the benefits of new drugs is also beginning in France (Drummond et al., 2014). In Italy, the assessment of innovativeness and the negotiation are conducted by the same authority (*Agenzia*

Italiana del Farmaco/Italian Medicines Agency), which has more discretion in negotiating the final price. For Italy, the cost of cancer drugs also represents a significant and growing part of the overall medical expenditure. It has been suggested that more stringent criteria should be introduced to define what drugs represent a relevant therapeutic innovation so as to reduce the financial pressure on governments, especially in countries like Italy, that in the last years have tried to reduce their expenditures (Andria et al., 2013). Several medical professionals whom I met during the fieldwork also questioned the long-term financial sustainability of targeted therapies.

Among the proposed solutions is the use of biosimilar medicines, biological drugs similar to an original one, the patent of which has expired. Biosimilars are not a perfect replica of the original treatment, but they generally offer the same results with reduced costs. Since 2004 the EMA has had a regulatory framework for biosimilars, and European countries have approved the highest number of biosimilar drugs in the world (Patel et al., 2018). However, this seems to be a solution that can only partially contain the problem of the increasing cost of anti-cancer therapies. Biosimilars are based on much larger molecules than traditional generics, and efforts to reduce the costs are hindered by the complexity of the approval process and the original developers' claims to ownership of development data even after the patent on the drug has expired (Greene and Riggs, 2015; Greene, 2018). Moreover, one of the main problems, as we will see later, is the incremental nature of the benefits brought by the new drugs (Bouvenot, 2018). The presence of new and increasingly expensive drugs impacts on not only public finances but also the everyday management of disease by medical professionals, and patient experiences. As we will see in Chapter 3, this situation has a significant impact, especially in the case of breast cancer, for which numerous treatments are available.

Assemblages of treatments and navigating healthcare systems

The organisation of the different healthcare systems presented in the preceding sections allows us to understand better the similarities and differences between the three countries. One of the ways in which different forms of healthcare organisations can shape patients' experiences is by defining how the patients move from one treatment to the next and whether and how they move between facilities and specialists.[5] These experiences can be understood through two different approaches, although with significant overlaps between them.

The first approach is to consider the practices of navigation of the healthcare system: what the patients need to do to access the different diagnostic and treatment services. Navigation can be extremely difficult in low-resource contexts (e.g., Molina and Palazuelos, 2014) or for categories excluded from healthcare, such as the uninsured or under-insured in healthcare contexts without universal coverage (e.g., Getrich et al., 2018) or categories of migrants without the right to healthcare (e.g., Larchanché, 2012). Navigating healthcare systems can also be difficult for groups subject to frequent discrimination, such as trans people (Edmiston, 2018). However, even when healthcare resources are available, and patients have a right to access them and are not discriminated against, navigating healthcare systems involves significant work that can influence the illness experience. Working on rural Missouri, Hunleth and Steinmetz (2022) have argued that such experiences should be understood as social navigation (Vigh, 2009), i.e. as the encounter between a dynamic social context of healthcare provision and conditionality of access, and patients with their own fluctuating resources.

The second approach includes considering the type of mobility: patients have to physically move to reach the place in which they receive diagnosis and treatment, and often the different steps can be in different locations. International movements for health reasons have attracted the most attention, and medical travels or medical migrations have been explored in a large number of works (e.g., Kangas, 2002; Whittaker et al., 2010; Roberts and Scheper-Hughes, 2011). Several analyses of the phenomenon (Sobo, 2009; Whittaker et al., 2010; Roberts and Scheper-Hughes, 2011) have explored the social inequalities and individual experiences of suffering characterising medical travel and have produced a nuanced picture of the phenomenon that contradicts the idea that people moving abroad for health reasons are only medical tourists looking for places where they can undergo elective and cosmetic procedures, paying lower prices than they would do in their country of origin (Sobo et al., 2011). However, mid-range intra-national mobilities, between regions or cities but still within national borders, also involve significant work (e.g. Vindrola-Padros and Brage, 2016; Greco, 2019), and even short-range micro-mobilities (Vindrola-Padros and Johnson, 2017), for example within the same urban area, add to the effort of navigating healthcare and dealing with an illness. Further, while healthcare is mostly organised through patients' mobility, the mobility of medical professionals can also be important (cf. Dalstrom, 2013), as I discuss in this section, particularly in the UK. As I have discussed elsewhere (Greco, 2019; 2021), the reasons for the mobilities of patients, and the aims they pursue while navigating healthcare systems, can be understood in terms of logics. Following Mol's (2008) distinction between a logic of choice and a logic of care on the part of medical professionals, in my analysis logics can be understood as categories of aims that patients try to pursue within their therapeutic trajectories. Such logics and aims can also be understood as different approaches which patients can follow to take care of their health, for example seeking professionals and institutions they consider more capable and trustworthy (logic of cure), with whom they can have a better relationship (logic of care), or pursuing the treatment they consider most appropriate to them (logic of choice).

Organisational elements within specific healthcare systems can define the breadth of both mobility and navigation. The movement of patients across the territory is generally discouraged in the UK, which limits the choices available to patients. In the French or Italian context, patients are freer to move between provinces/departments or regions, and this extends the combinations of services and specialists that patients can use. The standardisation of patients' pathways attempts to reduce the navigation work of patients, but such standardisation is usually more straightforward in contexts in which patients' choice is limited through the referral system (and, in any case, some degree of navigation on the patient's part is always necessary). Further, the presence of a relevant private healthcare sector (as in Italy and France), along with the public healthcare system and the possibility of accessing experimental treatments, can complicate the navigation (Besle and Sarradon-Eck, 2022).

In my fieldwork, intra-national mobility, particularly in the Italian context, has emerged as an important component of patients' illness experiences. As mentioned, patients in the UK have limited choice as to which public healthcare institutions they can be treated in. For some patients, the simple access to cancer screening may be limited by the GP acting as gatekeeper (Greco, 2020a). While these decisions are certainly motivated by the desire to preserve the sustainability of the medical system, they can be stressful for patients. In France, there is a wider choice, but, as my interviewees were living in the capital Île-de-France region, they had little interest in being treated in a different region, and their movements were intraregional, often between private and public facilities.

As discussed above, in Italy, territorial inequalities are one of the main factors structuring patient mobility (Greco, 2016a; 2019). Differently from other contexts in which cancer treatments are available, but concentrated in specific regions (e.g. Vindrola-Padros and Brage, 2016), in Italy the standard range of treatments for breast cancer is available across the national territory. Despite this, several interviewees moved to another city or region, especially for their tumourectomy or mastectomy, rather than undergo the operation at the closest hospital offering cancer treatments. It is important to underline that internal mobility to obtain health services is a phenomenon affecting not only the southern regions but also the northern regions. What changes is the type of mobility: in the regions of the north, movements are mainly between neighbouring regions.

The most common logic behind such mobility was a logic of cure: patients were looking for institutions and medical professionals that inspired more confidence, attempting to improve the outcome of their treatments (Greco, 2019; 2021). I have already discussed how the geographic and symbolic inequalities linked to the southern question are a major structuring dimension of the Italian healthcare system and how they fuel health-related mobility within the country, particularly from the south to the north. The interviewees whom I met in Italy gave different meanings to their mobilities. I met patients both in the north (Emilia-Romagna) and in the south (Apulia) who had had part of their treatments in a different city or region. However, for the interviewees in the south, moving for treatments was considered 'normal' and part of consolidated practices, while it was more unusual for the interviewees in the north. One of the consequences was that the same distance in kilometres (for example, from one province to another) was described as 'having moved' by interviewees in the north, and as having been treated locally by those in the south, for whom only 'going north' was considered proper mobility. Further, the interviewees in the south who stayed close to home to be treated often discussed the advantages and the capacities of the local doctors, as they felt they had to justify their choice (Greco, 2019). The case of south–north mobility in Italy shows how internal inequalities in healthcare – even when they do not impact on the availability of specific treatments – or 'postcode lotteries' can significantly shape illness experience, especially when intersecting with wider social inequalities and territorial stigma. Along with the logic of cure, however, my interviewees in Italy, and more so in France, presented a second logic: to find not only a capable doctor but also one they could talk with and who could give them attention and respect – a logic of care (Greco, 2021).[6] In the case of French interviewees, the micro-mobility between different institutions, including both public and private ones, was also driven by the logic of choice (Greco, 2021), in particular, to access specific reconstruction techniques.

In the UK, while the referral system limited patients' mobility, there was still something similar to a managed mobility, both of patients and of medical professionals. The organisation of cancer treatments was more often decentralised: while diagnosis, surgery and radiotherapy were concentrated in a smaller number of hospitals, chemotherapy teams were posted from specialised institutions to a number of hospitals that otherwise did not have an oncology department. In that way, patients could limit their micro-mobility, undergoing closer to home a part of the patient pathway that entails several appointments. As Sandra,[7] a British nurse, explained during the interview:

> They [a Foundation Trust specialised in cancer] commissioned us to provide on their behalf. They give us a block of money, and we provide on their behalf, and they send the doctors out here, [because] as a patient that's a lot of travelling to do. So we try and do as much as possible here.

For patients, navigating the healthcare system was linked to micro-mobility and, in some cases, to mid-range mobilities, but it did not stop there. Having collected interviews relative to different contexts, and in a number of cases with experience going back several years, I encountered instances in which making the link between the different steps in the diagnosis and treatment was entirely left to the patient. Claudia, an Italian patient diagnosed with breast cancer at a very young age, told me that after the diagnosis, the only indication she had received was to contact the oncology department, and she recalled that the lack of a clear pathway had increased the anxiety related to the diagnosis:

> There was no link. They told me to go to oncology … They gave me a photocopied sheet and told me to go to oncology. And then everything happened from there: in the two following days […] starting from there, within 24 hours I went to Mantua and then to Pisa. Meanwhile, [the oncologist in Mantua] he was a physician, he told me: 'You should know that, whatever the diagnosis, there will be another surgical intervention,' and he wisely told me: 'Start looking for a surgeon.' And so the next stage was to go to Pisa, because some friends had recommended a surgeon there.

As emerges from this excerpt, Claudia built a personalised and interregional treatment pathway based on the advice she received from medical professionals and friends. As mentioned, patients in Italy have a greater freedom to move, as compared to the UK; however, the downside is that the responsibility for organising this personalised pathway falls on the patients and their families, or, as in the case of Claudia, their friends. The opposite of such an approach are structured patient pathways, which standardise the steps to take, depending on the patient's profile, as well as the location in which each diagnostic, treatment and follow-up should occur. Internal movements are increasingly codified in standardised pathways, especially in the UK; however, more complex situations, such as those of patients with metastatic breast cancer, are more difficult to fit into a standardised pathway. Viney and colleagues (2022) have shown how, from the point of view of breast cancer services, the segmentation of treatments, innovations in treatments (and the delay in incorporating them fully into protocols and pathways) and lack of capacity in specific services mean that medical professionals need to tinker actively so that patients can complete their pathways. Literature focusing on other types of cancer (e.g., Llewellyn et al., 2018, on brain cancer) has further shown how the patient pathways are often approximations that do not capture the complex trajectories that patients actually follow.

I met some interviewees for whom the diagnosis of metastasis, among other more important issues, also meant changing medical professionals and losing the established points of reference. Camilla, a British patient in her early forties who had received a diagnosis of metastatic breast cancer several years after her diagnosis of early-stage breast cancer, said that for the metastatic disease she was treated not in the breast care unit but in general oncology, and that the change was very difficult for her:

> As soon as you are re-diagnosed with secondary [in my hospital] you go back straight to the oncology department where you are with everyone for all types of cancer, so all the people that I have got to know [for the previous diagnosis] I didn't have access to those people anymore and that was another loss.

Camilla's experience shows the limits of a healthcare pathway that can work if there is a clear sequence of treatments for a patient to follow, as in the case of early-stage breast cancer. But the path for patients with metastatic breast cancer is more complex and less straightforward, and patients can feel isolated as less support is available for them.

The search for innovative treatments, whether through clinical trials or through ordinary use of newly introduced (and not always fully approved for public coverage) drugs, required the patients, as well as their treating doctors, to combine different options.[8] In France and Italy, the possibility of changing medical professionals or institutions, discussed above, also brought complex bricolage-assemblages beyond the standardised pathway. Finally, the elective component of breast cancer treatments, breast reconstruction, brought a significant complexity to the navigation of the healthcare system. Among the interviewees whom I met and who underwent reconstruction, especially in France, several navigated complex choices between different available reconstructive techniques. In many cases, this also involved a search, often prolonged, of institutions that offered the specific technique and surgeons who were both able and willing to use that specific technique for their case (Greco, 2020b). In some cases, the navigation and the negotiation did not apply only to the elective reconstruction, as I also met patients who struggled to obtain a diagnosis, especially when they suspected a relapse or a metastatic development (Greco, 2020a).

The aspects discussed here show some of the different assemblages linked to breast cancer. While the standardisation of treatments connects the patients' bodies with specific organisational schemas, gaps and rigidity in the actual implementation of the pathway (organisational assemblages) and patients' own initiatives to pursue a desired outcome produce further bricolage-assemblages. In these cases, patients assemble their treatment trajectory, either to fill in blind points in a pathway or to seek specific results. In both cases, patients further need to mobilise different forms of capital – cultural capital to decipher information; social capital that can help reach specific medical professionals and/or help from one's personal network; economic capital to access techniques that come with an individual cost, as well as to manage costs associated with micro-mobilities.

Conclusion

Marchesi (1999), in his analysis of *Caro Diario*, underlines how, in *Medici*, the detailed narration of the facts does not show the 'achievement of an order' and, the critic continues, the chapter 'remains a path between discrete events, between data of a reality that seems to escape any definition' (Marchesi, 1999: 79). The choice not to transform the story into a 'progressive account' illustrates the disorientation with which patients often move within the medical system. In this chapter, I have shown how disorientation is an element that characterises the experience of many patients, not only in Italy but also in France and the UK. Creating standardised healthcare pathways is only a partial response to this disorientation; a fundamental element influencing how patients navigate the medical system is the resources available to patients (as we will see also in Chapter 3). In the US, where health insurances dominate the for-profit healthcare system, a 'low health-insurance literacy', that is, a limited knowledge of how to navigate the insurance system, can negatively impact on health outcomes (see Williams et al., 2020). In the countries I have studied, private insurances are significantly less present or play a less important role. However, while the British, Italian and French healthcare systems are still universal, this chapter has discussed the presence of different forms of privatisation in these three countries. In Italy, there is a strong integration between private and public services. In France, the presence of medical insurances can push some breast cancer patients towards the private sector, in particular for breast reconstruction. The NHS is also gradually creating separate routes for patients willing to pay (see also Chapter 3).

Moreover, universal systems are not necessarily easy to navigate, and the availability of financial resources and the opportunity to learn about the functioning of the healthcare system were also crucial for the women I interviewed. In this case, the resources that patients employ are varied. In Italy, they moved along a north–south axis of the country, trying to circumvent the actual or perceived disparities between the south and north. However, many women also moved between regions to consult different doctors and try to put together therapeutic pathways that met their needs. French patients also moved between different institutions, often combining public and private provision. British patients also implemented, as far as possible, forms of mobility and re-assemblage of care through bricolage. Healthcare systems, already the product of global and local organisational assemblages of biomedical knowledge (Collier and Ong 2007; Ong 2016), require a different kind of assemblage on the part of patients to navigate and access the different treatments available. These bricolage-assemblages of knowledge and information, and rearrangements of the available care, serve mainly to overcome the limitations of systems increasingly subject to cuts.

In 2020, following the acute phase of the COVID-19 pandemic, healthcare systems experienced great strain. Patients who started their cancer treatments with months of delay or had difficulties contacting overworked professionals and congested facilities have attracted public attention. The problems that exploded forcefully during the pandemic were not new. They had already emerged in the stories of the patients whom I met in the decade covered in my research projects. It is difficult to say how these problems will be addressed, whether European universal healthcare systems will see an increase in resources to maintain their universal approach, or if policy decisions will accelerate the already existing forms of privatisation, thus aligning European universal healthcare systems with the US model, as Roderick and Pollock (2022) suggest. What seems clear is that learning how these systems work is pivotal for patients in Europe as well. This is an often invisible work that adds to the heavy burden of dealing with cancer, negatively affecting the lives of patients. As I will discuss in the next chapter, public discourses are an essential factor in shaping the landscape of breast cancer.

I will show, in particular, how patients respond collectively and individually to the organisation of treatments and the cultural discourses about breast cancer.

Notes

1 The Health and Social Care Act of 2012 divided the territory into several NHS local bodies, the Clinical Commissioning Groups (CCGs), responsible for delivering healthcare services in the designated area (Checkland et al., 2013). However, the Health and Care Act of 2022 abolished the CCGs and replaced them with the Integrated Care System (ICS) model discussed in this section.
2 See NHS Choice Framework, January 2020, https://www.gov.uk/government/publications/the-nhs-choice-framework/the-nhs-choice-framework-what-choices-are-available-to-me-in-the-nhs (accessed 8 August 2024), where it is stated that patients may not have a choice when 'in need of emergency or urgent treatment, such as cancer services where you must be seen in a maximum waiting time of 2 weeks'.
3 Cf. www.bma.org.uk/advice-and-support/nhs-delivery-and-workforce/integration/integrated-care-systems-icss (accessed 8 August 2024)
4 The translation from the French of this extract is mine, as are all the other translations in the book, unless otherwise stated.
5 I have discussed the health-related mobilities and the navigation of healthcare systems that patients with breast cancer experience in Italy and France in more detail in Greco (2019; 2021).
6 Hunleth and Steinmetz (2022) also show different logics among their interviewees. Patients in that case mostly showed a logic of access (in the US, mainly using the institutions which one's insurance provides cover), but in some cases they also avoided some rural medical professionals because of lack of trust in their competence or because they demanded an excessively deferential attitude from patients.
7 All the names used for interviewees are pseudonyms.
8 It is important to note that clinical trials are becoming a relevant segment of the treatments that many cancer patients can receive (see Kerr et al., 2021 for an overview of the role of clinical trials in the UK; Arteaga Pérez, 2022a and Llewellyn, 2022 for, respectively, colorectal and brain cancer). Clinical trials can also be important for patients with metastatic breast cancer; however, they are less relevant for early-stage breast cancer patients, whose treatments mostly include established and effective drugs.

2

The cultural landscape of breast cancer

At the beginning of my fieldwork, a colleague who knew of my work on breast cancer sent me a link to the website of David Jay, a fashion photographer and author of the SCAR – Surviving Cancer: Absolute Reality – Project (www.thescarproject.org/). This photographic project aims to provide an honest image of breast cancer by portraying women with reconstructed breasts or asymmetrical bodies following a mastectomy (Jay, 2012). The photos were intense and honest, and it is no wonder the project earned the artist a Pulitzer Prize nomination (Ryan, 2011). But, following the link I had just received, one detail caught my attention, the subtitle: 'Breast cancer is not a pink ribbon'. It occurred to me at that moment that that phrase, so meaningful to me, would make no sense to my mother and the many older women in my family who, while being well aware of the harsh reality of breast cancer, did not know why a pink ribbon should have anything to do with it. In the space of a generation, a semantic and iconographic shift has taken place, completely altering the way the disease is perceived. The SCAR project is not the first example of photos showing the traces of breast cancer. In 1993, for example, the *New York Times Magazine* published 'Beauty Out of Damage', a picture in which the US artist Matuschka showed her asymmetrical body and that is now considered one the most powerful images of breast cancer (Petersen and Matuschka, 2004). However, in David Jay's project there is a direct reference to the pink ribbon, and the photos are intended to contrast with the glamorous image of the disease that this symbol evokes.

In 1992 a pink ribbon became the symbol of Breast Cancer Awareness Month, with the cosmetics company Estée Lauder producing over 1.5 million ribbons to be distributed as a visual reminder to accompany the simple message conveyed in awareness campaigns: that early diagnosis saves lives (Selleck, 2010).[1] Since then, the pink ribbon has become a metonymy for breast cancer. Even though these events are deeply embedded in North American biomedical and cultural history, the spillover has been global. The pink ribbon is also a powerful reminder of how neoliberal ideology infiltrates biomedicine and healthcare as it evokes a specific construction of breast cancer in which patients remain consumers, especially of products that enhance femininity and traditional roles within the family (King, 2006). The pink aesthetic invokes not only a particular way of presenting breast cancer but also a way of mobilising public opinion against the disease – by participating in races and buying products painted in pink (Sulik, 2011). Activism and participation in community activities centred on breast cancer are part of the resources that patients can mobilise. Some groups explicitly reject the pink rhetoric, but, as we will see, some can use it superficially and instrumentally. Moreover, the history of health activism unfolds in different ways in different countries, shaping the perception of the disease and opportunities for action (see, e.g., Klawiter, 2008 for the US; Knobé, 2009 for France; Porroche-Escudero, 2014 for Spain; Batt, 2017 for Canada; and Hamarat, 2020 for Belgium).

In the previous chapter, I explored how healthcare contexts shape breast cancer experiences. In this one, I discuss the cultural discourses on breast cancer, the different kinds of associative work around the disease and how individual women negotiate hegemonic cultural images of breast cancer. I explore such negotiations through the concept of cultural-political assemblage. The other kinds of assemblage explored in this book are all, to a certain degree, both cultural and political. However, with this term, I am focusing on the cultural politics of breast cancer (e.g., Nielsen, 2019), that is, on how public discourses on breast cancer, including those beyond the biomedical realm, are negotiated both collectively and individually. Previous analyses have dealt with political assemblages as a way to conceive collective action beyond both formal and identity politics (e.g., Amironsei and Bialecki, 2017). Breast cancer-related movements have been the object of several analyses, mostly focusing on North America (e.g., Klawiter, 2008; Ley, 2009). Here, I also analyse how associations with varying degrees of politicisation negotiate the discourses of breast cancers and how individual patients choose to what degree to participate in this kind of collective action. The associative context indeed can itself be considered a product of the cultural-political assemblage between the sick body and local cultural systems, and for patients the associations can represent a way of rearranging their own biographical assemblage in relation to the experiences of other patients.

While, in the last decade, the pink rhetoric has received many criticisms, this does not mean that moralistic injunctions around cancer have disappeared. After all, as Sontag (1978) showed over forty years ago, our understanding of cancer has been filtered through metaphors of repression, but also of 'idleness' and opulence, and it is difficult not to read in this the reference to the contemporary debate around lifestyle and cancer. The contemporary injunction to self-improvement taps into this cultural imaginary and redefines the moral boundaries of cancer. Here I am interested in exploring how rhetorics around breast cancer are adapted and transformed in Europe and how they affect the experiences of patients living with breast cancer.

The pink ribbon comes to Europe

The fortunes of the pink ribbon are strongly linked to the US Susan G. Komen Foundation, one of the most prominent breast cancer associations. Founded in 1982 by Nancy Brinker, the Foundation is named after Brinker's sister, who died of breast cancer in 1980, at the age of thirty-six. The Susan G. Komen Foundation is praised for being one of the first organisations to have spoken explicitly about breast cancer at a time when women and their families were living the disease in silence. Komen's activities aim to reduce mortality by increasing early detection of the disease, and the Foundation has been a leading advocate for expanding breast cancer screening programmes in the US. The success and longevity of the Komen Foundation can be attributed to its ability to spread the simple and optimistic message that early detection can save lives and to promote prevention campaigns (see Braun, 2003). Since the beginning, the Foundation has organised fundraising activities, including the well-known Race for the Cure, the first edition of which took place in October 1983, before October became Breast Cancer Awareness Month in 1985. Another aspect that has played a pivotal role in its success is the partnership with various businesses – from cosmetics companies to car manufacturers to airline companies – which, over the years, have spread the simple message of 'prevention' (Braun, 2003; Selleck, 2010). By donating a portion of their proceeds to breast cancer research, these groups have presented a charitable and progressive image to customers through a process known as 'pink-washing' – a term coined by the grassroots association Breast Cancer Action.[2] This definition refers to a specific aesthetic of breast cancer, characterised by the omnipresence of the pink colour and the pink ribbon, which has gradually taken hold. Several analyses have criticised such an approach, defined as cause-related marketing, in which social problems, such as breast cancer, become a marketing strategy to sell products of all kinds, from cosmetics to cars to detergents. In particular, these forms of associationism have been linked to the general backlash against feminism that characterised the late 1980s and the 1990s (King, 2006). This interpretation of the phenomenon helps us to understand how cause-related marketing strategies contribute to extending the expectations that a patriarchal society imposes on women in their everyday life – to be excellent wives and mothers without forgetting to be attractive – to the oncological context so as to build a gendered image of breast cancer (Sulik, 2011). Moreover, the message of optimism and the emphasis on the benefits of early diagnosis excludes the experiences of women with metastatic breast cancer (Sulik, 2014; Davis, 2016). However, this latter point is changing, and, as we will see in Chapter 3, public messages about breast cancer are starting to address the metastatic stage of the disease.

Other breast cancer organisations have challenged the simplistic discourses that emphasise prevention through early detection, overshadowing the environmental causes of breast cancer and the discriminations based on race, class and gender that the disease highlights (Klawiter, 2008). Among the associations promoting a critical stance on breast cancer, one of the most prominent is Breast Cancer Action (BCA; see Klawiter, 2008; De Michele, 2016). Under the direction of the late Barbara Brenner, BCA has led initiatives exposing how cause-related marketing involves brands whose products – such as food containing hormones linked to breast cancer and cars fuelling environmental pollution – increase the risk of developing breast cancer. The activities of BCA have been instrumental in deconstructing the pink-washing phenomenon.

If the pink ribbon rhetoric and the imposition of an optimistic tone surrounding breast cancer originated in the US, they have spread quickly in other countries (see, for example, the analysis of Porroche-Escudero, 2014 for Spain). The Komen Foundation has established local chapters in a number of countries, and the Race for the Cure has involved millions of participants worldwide (Braun, 2003). October is now internationally recognised as Breast Cancer Awareness Month, and initiatives, often characterised by the colour pink and pink ribbons, are spread worldwide.

In Italy, where Komen has a national chapter, the Race for the Cure takes place in various Italian cities at different times of the year, with the involvement of local groups and the creation of prevention programmes. Always in Italy, several companies use breast cancer to boost their sales. In France and Italy, a number of public monuments are illuminated in pink in October, following the example of initiatives already widespread in the US. As in the US, these forms of activism have also generated criticism and negative reactions in Western Europe.[3] In France, for example, a part of public opinion is critical of exploiting a disease for commercial purposes and using simplistic messages that push women to have a mammogram by making them feel guilty (Omrane and Mignot, 2018). Similarly, research conducted in 2015 showed that Italian consumers tend to perceive cause-related marketing negatively (Schoier and de Luca, 2017).

However, in Europe there are several types of associations against breast cancer and cancer in general (see, e.g., Knobé, 2009 for an analysis of the situation in France), and in several instances the pink ribbon rhetoric and aesthetics were not simply imported, but have been adapted to the local contexts. Several patients whom I met in France mentioned the work of the association *Vivre comme avant*, a branch of the Reach to Recovery Association, founded in the US in 1953. The women volunteering in this group have all experienced the disease at first hand, and they share their experiences to support women who have just received the diagnosis. The main activities of *Vivre comme avant* are hospital visits to support patients facing treatments and out-of-hospital support to patients who turn to the association, responding to their doubts and questions about treatments or other aspects of the disease. Another association that plays an important role in France and Italy (and elsewhere in Europe) is Europa Donna, created in Milan in 1994 following an idea of the Italian oncologist Umberto Veronesi (see Chapters 4 and 5). The priority of this association includes the 'harmonization of standards of treatment throughout Europe, emphasis on education and training for health professionals, increases in research funding, and increased diffusion of screening programs' (Buchanan et al., 2004: 148). Europa Donna also offers phone support and organises information meetings for patients. During the interviews with metastatic patients, it emerged that Europa Donna was among the first to bring attention to metastatic breast cancer.

Alongside these larger associations, in both countries several small groups have been established with a specific rooting in local areas (see Mosconi and Kodraliu, 1999 for the Italian case). As I will discuss in the next section, these groups support patient needs on a local level. Further, some of these smaller groups are organised around specific aspects of the treatment pathway. Smaller groups can, for example, focus on disseminating information around specific reconstruction techniques, and their efforts are directed toward making a specific technique available in the national area and supporting patients pursuing that reconstructive approach. There are also groups focused on changing some aspects of the social perception of breast cancer, such as raising public awareness regarding the choice not to carry out a reconstruction (Greco, 2016c; Fortier, 2020).

The British context is more strongly characterised by large national cancer organisations, usually registered as charities (cf. Allsop et al., 2004). Along with the more common role of funding research (particularly Cancer Research UK), cancer charities in the UK are notable for more direct intervention in providing services. Macmillan Cancer Support and the Marie Curie charity fund nurse posts directly, while Maggie's funds support centres. Several patients and medical professionals have highlighted the role of such centres – usually located close to hospitals specialised in cancer care, and characterised by warm and welcoming architectures (Martin et al., 2019). They offer a place for patients to relax and meet others going through the same experience, but they can also offer advice on practical matters such as how to claim benefits.

In the field of breast cancer, the main national charities in the UK (Breakthrough Breast Cancer, Breast Cancer Campaign and Breast Cancer Care) have undergone a series of mergers, forming the current Breast Cancer Now. Charities in the UK have historically been central in funding and shaping cancer research (see Gibbon, 2007, who also noted how most of the fundraising advocates she met were relatives of patients) and in bringing attention to the disease in the social and political arena. Although these charities have used the pink ribbon imagery in some of their campaigns, the UK's associative landscape seems to have retained its identity and has never fully adopted the message from the US.[4] Outside the national charities, patient activism and advocacy are represented mainly by specific advocacy groups (such as MET UP UK, for metastatic breast cancer), with a further space created by requirements for patient involvement, which has led to individual NHS Trusts creating their own patient advisory groups.

In the three countries, it can be difficult to map the rich associative panorama, since many small groups are linked to the efforts of a few patients, and these groups can sometimes be active for only a short time. Nonetheless, smaller, local initiatives are pivotal in supporting women living with breast cancer. They can offer tailored information and support and help women find a network that includes other breast cancer patients. Some of these groups may tap into a pink aesthetic without necessarily sharing its values or messages, simply exploiting the metonymic value of a colour or a symbol that, in the public imagination, is immediately associated with breast cancer. Given the variety of associations and groups, patients can often contact several for different purposes and at different moments of their experience, as we will see in the following sections.

Changes and adaptation: how women navigate the associative landscape

Associations and support groups act at multiple levels and are organised differently in the three countries, albeit with similarities, as seen in the previous section. Here, I focus on how patients use, combine and innovate the different forms of advocacy and support available to them. As we have seen, in addition to the more prominent associations organising national initiatives, numerous local groups pursue different aims through different activities. The participation of patients in association activities can take several forms. A first and essential distinction is between activities in which patients have an active advocacy role (which can range from promoting a specific treatment to more general political positions about the disease) and activities in which patients benefit from services aimed at improving their experience of illness.[5] The profiles of these two activities can overlap, and the social and political organisation of the healthcare system can also influence their distribution. In France,[6] I have encountered both types of involvement, while in Italy and the UK, I have mostly encountered patients focused on sharing and receiving information about the functioning of the healthcare system and on how to manage some aspects of their disease.

Local groups often aim to create a place where patients can meet to reduce the isolation that can be part of the breast cancer experience. During my fieldwork, I met several women volunteering in smaller groups, like Marguerite, a woman in her late fifties and member of a group located in a suburban area on the outskirts of Paris. Marguerite told me that the *bénévoles* (volunteers) carry out various support activities, including visiting patients in hospital. During the interview, the woman told me that at the moment the group was preparing to stage a theatrical piece for *Octobre rose* (Pink October, the name given in France to Breast Cancer Awareness Month), the aim of which was to '*dedramatiser le cancer*', that is, to defuse the dramatic tones around breast cancer, but also to offer information on prevention and treatments. The members of the association highly appreciated the initiative, and what mattered most, according to Marguerite, was that they were creating a welcoming and engaging space 'so that people have a reason to get out'. Marguerite underlined the convivial and relaxed atmosphere that the association offered. Although the event that the group was preparing was part of the *Octobre rose* activities, the Breast Cancer Awareness Month seemed just an excuse to engage the women in the association and allow them to work towards a common goal.

For many, participation in advocacy activities was motivated by a willingness to 'use' their illness experience to offer support and improve the medical services for breast cancer. This came out clearly in my French fieldwork, as I observed the meetings of a project established by a Parisian medical institution that aimed to improve communication on mastectomy and reconstruction options by producing new informative tools for patients. The participation of the patients who, meeting after meeting, presented their experiences, proved to be central in shaping the new communication strategies and materials. Among the changes introduced were the choice to no longer define mastectomy as mutilation and new communication strategies that include understanding why women do not undergo reconstruction, including cases in which they come to terms with an asymmetrical body (Greco, 2016c).

To fully understand the advantages and limitations of patients' advocacy, it is important to analyse the imbalance that the collaboration between patients and medical professionals can produce. As mentioned, some smaller advocacy groups can revolve around specific aspects of the medical pathway, such as the associations promoting specific reconstruction techniques. Women in such associations wanted to support others in obtaining the best reconstructive option. However, volunteers often worked closely with surgeons and other medical professionals. The alliances between doctors and patients were organised according to an unbalanced and gendered division of roles. For example, it was made explicit that the information volunteers gave could not replace a medical consultation. Medical professionals were those with expert, 'objective' knowledge, while volunteers shared their 'experience', which was presented as a partial, limited expertise from which no general inference could be derived.

For some patients, participation in such activities can be a way to rediscover some forms of sociality altered by the disease. Several cancer groups and charities met these needs by offering a range of patient-focused activities such as Pilates, gentle gymnastics, Nordic walking or forms of psychological support. Many women whom I interviewed in France participated in and often benefited from these workshops. For many, these dedicated activities represented a way to confront aspects of the disease, obtain information and meet people with similar experiences. However, these initiatives also offered the opportunity to try out new activities, such as theatre and other forms of artistic production, that could bring some solace in a difficult moment. Brigitte, a French woman in her late fifties (whose story I discuss more in detail in Chapter 5), had a great passion for sewing and knitting. Through an association, she participated in a project that involved the creation of dresses for asymmetrical bodies. The engagement in this project, the woman told me, was an essential step in addressing the physical changes caused by the surgery.

Sally, a British woman diagnosed in her thirties, told me that she decided to participate in a conference organised by a breast cancer charity dedicated to young patients with breast cancer because most patients in the clinic where she was being treated were significantly older than her. She felt the need to exchange with women who, like her, were dealing with cancer while supporting a young family. Sally described the conference as a positive experience because it allowed her to connect with women in a similar situation who could help and support each other. After the diagnosis, Sally decided to launch a website with medical information and to use social media to create spaces for discussion between women. During the interview, Sally repeatedly emphasised how her online activism aimed to create new spaces where people could talk and offer peer-to-peer support. Several interviewees have underlined the importance of being able to share their experience with women in the same situation. For example, Franca, an Italian woman in her mid-forties, said that she felt welcomed in the association in Northern Italy where I met her:

> [the association] is a point of reference, you feel welcomed, the women there give you advice, they understand, you don't need to give a detailed story. The association is a place where you can go if you need something because maybe they can give you advice, they can tell you: 'see that person, do this or do [it] there, that's what happened to me'.

Franca underlined how it might be easier to talk to people who share the same experience and understand the difficulties without her necessarily having to provide too many details about her condition. But the women whom she met at the association could also advise on specialists to consult and facilities to contact (knowing the 'right' specialist is particularly emphasised in the Italian context – Greco, 2019). During these meetings, patients exchange their experiences on the type of therapy they are undergoing, their relationship with the medical staff and the quality of their care. This knowledge from other patients' first-hand experiences with the disease and the healthcare system is important for many. Several patients whom I met, in all three countries, underlined that visits with surgeons and oncologists are often short, and it is difficult to have a detailed discussion and obtain all the information patients need. The horizontal sharing of knowledge that patient groups can offer represents a way to overcome the limits of healthcare systems in the three contexts explored. However, several patients also highlighted the limitations of patient groups. Poppy, a British interviewee in her late forties, told me she attended only a few meetings of a nearby support group because she did not want to 'hear everyone else's horror story'. Other women expressed the same doubt, stating the importance of balancing involvement in associations with the need not to be absorbed by the disease.

Additionally, many patients with metastatic breast cancer expressed greater distress. We have already seen how many of the messages around breast cancer revolve around early detection and treatments aimed at curing the disease. Women with metastatic breast cancer, who are therefore in a terminal stage and aware that they cannot recover, are excluded from these messages, and this limits their participation in the activities of some of the main associative groups. Alfieri and colleagues (2022), in particular, highlight the need for a greater engagement with the needs of patients with metastatic breast cancer among Italian charities. Florence, a French woman in her late forties, said that since her diagnosis, she had participated in several events. Still, they did not focus on metastatic breast cancer, except for a few more recent conferences finally starting to address the experiences of patients living with metastatic breast cancer. Describing one of those events, she said:

> It was the first time that we spoke freely about metastases in front of an audience of all kinds because I, for example, in [other support group meetings], I always had trouble talking about it because I had other women in front of me who didn't have metastatic breast cancer and I was afraid to let them know that there was the possibility of having a relapse.

Florence appreciated the opportunity to participate in an event focused on her situation and to be able to speak freely about her experience, because for her was difficult to talk about metastatic breast cancer in the presence of women with early-stage breast cancer and in contexts where breast cancer is presented as curable. The experience of Camilla was in many respects similar to that of

Florence. The young British woman said it was easier to find support after being diagnosed with early-stage breast cancer than when she was diagnosed with metastatic breast cancer. Camilla was able to find support through online activism, which often enables connection with patients with similar but less visible experiences, and creates communication spaces that can bypass traditional initiatives focused on extremely simple messages that do not find a place in the lives of many patients.

Bell and Ristovski-Slijepcevic (2015) have analysed the communication strategies used in cancer prevention conferences aimed at the general public. The goals of the initiatives observed by these researchers were to present the connections between diet, physical activity and cancer and to offer strategies for implementing lifestyles to reduce the risk. The researchers underline how communication strategies aim to simplify the messages they provide, even in the face of much less clear scientific evidence. One result of this type of communication is the emphasis on the link between cancer and lifestyle and the possibility of reducing cancer risk by adopting appropriate lifestyles (Greco, 2016a). Encapsulating the complexity of the disease in simple messages seems to be a common element in the communication between patients and medical institutions. In my fieldwork, it emerged that several patients participated in workshops and initiatives organised by medical facilities and hospitals which aimed to provide information for patients who are about to finish or have just finished their treatments. Sandra, a British nurse involved in these initiatives, said their goal is to 'make sure that they're able to self-care rather than being so reliant on hospitals'. These initiatives usually include information about nutrition, sports activities that can be undertaken and techniques to manage anxiety. Similar initiatives are also present in Italy and France, and many patients have attended them and said they have received helpful information and guidance on improving some aspects of their lives after their diagnosis. However, these initiatives, while certainly beneficial for some patients, encourage a vision of the disease as a finite episode in life, after which patients will have a decreasing need to maintain a relationship with medical facilities and should instead focus on improving their lifestyle.

While helpful for some, these forms of support foster a vision of the disease as a catalyst for self-improvement, which, as we will see in the next section, has an ambiguous role. This approach is an example of how the emphasis on individualisation aims at constructing an ideal patient capable of managing their health problem independently, thus limiting the burden on healthcare services. Cuts to health expenditures drive the individualisation of care. As we will see in Chapter 3, cancer care is made more complex by the introduction of new drugs, and the demands that new treatments introduce are not sufficiently balanced by additional new resources for healthcare institutions. The risk is an overall reduction in the quality of patient care. Moreover, as Florence and Camilla pointed out, patients with metastatic breast cancer may not recognise themselves in these messages because metastatic breast cancer is a terminal disease, cannot be managed outside of the hospital (Greco, 2022a) and does not fit into the optimistic rhetoric of cure (see Chapter 3). Daisy, a British woman in her sixties, described in this way her experiences with events of this kind organised by the NHS Trust in which she was treated:

> I was never told that I was cured, I am not saying that, but I was given the impression that … the hospital offered a 'survive after cancer' course that kinda of gave the impression that you had cancer, you have done the treatments, and off you trot. I don't know if this would have made it any easier, but I would have liked to have known that there was more of a chance that it would come back.

Daisy's experience shows how the desire to produce patients able to manage their post-cancer care independently is not always in line with the risks of breast cancer, and, as many patients have underlined, it would be essential to include more balanced and honest communication on metastatic cancer.

Negotiating the optimist rhetoric

Several scholarly and activist analyses have criticised the dangerous implications of the cheerful and glamorous pink rhetoric surrounding breast cancer (Ehrenreich, 2001; Sulik, 2011). These concerns have finally gained traction among the general public. An article published in 2017 in the British newspaper the *Guardian* criticised fundraising strategies using pinkwashing practices and encouraged us to 'sink the pink' (Boyd, 2017). However, the same year, the same newspaper published an article in which a well-known British presenter diagnosed with breast cancer stated: 'After cancer, I'm squeezing life out of every second' (Kellaway, 2017). British journalist George Monbiot wrote the following year about his prostate cancer: 'Through my cancer, I have found the key to a good life' (Monbiot, 2018).[7] Articles and books presenting cancer as a rebirth experience abound. Accepting cancer as an opportunity is increasingly becoming part of the social script of the disease, and while it might not include a glamorous presentation of breast cancer, the new script is still limiting for many women. If patients can today express temporary anger and fear, this possibility seems conditional on the need to transform the disease into an occasion to improve oneself and one's life.

One of the possible reasons for this paradigm shift is that, despite the undeniable improvements brought by therapeutic innovations, for most patients, surviving cancer does not mean having a cancer-free life. The consequences of the disease and the risk of relapse mark patients' lives permanently. For many, finding a way to come to terms with these changes is an important step. The modification brought by the disease has been described as a 'new normal' (Trusson et al., 2016). For many patients, accepting a new, altered life is essential to regaining the quality of life after cancer, to the extent possible. However, discourses of renewal are an invitation not just to accept life's changes but to use them to create a new and enhanced version of the self. Bell (2012) has shown how psycho-oncology presents a traumatic experience, such as cancer, as an opportunity to adopt healthy lifestyles and reach psychological growth using the traumatic experience.

The construction of this enhanced and wiser self involves learning, thanks to the disease, how to appreciate life more. In my fieldwork, some patients have described how cancer has given them a more critical and radical outlook on life (see Chapter 6); however, this political growth is rarely discussed, either in psycho-oncology or in general cultural venues. Another aspect of this post-cancer enhancement rhetoric is that patients, as seen in the previous section, are encouraged to change their lifestyles. While adopting a new diet or taking up sports can benefit individuals, there is no guarantee that these changes will prevent a relapse. Moreover, not only is the possibility of adopting a certain lifestyle strongly linked to people's income and type of job, but discourses emphasising the role of individual behaviour obscure the environmental and social causes of cancer (Brown, 2007; Greco, 2016a).

In Chapters 5 and 6, I will discuss how women respond differently to life-altering experiences like serious illness. In some cases, they may gain courage and a new, brighter outlook on life. However, the univocal portrayal of cancer in the media as a source of moral strength or inner peace significantly influences patients' experiences and expectations.

I met Mélanie, a French woman in her fifties, in a café on the outskirts of Paris. She was nearing the end of her treatments, and she told me that the diagnosis had been a shock and the disease had caused professional and personal disruptions. She also added that she was still looking for the sense of her illness:

> One always finds a sense in the disease […]. But I should tell you that the sense of my disease, I am still looking for it. I look for the sense of my disease: what will I get from this disease? Because I also worked [with cancer patients] and I remember a woman, who had a son, who was her adoptive son, and [she] had a lot of relational difficulties with her adoptive son, and one day she told me 'the disease gave me something, it allowed me to settle all the accounts and now it's great'. I cannot get to see what I have got from the disease […] I think that it's also this, that I am looking for a sense in my disease and I cannot find it. […] I would like to find a sense in this disease and see in what way it makes me go forward.

Illness has already been analysed as biographical disruption (Bury, 1982), as an event separating the present from the past and introducing uncertainty about the future. However, Mélanie was not just trying to recompose the fracture between her pre- and post-diagnosis life: she hoped to obtain positive changes. The contemporary construction of cancer fostered her expectations that her illness might be a catalyst for improvement. However, in her case, these changes were slow to manifest, and the fact that she could not see the positive outcome that would have given a new meaning to her cancer made the overall experience – the diagnosis, the difficulties and the pain linked to the therapies – harder to accept. This story is a way to explore how messages of post-traumatic growth and transformation can permeate the lives of patients. Mélanie's expectations echo what Berlant has defined as cruel optimism, i.e., 'when something you desire is actually an obstacle to your flourishing' (Berlant, 2011: 1). The injunction to optimism introduced around breast cancer takes something intuitively negative – illness – and builds expectations that it will improve one's life. Berlant analyses the aspirations for the good life and how the elements that can characterise a life as good are determined by what she defines as the 'neoliberal restructuring within the ordinary' (Berlant, 2011: 16). A disease like cancer goes beyond the ordinary and enters the realm of the tragic, but its tragic nature does not prevent neoliberal ideologies from shaping our ideas of the disease. In this situation, a cancer diagnosis is rearranged as an event from which one can gain something,[8] on which one can capitalise. And the gain of this capitalisation is a new, brighter outlook on life and a healthier lifestyle. However, many women whom I met did not fit into this vision. The construction of cancer as a transformative event is grounded in the image of a patient who not only adheres perfectly to treatments but also has an early-stage diagnosis and no relapse. Further, it is grounded in the image of a white, middle-class woman living in the Global North. For this ideal patient, cancer is a tragedy that strikes in an otherwise happy life. And while many women might recognise themselves in this description, it finds limited application in other social, cultural and economic contexts. New theoretical frameworks have emerged to provide more accurate interpretations of these experiences. For example, Banerjee (2020), in his research, analyses the experiences of cancer in India as forms of endurance, situations in which the diagnosis of cancer takes place in a context of precariousness and difficulty and 'put[s] further pressure on already frayed social relations' and in which 'living with cancer entailed living with a pervasive doubt about the viability of such relations' (Banerjee, 2020: 4). The women whom I interviewed in southern Italy had greater financial and social stability than the patients Banerjee interviewed. However, they too found themselves in the situation of having to include the disease in an already difficult life characterised by challenging work and personal situations that reduce the space they can give to their illness. Elsewhere I have analysed these struggles, and the strategies women employed to deal with cancer, as forms of 'biographical containment' (Greco, 2023). The concept starts from previous literature (Manderson, 2011) on how people react to traumatic events by attempting to build identities beyond their illness. Containment (see also Alonzo, 1979) indicates cases in which patients limit the space given to the illness in their life. By biographical containment, I refer in particular to cases in which they either can rely on resources to limit the impact of the illness or have to limit the space given to the illness because of other co-occurring problems. Many women whom I met stressed that they had been dealing with other serious health problems before the diagnosis, in some cases as patients, in others as caregivers for family and friends. For many women, the need to contain the impact of breast cancer in their lives was linked to the need to protect the stability of their family, which was simultaneously a source of support but also a structure whose stability relied heavily on women. Many interviewees were extremely grateful for the support they received from their adult children, husband, sisters or, for younger women, parents. However, they also insisted that they needed to be strong precisely so as to preserve the well-being of other family members and the stability of the family itself. Catholicism, permeating the life of many people in southern Italy, also played an important part in the practices of containment. Religion indeed emphasises the redeeming role of suffering and offers a positive vision of the moral strength which characterises the approach to suffering in southern Italy. This shows the fragile balances on which containment practices are based and their crucial role in limiting the impact of the disease when it occurs in a situation of fragility and difficulty (Greco, 2023).

If containment strategies were more marked in southern Italy, ways of redefining breast cancer diagnosis that challenge the idea that an enhanced self should emerge from cancer were also present in northern Italy, France and the UK. Many women in these contexts have expressed a pragmatic attitude towards the disease. Clothilde told me that, despite the initial shock of the diagnosis, she had always considered breast cancer an event that can occur in a woman's life: 'I never thought "why me?" It's a question I've never asked myself. It's one woman out of nine, it can be you, it can be me or your sister. Or it's me today and you tomorrow. We don't know anything, I never asked myself the question in these terms.' This way of thinking about cancer was common among the women whom I interviewed, and it was not a way of trivialising the disease and the difficulties it causes but an attempt to reject the singularity of the diagnosis by emphasising how widespread breast cancer is.

As we have seen, some patients expressed their disappointment at the lack of information on the possibility of relapse. Daisy, who, as we saw in the previous section, was given the impression that she was cured, said that she would have liked to know 'that there was more a chance that it was gonna come back' and that after the diagnosis of metastatic breast cancer she had to adjust to a new mindset:

> the first time I was looking at a cure, it's different how you approach [metastatic breast cancer], I still try to look at it [the fact that the disease is manageable] as being a positive thing, but sometimes is more difficult because I know this [the treatment] is not gonna cure it.

Like Daisy, many women with metastatic cancer tried to have a pragmatic and realistic approach to their situation. As I will discuss in Chapter 5, they were aware of the diagnosis, they knew that the effects of the disease were irreversible and that they needed to take into account the terminal nature of metastatic breast cancer when planning the next steps for them and the people close to them. But this important work was often conducted outside of the main cultural and social script available for women with breast cancer, which is still largely based on the idea of survivorship.

The women whom I met recognised that breast cancer is a life-altering experience, but they rejected its optimistic image and refused to consider it an opportunity for improvement. They were trying to insert their diagnosis into their lives, and they were aware that its presence was indelible and were honest about the fact that their post-diagnosis life did not improve. Although varied, and influenced by cultural and social contexts, the strategies that the women displayed show the limit of the optimistic cancer rhetoric, which is strongly individualistic and rooted in the neoliberal ideology of turning adversities into opportunities. Patients often felt that viewing illness as a transformative event with profound meanings did not align with their personal experiences. The rhetoric of moral growth discussed here may not provide a helpful framework for interpreting their illness. As a result, many patients are moving away from the optimistic perspective and instead seeking practical strategies to manage and cope with their illness. In doing so, they are disarticulating the social script of the disease and producing biographical assemblages around ideas and experiences that include breast cancer as a negative event from which it is not always possible to gain anything.

Conclusion

When David Jay started shooting the SCAR project in 2005 – also to criticise the pink ribbon discourse – images of the mastectomised body were hardly part of the public discourse. Mastectomised bodies are still far from being normalised (as I discuss in Chapter 4), but photographic representations have risen in number. Similarly, when I started working on breast cancer in 2011, the pink ribbon discourse was stronger than it is now. Activist and academic criticism of the discourse have had an impact on some aspects of the pink ribbon, redefining the cultural-political assemblage of breast cancer. In the associative contexts I have studied, the colour pink was often used because that colour is now strongly associated with breast cancer, but it did not necessarily indicate adherence to a glamorous and highly feminine vision of the disease. However, other social scripts are gradually spreading: cancer is increasingly presented as an opportunity for growth and a 'teaching moment' (Bell, 2012). The idea that cancer should produce positive changes has tangible effects on patients' lives, with some expecting changes and improvements that might not occur. This vision of the disease as a moment of growth and progress can be linked to a presentation of breast cancer as an individual problem that can be solved with personalised therapies (as we will see in Chapter 3) or with lifestyle changes to prevent the return of the disease.

Patients' groups and associations can have different aims. I mostly met smaller groups for whom fundraising and campaigns, if part of their activity, were not professionalised or on a large scale, and therefore some aspects of the pink ribbon discourse were not particularly relevant. Some groups were openly critical of the pink ribbon and of other aspects of the public discourse. Such groups often aimed to help patients to confront the experience of breast cancer and to offer informal support, activities that often feed into the assemblage processes that women put together.

Initiatives organised by medical institutions and charities are also considered sources of help. Still, they often refer to models of patienthood that can continue to emphasise optimism and self-reliance, if not self-improvement. Crucially, while screening programmes are based on regular contact with the institutions, some post-diagnosis approaches can encourage relying less on medical institutions' support. Patients with early-stage breast cancer are often encouraged to self-manage their disease, and some patients whom I met reported that the emphasis on being able to leave cancer behind decreased the amount of information received about the risk of relapse and metastasis. As we will see in the next chapter, the introduction of new treatments is changing the organisation of individual institutions and increasingly contributing to the presentation of breast cancer as an individual problem with individual medical solutions.

Notes

1 The well-known history of the pink ribbon is that it was initially created as a peach-coloured ribbon by Charlotte Haley in the early 1990s for a more grassroots campaign aimed at the National Cancer Institute. When Haley refused *Self Magazine*'s proposal to make the ribbon part of a national-scale campaign, the magazine changed the colour to pink and partnered with Estée Lauder (Selleck, 2010).
2 The association gives the following definition of 'pinkwasher' on its website: 'A company or organization that claims to care about breast cancer by promoting a pink ribbon product, but at the same time produces, manufactures and/or sells products that are linked to the disease' (www.bcaction.org/about-think-before-you-pink/ [accessed 8 August 2024]).
3 For some examples from France, see https://leplus.nouvelobs.com/contribution/1248222-octobre-rose-j-ai-le-cancer-du-sein-votre-marketing-me-rend-malade.html (accessed 13 July 2023) and www.nouvelobs.com/rue89/nos-vies-intimes/20170925.OBS5126/octobrerose-revoila-la-guimauve-rose-culpabilisante-contre-le-cancer.html (accessed 8 August 2024).
4 It is also worth noting that the history of cancer campaigns in the UK shows a delayed start when compared to the US, as in the 1950s there were doubts about the impact of 'educating' the general population about cancer, and the orientation was towards local, rather than national, campaigns (Toon, 2007).
5 Hamarat (2020), focusing on two associations in Belgium, also shows the tension between the experiences of individual patients that do not

match hegemonic discourses about breast cancer and associations that tend to produce a collective discourse reconciled with the dominant one – see Nielsen (2019) for some similar insights on North America.
6 It is important to note that in France I conducted my fieldwork in the area of Paris, which, as a capital city, was more likely to have a wider range of associations.
7 There are many examples of articles in other British, Italian and French newspapers presenting cancer as an opportunity to appreciate life more. However, some exceptions stand out, such as the interview with the Irish writer Colm Tóibín published in the Italian newspaper *La Repubblica*, the title of which states that, according to the writer, 'cancer is not a life teacher' (Guerrera, 2019).
8 In Chapter 4, we will see how this also applies to the body and how breast reconstruction is presented as an opportunity to have a 'better' breast.

3

Biomedical innovations and the redefinition of breast cancer

The Buy My Cancer project (www.buymycancer.org), launched in Poland in 2022, seems to be a logical development of several tendencies in the recent transformations of cancer. The project aims to raise funds for CAR-T cells therapies for blood cancer patients, a therapy presented as highly innovative and promising and, as other therapies of this kind, involving very high costs (estimated in this case to be around $400,000 per patient). To raise funds, the cancerous cells of the patients selected are photographed and transformed into works of art and then sold as NFTs ('nonfungible tokens' – an experimental procedure to assign value to digital images by making them non-replicable). It is striking how not only is the illness located clearly at the level of the cancerous cells, but there is also an attempt to extract value from the cells themselves (or, at least, their image). Further, CAR-T cells therapies are part of a broader range of therapies in which the approach is to target specific markers in the cancerous cells, in this particular case by engineering lymphocytes aimed at the target. The success rate of the treatment is estimated to be around 40% for patients for whom other therapies do not work, and, in this sense, CAR-T cells are part of a wider discourse of hope in cancer therapeutics.

In 1990 Del Vecchio Good et al. described a transition, which began with the War on Cancer in 1971, from cancer as a diagnosis leading to a social death to a more optimistic approach to the condition. Greater availability of funds, resulting in more research and more cancer treatments, has promoted over the years what Del Vecchio Good and colleagues define as an 'economy of hope' (Del Vecchio Good et al., 1990: 60). Breast cancer, more than other types of cancer, seems to be the perfect example for a story of hope, as several new treatments have increased the survival times of patients. A woman who, after a breast cancer diagnosis, decided to look for information online would find encouraging data, with many websites of major charities and associations describing survival times for the condition as good. The pharmaceutical landscape includes several treatments that can keep the disease at bay for longer periods. It is difficult, however, to know whether a patient can be considered cured, because with the current knowledge and diagnostic capacity the best result that can be achieved and shown is that someone is not presenting any evidence of disease. New treatments are indeed developed with the hope of reducing the risk of relapse for early-stage disease, and to extend survival times for patients with metastases. However, most new treatments are not developed for all breast cancer patients, as an increasing number of newly introduced drugs target just specific subtypes of tumours. This segmentation, according not only to stages but also to the biological profile of the tumour (see Ross et al., 2021, and below), redefines breast cancer as a group of diseases occurring in the same bodily location – the breast.

In previous literature, the concept of assemblage has been used to theorise how biomedicine conceptualises the human body, its parts and its functioning (Johnson, 2018). However, there is reason to push the concept of the assemblage beyond the *internal* workings of the body and how biomedicine conceptualises them. For instance, a new definition of breast cancer as a plurality of conditions not only creates a reconceptualisation of the disease but entails further new relationships between the ill body, the biomedical categories defining the disease and the healthcare institutions treating it. One aspect of such relationships can be partly understood through the assemblage of the 'techno-body' of the cyborg – how different kinds of prostheses transform the body (e.g., Gibson et al., 2007; Shildrick, 2013; 2015). I propose the concept of medical-bodily assemblage to indicate how the biomedical conceptualisation of the human body simultaneously redefines the body itself and opens up different kinds of management (diagnosis, monitoring) and transformation (treatment) of the same body. Moreover, how medical professionals and patients reappropriate, use or reject these ideas is central to understanding the current transformation of breast cancer. In this chapter, I discuss how these new biomedical approaches are reassembling the experiences of illness and the pharmaceutical promises of regaining a healthy body after a diagnosis. The introduction of new drugs and surgical techniques, which can see delays in approval or unequal geographic distribution, has created a complex therapeutic landscape that patients can find challenging to navigate, as well as inequalities in access to specific treatments (Kerr et al., 2021; Greco, 2022a; 2024; and Chapter 1 of this book). New definitions of early-stage and metastatic breast cancer and therapeutic approaches are creating new assemblages between biomedical tools and patient's bodies. How do patients deal with medical innovations? How do they negotiate access to specific treatments with the biomedical establishment? What impact are new targeted treatments having on the daily activities of medical professionals? Guided by these questions, in the following pages, I discuss how biomedical innovations are reshaping our understanding of breast cancer.

Between early diagnosis and breast surgery: how to assemble a healthy body

The history of breast cancer has been marked by a series of breakthroughs, including the evolution of the surgical treatments of the disease, innovations in radiotherapy and the inclusion of hormonal treatments and new targeted therapies. These changes and innovations have contributed to lengthening survival times (Youlden et al., 2012), particularly for patients whose cancer has not spread outside the breast involving vital organs. Early-stage breast cancer is now defined as 'curable', and, as we will see, through a redefinition of the concept of chronicity, the encouraging vision of a curable disease has also been rearranged to include the situation of (some) patients with metastatic breast cancer. Therapeutic successes for breast cancer are presented as effective, especially when coupled with an early diagnosis. As Löwy writes '[c]ancer experts stipulated that the only way to transform a fatal disease into a treatable condition was to be "faster than the cancer"' (Löwy, 2010: 2). According to the linear model of cancer progression discussed in the Introduction, tumours of small size can be successfully treated, and this representation underpins the organisation of information campaigns urging women to check for changes in the feeling and appearance of their breast (Gardner, 2006). It also underpins the choice to organise screening campaigns for specific segments of the population – that is, post-menopausal, middle-aged women – that are considered to be particularly at risk. In the UK, in 1986, a commission headed by breast surgeon Patrick Forrest recommended the introduction of an NHS-supported triennial screening for British women between the ages of fifty and sixty-nine. The first British screening programme started a couple of years later. During the 1990s, screening programmes were also consolidated in Italy and France. In Italy, these programmes began first in some regions of northern Italy, and then gradually spread to the centre and south of the peninsula, but it is only since 2007 that all Italian regions have a screening programme, with Puglia and Sardinia among the last to activate one (Giordano and Giorgi, 2011). In France, screening programmes started earlier, in 1989, in some departments of the country, and despite the efforts to extend screening programmes throughout the country, it was only in 2004 that this goal was achieved (Philip et al., 2005). In each of the three countries, a large amount of financial and organisational resources are directed into screening campaigns, especially to extend the number of women taking part in them and to make sure that the hard-to-reach population that could benefit most from them will take part (see Fagan Robinson and Arteaga Pérez, 2023 for an analysis of care for hard-to-reach groups). However, breast cancer screening efforts and the linear model of cancer progression supporting them are not exempt from criticism. Several medical professionals and public health experts have pointed out the low effectiveness of early diagnosis as the preferred approach to tackling breast cancer (in this regard, see among others, Baum, 2015). Azra Raza, oncologist and author of the bestseller *The First Cell*, summarises in this way the contradictions of breast cancer screening: '[e]arly detection of more aggressive breast cancer [is] not helpful because by the time the tumor appeared on a mammogram, it had already spread and was incurable' (Raza, 2019: 218).

Despite the doubts about its usefulness, breast cancer screening and early diagnosis have become the pivotal aspects of the biomedical and social approach to the disease. As I discussed in Chapter 2, several charities and patient groups have contributed to spreading the simplified message that breast cancer screening 'saves lives' (Sulik, 2011; Carter, 2015). The innovations that characterised breast cancer surgery in the 1980s reinforced the idea that early detection is the key to treating breast cancer satisfactorily and avoiding the surgical removal of the breast. Tumorectomy has contributed to the presentation of breast cancer as a surmountable experience that leaves minimal or no traces at all in women's lives. As we will see in Chapter 4, technical improvements in the surgical treatment of breast cancer are slowly introducing the idea that the removal of a breast tumour is not necessarily a mutilating experience but that, for some patients, it can be the occasion to improve the appearance of the breast (see also Greco, 2016d). However, the extension of screening programmes is also linked to an increase in the diagnosis of *in situ* cancers. These are slowly developing indolent lesions that do not spread to other organs and often do not threaten the woman's life. However, they are in many cases treated with a mastectomy, thus creating a contradiction that fractures the relationship between early diagnosis and conservative surgery (Löwy, 2010). Dr Isabelle, a French oncologist, explained why a mastectomy is often performed to treat what she defined a cancer with a good prognosis (*cancer de bon prognostic*), that is, intraductal or *in situ* tumours:

> In [these cancers] with a good prognosis, the breast is almost always removed, because sometimes there are lesions that are diffused in the breast, compared to invasive cancer or other cancers, where sometimes there are small tumours but for which we do radiotherapy, chemotherapy, etc. Patients sometimes say: 'I don't understand, you say it's a good prognosis and remove my breast, while my neighbour, who has cancer and who has undergone chemotherapy, etc. she kept her breast.' That is to say that keeping the breast or not is not linked to the prognosis of cancer. So here it is, *in situ* cancer is a cancer with a good prognosis, but *in situ* cancer is less sensitive to radiotherapy than fairly serious invasive cancer ... so there is still a tendency to relapse, and as it is a cancer with a very good prognosis, we must not miss the boat [*rater le coche*], as they say, to treat it really well so that it does not relapse in an infiltrating form. Because that means that there we failed ... [So there you go, there's this] apparent contradiction between surgery which can be radical when the cancer has a good prognosis.

This excerpt shows how difficult it is to establish a correlation between the radicalness of the surgery and the severity of the disease. According to Dr Isabelle, a mastectomy is in many cases sufficient to eliminate the risk that an *in situ* or intraductal tumour might develop into a more severe form. However, the medical opinion about *in situ* cancer is divided. Esserman and colleagues presented in 2013 a variable model of progression, according to which only some types of cancer have the linear progression that predicts the evolution of an *in situ* cancer into an invasive one. Other types of indolent lesions will never develop into an invasive form. According to Esserman and colleagues 'Ductal carcinoma in situ is a pathological entity that is an unintended result of breast cancer screening, rarely diagnosed before screening was adopted. Diagnosis of ductal carcinoma in situ results in immediate treatment with aggressive locoregional therapy.' The authors further write that '[r]esults of studies suggest that only a subset of ductal carcinoma in situ progresses to clinically significant invasive cancer during a patient's lifetime.' (Esserman et al., 2014: e238). However, it is difficult to predict the evolution of an *in situ* lesion (Sakorafas and Tsiotou, 2000), which can explain the surgical approach described by Dr Isabelle. Even when associated with a low risk of developing metastases, mastectomy is experienced differently by patients. Some find it difficult to consider breast removal a treatment corresponding to a cancer of good prognosis. Other therapies (chemotherapy and radiotherapy), often associated with surgery, are also mentioned in this excerpt, and systemic therapy is used to stem rapidly evolving infiltrating tumours. According to Dr Isabelle, many patients interpret this combination of treatments as less debilitating than mastectomy because, in many cases, the breast, and the body integrity associated with it, can be preserved. Patients and doctors can attribute different meanings to treatments. For oncologists, the main objective is to avoid the development of metastases, that is, the extension of the cancer to other organs.

A situation similar to the diagnosis of an *in situ* cancer is that of women with BRCA 1 and 2 mutations. Identified in the 1990s, these mutations are associated with a high risk of developing breast cancer. There is, however, a 'contrast between the sophistication of a diagnostic technology grounded in the latest developments in molecular biology and the crudeness of the solution to the diagnosed gene mutation – the mutilation of a healthy female body' (Löwy, 2010: 1). Options for patients with the gene mutation are indeed limited to a preventive bilateral mastectomy, close screening appointments or, in the UK but not in France and Italy, the possibility of taking tamoxifen or raloxifene. However, preventive hormonal therapy has limited effectiveness in this case, as BRCA 1 and 2 mutations are often associated with non-hormone-responsive cancers.

The possibility of diagnosing indolent lesions and genetic mutations fuels, in some cases, a return of surgical radicalism (Löwy, 2010), which, as we have seen, is in opposition to the objectives of early diagnosis and recalls the apparent contradiction mentioned by Dr Isabelle. However, the evolution in surgical approaches to breast cancer represents only one aspect of the treatment. As Dr Isabelle reminds us, different treatments are often necessary to keep the disease at bay in the most complex cases, even in the presence of early-stage breast cancer, which is usually defined as curable. To achieve the balanced situation that can be defined as a cure, a complex mosaic of treatments – surgery, chemotherapy, radiotherapy, hormonal therapy and monoclonal antibodies – are currently used. Some have been introduced more recently, while others have been used for decades. In the case of breast cancer, where the best result that can be obtained is a temporary NED (No Evidence of Disease) status, the concept of cure is inappropriate, as for many patients being cancer free can be a precarious and sometimes temporary condition (see Greco, 2022c; and Chapter 5). The absence of the disease is never certain but must be confirmed through periodic screening. A diagnosis of breast cancer that is still in an early stage amplifies significantly the biomedical promise of being able to keep cancer at bay and prevent its return. Hormonal therapies, which we will describe in the next section, are often prescribed for several years after the acute phase of the treatments, extending the possibility of avoiding a relapse. A characterising trait of the current therapeutic approach to breast cancer is that it is increasingly presented as a linear and personalised pathway. A life without cancer is a complex assemblage of knowledge about the disease, relations with medical professionals and therapies that follow one another at different points in the therapeutic pathway.

The personalised approach to breast cancer and its limits

Since the 1990s, oncology has tended to develop drugs capable of targeting specific reproductive mechanisms of the tumour and attacking cancerous cells with minimal damage to the surrounding organs and tissues. This approach has been defined as 'personalised' medicine, and the new class of targeted drugs is often described as highly effective while causing fewer side effects, particularly when compared with chemotherapy (Schirrmacher, 2019). The concept of personalised medicine is also being used to underline that this approach can offer tailored treatments for groups of patients, thus improving the benefits. However, commentators have also highlighted the limits of this approach, characterised by high prices of targeted therapy not often justified by the results that it delivers for small numbers of patients and the fact that they may subtract resources from less innovative approaches that could benefit a wider number of patients (e.g., Sturdy, 2017). Moreover, the term 'personalised' itself is misleading, as the approach rarely entails, as the term would suggest, offering ad hoc treatment for each patient, but instead focuses on standardised treatment for all patients whose tumour presents the same biomarker. In this sense, 'targeted' or 'stratified', often used as synonyms, are more appropriate descriptors of the approach. Targeted therapies are an important component in the treatment landscape for breast cancer, where the possibility of locating new molecular subtypes is changing how this cancer is considered and treated. Among the oncologists whom I have interviewed, there is a common view that can be summarised in Dr John's words: 'Breast cancer isn't just one disease, it has been recognised that there are different kinds of disease.' The segmentation into subtypes at a molecular level is an essential aspect of the current understanding of the disease, up to the point that it has been argued that 'breast cancer' should be considered an umbrella term including different subtypes of disease, some of which can even be seen as rare diseases (Bartlett and Parelukar, 2017; see also Harbeck and Rody, 2012).

The salient characteristics of cancer biology have been known for several decades. The relationship between breast cancer and hormones began to be understood as early as 1896, when Beatson published an article discussing how three patients with advanced breast cancer benefited from an oophorectomy (Love and Philips, 2002). The fact that some types of cancer had receptors that made them more susceptible to hormones such as oestrogen and progesterone has been known since the 1970s, and this awareness led to the creation of tamoxifen, a landmark treatment for breast cancer.

Tamoxifen was among the first hormone-focused drugs used to treat metastatic breast cancer, and the first to greatly impact on the condition, as it aims to modify the endocrine environment that increases the growth of hormone-responsive tumours.[1] Pharmacologist Craig Jordan played a leading role in its development, as he was one of the first to see that the drug, initially synthesised as a post-coital anti-conceptional, could be turned into a hormonal treatment for breast cancer. Tamoxifen was more tolerable and less toxic than chemotherapy. It laid the foundation for the idea that some specific therapies could tackle specific cancer subtypes, thus slowly shifting the treatment paradigm at a time when chemotherapy was receiving most of the attention. The first cancer drug to introduce some traits of what is now considered targeted therapy[2] (Jordan, 2006; see also Hedgecoe, 2004), tamoxifen revived the interest in hormonal cancer treatments. Since then, various hormonal drugs, such as the more recent aromatase inhibitors (Eraso, 2020), have been developed. However, Jordan writes that in the 1970s, when tamoxifen was introduced, it was 'not hailed as a breakthrough by the clinical community' (Jordan, 2003: 205). He continues:

> By contrast, there was enormous enthusiasm for the discovery and application of cytotoxic chemotherapy. Some 30 years later, enthusiasm for the nonspecific approach of chemotherapy has waned and has been replaced by the anticipation of a new generation of targeted therapies. Tamoxifen, an agent kept on life support for the first 20 years of its existence (1962–1982), evolved into the first targeted medicine for breast cancer.

The history of tamoxifen, according to Jordan, illustrates the evolution of biomedicine's understanding of breast cancer and the treatments against it. The shift of tamoxifen from a drug 'on life support' to the 'first targeted medicine' can be better understood if we consider that the approach towards breast cancer in the 2000s has been characterised by what Keating et al. define as 'a progressive dismantling of a common pathology' (Keating et al., 2016: 22) in which breast cancer as such has become less relevant, with more prominence given to the biological characteristics such as biomarkers, the analysis of gene expression profiles or DNA mutations, that characterise it. Breast cancer subtypes can be considered as 'bio-clinical objects' (Keating et al., 2016) emerging from the encounter of a redefinition of tumours and the availability of new chemotherapeutic agents that can target tumours expressing certain biological characteristics. These bio-clinical objects appeared in a period of attention to stratified approaches against cancer, as opposed to the priority given to systemic treatment, such as chemotherapy, prevalent in the 1970s. That explains why, today, tamoxifen is considered the first 'non-toxic targeted treatment for breast cancer' (Jordan, 2003: 205). Still, despite tamoxifen's longevity and wide use against the disease, it is another drug that is universally regarded as a game changer: trastuzumab. In addition to oestrogen and progestogen receptors, a third receptor, the HER2, had already been known since the 1980s, and for decades its presence was considered an indicator of poor prognosis for patients (Ménard et al., 2002; Figueroa-Magalhães et al., 2014). However, the situation changed in the late 1990s with the introduction of trastuzumab, one of the first monoclonal antibodies, a class of drugs capable of targeting specific proteins in cancer cells. The drug, marketed by Roche under the name of Herceptin, is considered one of the most important breakthroughs for the treatment of breast cancer and has been described as the 'poster child' for targeted therapeutics (Issa, 2007). The introduction of trastuzumab caused 'a shift in expectations as to what benefits these drugs could deliver: neither just palliation nor quite a cure. Rather, like insulin for diabetics, or some of the new AIDS drugs, these compounds would turn cancer into a chronic disease, which could be managed over long periods of time' (Timmermann, 2019: 125). The innovation represented by trastuzumab – that is, the possibility of extending survival times not by eliminating cancer once and for all, but by keeping it at bay thanks to prolonged use of the drug – combined with its extremely high cost, was a shock for several healthcare systems (for the UK, see Barrett et al., 2006). As one of my interviewees, Dr Harry, a British consultant, mentioned:

> [Herceptin/trastuzumab] was very controversial when it was first identified, because it is a very expensive drug […]. When we first got Herceptin, [it was a] very expensive drug, so our finance department asked us to estimate what the survival rate would be, so that they could work out what the cost would be, so we estimated that it would be … because people already had treatments, this was going to do be second or third line treatment, so we estimated a three months' treatment. The first group, the finance team were horrified, because

their survival was beyond two years, almost three years, and that was the first group, and was very expensive. Good for the patient, bad for the hospital.

The approval of trastuzumab in the UK – which took place a few years after the creation of NICE (see Chapter 1) – was at the centre of controversy regarding the cost of the drug (Hedgecoe, 2004; 2006). The above interview excerpt shows the surprise at the drug's efficacy, initially prescribed as a second or third line of treatment for patients with metastatic breast cancer. However, the importance of trastuzumab for the survival of patients with metastatic breast cancer was unanimously mentioned by the doctors whom I interviewed.[3] Dr Maria, a breast cancer consultant, also noted the drug's role in extending survival times:

> The difference in treatments for MBC [metastatic breast cancer] has come with Herceptin or trastuzumab, once we had this [knowledge] to identify HER2-positive breast cancer. Trastuzumab, I think, has made a big difference to the treatment of those patients, and particularly when they had metastatic disease … if we use trastuzumab alongside chemotherapy or hormonotherapy we achieve quite long responses … and they live for months, they live for years after treatment, and we can continue to give them trastuzumab and change the chemotherapy if there is a bit of progression. So I think that is one group of patients where new advances have made a big difference in terms of the choices for that group. They are not huge, but we have trastuzumab, which we use alongside chemotherapy, we have Kadcyla, trastuzumab emtansine, which again can be used [for some] people for years. We have a few patients, once we establish them on a dose, they tend to keep going.

Today, trastuzumab is used in neoadjuvant therapy for early-stage breast cancer and metastatic breast cancer in the UK, France and Italy. While trastuzumab was a major innovation in breast cancer, a variety of new therapies were mentioned alongside it in the interviews I conducted with medical professionals. This growth of drugs targeting specific markers establishes a further medical-bodily assemblage between the patient's body, the tumour with specific markers and the complex created between biotechnologies, diagnostic procedures, biomedical treatments and the medical systems that regulate their administration.

While the literature discusses widely the impact of an extensive range of new drugs on patients, it discusses more rarely how these new therapies are changing how treatments are administered and how a large set of new personalised treatments can clash with the organisation of healthcare facilities. Dr Maria acknowledged that a new challenge for medical professionals is to learn how to manage new treatments, each with its potential sets of serious side effects. She mentioned that trastuzumab, for example, despite the good results that it can provide, can also cause heart problems, and that oncologists have to learn how to monitor heart function or treat heart failure. This also means engaging with cardiologists and other specialists. However, the interdisciplinary collaborations made necessary by the new drugs might not be straightforward, because, as Dr Maria mentioned during the interview, other specialists already have busy schedules, and it may be challenging to add the follow-up of breast cancer patients to their workload (Greco, 2024).[4] Other medical professionals also underlined the impact of new treatments on medical services. Isabella, a nurse and a cancer services manager whom I interviewed in the UK, said that while the lines of treatment for metastatic patients have increased, the oncological service in which she worked had had the same capacity for the last thirteen years. She added that 'all the new treatments are having a massive impact on that, so we are trying to respond by saying: "OK which patient do we really not need to see any more?"', indicating that the increase in therapies for metastatic breast cancer could mean decisions to have fewer follow-up appointments for patients with early-stage breast cancer.[5] The intersection between overstretched services and efficient but difficult-to-manage drugs for metastatic breast cancer can have an unforeseen effect on early-stage breast cancer, as the reduction of follow-up appointments for patients can further reinforce the perception of this stage as curable. Martin and colleagues (2017), who have analysed the impact of targeted therapies for metastatic breast cancer in France, illustrate similar difficulties. The high number of therapies and the range of side effects demand more effort from oncologists, as they have to familiarise themselves with new therapies and approaches to patient care. Targeted therapies also make it necessary to increase the collaborations between different professionals. These elements can disrupt the management of patients and delay the use of these targeted therapies (Martin et al., 2017). As seen in Chapter 1, targeted therapies can be costly, but they also alter the financial organisation of French healthcare facilities. In France, funding is provided 'according to the nature and volume of medical procedures performed [and a] cost-per-case mix (i.e. per-case payment system) is applied based on the type of medical activity documented in the French national hospital database' (Benjamin et al., 2014: 2). In this context, oral targeted therapies might shift part of the funds from the hospital to the community, and the disruption they bring to the organisation of local funding could potentially influence patient access to such medications (Benjamin et al., 2014; Martin et al. 2017).

Another important aspect concerning targeted and personalised therapies is that they have not supplanted the systemic therapies, in combination with which they are often used. As Dr Mark, another among my interviewees in the UK, underlined, differently from targeted therapies, chemotherapy is used for all subtypes of breast cancer, although at different points in the therapeutic pathways:

> People sometimes imagine that for hormone-receptor metastatic breast cancer the treatment is hormone therapy; that is usually true and they will have one, two, three types of hormone therapy, but eventually their cancer no longer responds to hormone therapy and if we want to give them further therapy that's chemotherapy … patients with HER2-positive disease, we give them Herceptin and other HER2-positive drugs, but we usually give them those alongside chemotherapy.

What emerges from the interview is that it is not so much the chemotherapy itself that has changed, but instead how it is administered and the availability and quality of drugs that can help patients with the side effects.

The approach targeting specific biomarkers is also extended to subtypes of tumours for which, until recently, no specific treatments were available. Tumours that do not present HER2 receptors or hormonal receptors are called triple-negative breast cancer, and until a few years ago the most common treatment for these was chemotherapy. But since the 2010s clinical trials have been testing targeted therapies for this subtype, such as PARP inhibitors, indicated in particular for treating triple-negative breast cancer in the presence of a BRCA mutation (Lyons, 2019). In 2022 the *Associazione italiana di oncologia medica* (Italian Association of Medical Oncology), together with biopharmaceutical companies and patients' associations, organised an event in Italy to discuss the new therapies for triple-negative breast cancer. An article describing the initiative emphasised how the introduction of new treatments can pave the way to chronicise triple-negative breast cancer as it is happening for the other subtypes of breast cancer, extending the survival times and preserving patients' quality of life (Quotidiano Sanità, 2022). Despite the efforts of individual healthcare facilities and governments to accommodate expensive new medicines in oncology (see Chapter 1), many difficulties persist.

The current construction of breast cancer as an individual problem that can be better faced with highly personalised therapeutic pathways while offering opportunities to improve the life of patients can simultaneously increase healthcare inequalities. Second-wave feminism has shown that individual difficulties are often rooted in social inequalities, and it has also shown how confining problems to a personal sphere limits the capacity to address their structural origins (Heberle, 2015). In this sense, the rhetoric of personalisation in oncology can be considered a sign of a broader social tendency to individualisation.

Moreover, the emphasis on a pharmaceutical approach is at least in part to the detriment of primary prevention, and efforts to reduce the incidence of the disease by tackling social and environmental inequalities are not prioritised. Further, presenting cancer treatments as highly personalised makes it more difficult to create common advocacy platforms for fairer access to treatments. The emphasis on personalisation in cancer care is not neutral, making it extremely relevant to explore the impact that new treatments are having on medical professionals and patients.

Breast cancer: almost chronic, but still not there

In the comic book *Cancer Made Me a Shallower Person*, Miriam Engelberg, a US graphic novelist who died from breast cancer in 2006, the same year in which the book was published, defines the difference between early-stage and metastatic breast cancer as the 'divide' in the breast cancer community. As we have seen in the previous section, metastatic breast cancer is increasingly presented as a manageable condition.[6] At the same time, tangible success characterises early-stage breast cancer where extended survival times have been obtained by moving drugs initially intended for metastatic patients – tamoxifen, aromatase inhibitors and more recently trastuzumab – to the adjuvant setting. The shift of drugs from metastatic to early state is common in the organisation of breast cancer treatments: drugs that give good results in the metastatic phase are regularly tested as treatments for early-stage breast cancer patients in order to avoid relapse (Greco, 2024).[7]

Preventing the spread or the recurrence of cancer in metastatic form is an important goal, and the number of drugs used to reduce this risk contributes to the construction of early-stage breast cancer as a treatable disease. Metastatic breast cancer, on the other hand, cannot be cured. However, the new image of this stage of the disease, increasingly defined as a treatable disease that can be kept at bay for several years, is paving the way toward a definition of metastatic cancer as a chronic condition. At the base of this vision, there is a new use of the concept of chronicity, linked to the fact that 'medical innovations have brought about changes promising to turn severe diseases into chronic ones via new long-term treatments' (Greco and Graber, 2022: 1). Dr Jessica, a French psycho-oncologist who has dedicated her career to supporting patients with breast cancer, said:

> When I started working, if you got the metastasis you would be dead within a year. The other day I got a phone call from a woman who had her first metastases six years ago. Well, she has chemo, she has treatments … but she's still here, she saw the birth of her grandchildren, she can take care of them. Well, I'm not saying that it's pleasant to live with metastases, but she's alive. She's chronically ill, like if you have severe diabetes, if you have heart failure, you're alive but you're bothered (*vous êtes embêtée*). So the big change is this, for the patients and for the doctors, that's huge, because they still have therapeutic weapons, they have more drugs … They can, like one of my colleagues says, look in [their] pocket … that means they [can prescribe a] certain number of treatments and they know that there are others [available in case of a] relapse. And that's, if you will, the major change.

In this excerpt, the introduction of new treatment options is presented as one of the most important shifts in metastatic breast cancer, which is starting to look similar to other chronic conditions. Significantly, the diseases chosen as a term of comparison are diabetes and heart failure, which are often considered (especially diabetes) manageable conditions. The breast cancer community is divided on whether metastatic breast cancer can be considered a chronic disease (see Greco, 2022a). Associations such as Europa Donna show more optimism about the possibility of keeping the disease under control for extended periods; however, other groups do not share this opinion. In 2008, the late Barbara Brenner, executive director of Breast Cancer Action until 2010, rejected the definition of metastatic breast cancer as chronic: 'Using the term chronic implies that breast cancer is a manageable disease, and downplays the reality that it is far too often fatal. It also diminishes the fact that we are in desperate need of better treatments' (Brenner, 2008). According to Brenner, breast cancer can be defined as a 'recurrent' disease; this is because 'recurrent diseases relapse repeatedly, with periods of remission in between' (Brenner, 2008, citing Wikipedia).

Dr Maria underlined during her interview that many patients, like Barbara Brenner, do not consider the term chronic adequate to describe metastatic breast cancer: 'patients don't like that. [There is a] research group of patients here who advise us [...] and they think it's undermining the severity of the condition, because you will call diabetes a chronic condition, but the perceived threat is not the same.' The idea that breast cancer can best be described as a recurrent disease was also mentioned by another consultant interviewed, Dr Luke, who said: 'another definition might be a series of acute episodes linked together by areas of more chronic stabilisation'. This description has the advantage of not erasing the difficulties of managing the condition, as recognised by reference to acute episodes. It also probably reflects that, while median survival times for metastatic breast cancer have increased since the 1990s, only approximately one third of patients survive five years after the diagnosis (see Sundquist et al., 2017). However, while important, survival statistics do not tell the whole story. As many of the medical professionals interviewed pointed out, biomarker-based diagnostic stratification is also crucial in the metastatic phase of the disease. For example, Dr Maria said: 'certainly hormone receptor-positive breast cancer can easily be called a chronic disease; the HER2 positive which responds to treatment probably falls into that group'. Dr Luke was even more explicit in this regard: during the interview, he said that it would be incorrect to 'lump all metastatic breast cancer together as one condition', and continued by saying:

> You could identify for example an older woman with metastatic breast cancer that's hormone receptor-positive, that's present only in the bones, whereby you could use hormone treatments to control that cancer sometimes for many years. And ... very much that cancer can be defined as a chronic condition, because women are living with that cancer on treatments ... Whereas a contrasting example would be a young woman in her thirties or forties with aggressive triple-negative breast cancer that's metastasised to the liver, that's not responding to the chemotherapy agents that we're using, where her prognosis might be measured in months, not years, and so in that situation that's not a chronic condition, that's a rapidly progressing terminal cancer.

In this extract, hormone-responsive and triple-negative breast cancer are presented as two different diseases, not only in the early stage but also in the metastatic phase, to the point that the first can be considered chronic, while the second is defined as terminal. In this case, a further element of stratification is mentioned to explain the differences between the two situations, namely the localisation of metastases, in the bones in one case and in the liver in the other. In the medical literature, the idea that metastatic breast cancer can be considered a chronic disease is often mobilised as an indicator of the successes and progress achieved in treating metastatic breast cancer (Greco, 2022a). Chronic is a term that can be used to describe a variety of circumstances, and chronicity in biomedicine is increasingly defined in multiple ways, even if the duration of the condition remains the primary aspect. Earlier syntheses present in the literature have found different criteria for the definition of chronicity, including duration, biological indicators, the impact on patient's lifestyle (Walker, 2001), slow onset, recurrent or deteriorating development and poor prognosis (O'Halloran et al., 2004).[8]

Several medical professionals whom I interviewed were uncertain about the chronicisation of metastatic breast cancer because they were unsure of how to define chronicity. Dr Trevor, for example, said: 'I don't even know what the definition of chronic disease is. When you think of chronic disease, you think of COPD [chronic obstructive pulmonary disease], you think of ... hypertension, you think of diabetes ...'. Some interviewees responded to the question of whether metastatic breast cancer could be considered a chronic condition by offering a more complex definition of chronicity itself. Dr Harry, for example, affirmed that metastatic breast cancer, while more serious than a diagnosis of diabetes, could be understood in the same way as a diagnosis of heart failure, adding that 'half the people with heart failure die within five to ten years, so [it] cannot be cured'. In some cases, the evolution of metastatic breast cancer was compared with conditions that have recently acquired chronic status, such as HIV/AIDS, underlining that future evolutions in the treatment of the disease might turn the condition into a more manageable problem as has been done with HIV/AIDS (as also suggested by Timmermann, 2019). Some other medical professionals interviewed mentioned disease management as a possible criterion for discussing the chronicity of metastatic breast cancer.

The fact that patients continue to need specialist care delivered in hospitals and that, in the majority of the cases, metastatic breast cancer cannot be managed at home or by general practitioners is, for many, a reason why it cannot be considered a chronic condition. These considerations echo Dr Maria's description of how new treatments can impact on already stretched services and professionals and present a multidimensional conception of chronicity that goes beyond survival times. Elsewhere (Greco, 2022a), I have used the comparison with a nebula to help understand the variable conceptualisation of chronicity that emerges from interviews with medical professionals (and patients). A nebula is a conglomerate of different interstellar materials with a fluid structure that can originate stars, planets or other planetary objects. Similarly to a nebula, in the different definitions of chronicity 'we can find different structuring principles that can push the concept in different directions' (Greco, 2022a: 110). As we will see in the final part of this chapter, the instability of the concept of chronicity is also a further element that adds to the medical-bodily assemblage, and leads patients to adopt different practices of biographical assemblage. It is thus important to explore patients' experiences.

Missing targets: the experiences of personalised medicine

Targeted therapies in cancer care have introduced what, following Klawiter (2008), I have defined a regime of personalisation, linked to the promises that patients would receive therapies that best suit their needs (Greco, 2024; and Introduction to this book). New tailored treatments should improve not only survival but also the quality of patients' lives. However, patients do not always find it empowering to have information about the molecular profile of their tumour (Kerr et al., 2021). Patients' narratives show us another, less widely appreciated, side of therapeutic innovation: the uncertainty of the condition and the limits of technical progress. Uncertainty, unpredictability and a complex relation with therapeutic options mark the experience of several of the patients whom I met (see also Greco, 2022a; 2022c). Natalie, a British woman in her early sixties, had received various therapies, and her therapeutic path was marked by uncertainties and difficulties, the first of which was trying to establish the exact nature of her tumour. A few years after being diagnosed with early-stage breast cancer, Natalie was diagnosed with bone and liver metastases in 2016. The examination showed that Natalie's tumour was back, that it had invaded the liver and also that the tumour was ER-positive. The medical professionals had reason to think that Natalie's tumour might also be HER2-positive, but the lack of a tissue sample meant that it was not possible to confirm that. Natalie was prescribed paclitaxel chemotherapy and was told there was a good chance that therapy could keep her situation stable for up to two years. However, after six months of treatment, the chemotherapy stopped working. At that point, Natalie explained to me, the doctors tried to perform another liver biopsy to gather more information about her tumour type. But a liver biopsy can be painful and tricky to perform, especially in cases like Natalie's, where the tumour is hard to reach. In Natalie's words:

> Anyway it didn't work, so they kept treating me on the basis of just the ER+ and then I was put on capecitabine … three weeks ago I was told it stopped working as well, and I have a new tumour in my liver, so meanwhile they have tried to biopsy me again a couple of times, and now I am waiting for them to have another go and do a biopsy, but they are not really sure that this [the new attempt at the biopsy] would work. I'm waiting for an appointment, they were talking about putting me on eribulin which is on the Cancer Drug List [the Cancer Drugs Fund], whatever it is called, but of course that would depend on what the biopsy shows so I am kind on no man's land of the moment.

This excerpt shows that Natalie had already received several treatments to keep her metastatic breast cancer at bay. However, these therapies were of limited efficacy. Although doctors were deciding whether to try a new drug – eribulin – the lack of information about the nature of the tumour made it difficult to plan the next steps. At the time of the interview, Natalie was waiting to try to have a new liver biopsy. She was in a situation of uncertainty and impasse that she defined as a 'no man's land'.[9]

Natalie was not the only woman I met whose pathway was complex and marked with uncertainty. The case of Kathy, another British woman in her fifties, shows how complex the management of innovative therapies can become for patients. At the moment of the diagnosis, Kathy's tumour had already spread outside the breast. Despite the shocking news, the fact that her tumour was HER2 positive was encouraging, as trastuzumab could potentially slow down the progression of the disease. She said this information gave her hope; however, the first treatment she received, chemotherapy combined with trastuzumab, did not provide the results the medical professionals hoped for. Kathy decided to try another treatment, Kadcyla,[10] which she had to self-fund because the NHS did not offer the drug at that time in the area where she was living. However, the treatment did not work and Kathy was 'running out of options'. She was resigned to undergoing another round of chemotherapy but was aware that the perspective did not offer her much hope. She was, however, able to find one of the last slots remaining in a clinical trial, and this time the treatment offered was able to effectively keep the disease at bay and improve her health and quality of life. Kathy's story also shows another side of the regime of personalisation: the increasing unaffordability of targeted treatments. The combination of increasingly expensive treatments and the opening of the NHS to private patients gives a new, probably unintended, meaning to the concepts of personalisation, in which patients' financial capacity may become a more decisive factor than their molecular profile (for other examples of privatisation of cancer care in the UK beyond breast cancer see Kerr et al., 2021 and Arteaga Pérez, 2022a).

Patients are aware of the financial stratification creeping in to cancer care, as this excerpt from Camilla's interview shows:

> A drug has been just approved by NICE, and it seems to give the best results for people like me, but it's only available as a first-line treatment, but I am past the first-line treatment, that's a drug that could potentially give me another year so and that shouldn't be just

about money, but if I was to put myself through that [it] would be three thousand [pounds] at month so …

NICE guidelines establish which patients are entitled to specific treatments; outside of that frame, private treatment is an option that only a small number of patients can access, and, as Kathy's experience shows, there is no guarantee that it will work.

These stories show not only the limits but also the dark areas of the regime of personalisation. Having a specific marker does not guarantee that the treatments will be effective, which also shows how the medical-bodily assemblage established by targeted treatments is not a simple biochemical relation between the marker and the drug, but involves probabilistic relations as well as financial factors.

Further, the idea that numerous lines of treatment for metastatic breast cancer represent different aces up the sleeve of doctors, which they can prescribe in sequence, and that each of them can keep the disease at bay, is a linear vision of how these treatments are used. *Mutatis mutandis*, this idea follows the linear cancer schemata mentioned by Löwy (2010), according to which detecting and intervening on small lesions is a guarantee of success in breast cancer treatment. Similarly to the early detection of small tumours, the possibility of offering different lines of treatment for metastatic breast cancer is the best approach that contemporary biomedicine can offer. Early diagnosis, the shift of drugs to the adjuvant setting and the development of multiple lines of treatment for metastatic breast cancer have certainly improved patients' prognosis and quality of life. However, this progress is not linear, nor equally distributed. Some patients benefit more than others: the characteristics of the tumour, and the possibility of accessing information and treatments, greatly influence the impact of medical innovation on their lives. As an alternative to a linear view of breast cancer, in this chapter and this book more generally, I propose instead the idea of medical-bodily assemblage as an analytical tool, aiming to capture the complexity and multidimensionality of breast cancer.

Other experiences of illness also show the inadequacy of linearity in the approach to breast cancer. Mariella, an Italian woman in her late fifties at the time of the interview, who had been living with metastatic breast cancer for several years, told me that up to that point her disease had been under control, thanks to an aromatase inhibitor. However, she also added that the therapy 'had to be done for life' ('è a vita'), and was scared that there might be a shortage of the drugs she used. She told me she was grateful to the doctors and the health facility who treated her, but she also noted how her link with the hospital was, like her therapy, for life. Muriel, a French woman similar in age to Mariella, also discussed feeling anchored to a healthcare institution, even without a metastatic diagnosis. She told me that, despite being cancer-free, she would no longer go to live in other countries, because this would jeopardise her access to follow-up care and treatment in case of a relapse. For both women, cancer was an experience that altered not only their present but their future life as well. In different ways, both metastatic and early-stage breast cancer inscribe themselves in patients' lives and limit them. The stories of the patients show how the experiences of illness are marked by unexpected difficulties, deviations from the expectations of biomedicine and new anxieties and fears generated by the intersection of complex therapies administered in functioning but imperfect healthcare systems. In this way, what seems personalised for the patients is the medical-bodily assemblage of what is available to them. What the patients find themselves doing is a biographical assemblage – a redefinition of their life expectations, not only in a chronological sense but also in an experiential, material and moral sense.

Conclusion

In this chapter, I have discussed how therapeutic and technological advances have changed the natural history and perception of breast cancer. As mentioned, cancer diagnosed in its early stages is considered curable, while metastatic breast cancer is increasingly being presented as a manageable condition that can be turned into a chronic one by using several lines of treatment. However, the difference between a tumour that has not spread outside the breast, and another that has metastasised involving other organs, is not the only one. Targeted therapies, together with a new understanding based on biomarkers and genetic profiles, are redefining breast cancer as a series of different diseases. Each of these diseases can be tackled with targeted treatments able to extend survival times. New treatments are also changing the status of cancerous cells, which now are not simply destroyed but need to be collected and identified in the hope that they might be the right kind of cells, those for which a treatment exists: as seen with the Buy My Cancer project, cancerous cells, while still dangerous, are now also becoming valuable.

However, at an individual level, there is no guarantee that these treatments will work, nor any way of knowing for how long. In the 1970s, the War on Cancer had raised hope that a single therapy for all cancers could be developed, but this approach has been sidelined. Instead, several therapies able to keep different types and subtypes of cancer at bay for longer periods have been prioritised. The presence of a number of treatments associated with some biological characteristics of the tumour defines the regime of personalisation. The economies of hope surrounding this cancer regime are circumscribed, fragmented and incremental, as the results in terms of survival times that new targeted therapies can offer for metastatic breast cancer are often measured in months and, only in the best of cases, in years. While new therapies have extended the survival of patients with metastatic cancer, biomedical progress has not yet significantly affected the terminal character of the disease.

The presence of multiple treatments is reshaping how healthcare systems deal with breast cancer: on the one hand, new treatments are creating new interdisciplinary collaborations necessary to manage complex side effects; on the other hand, their approval and availability take into account the financial pressure that these treatments put on universal healthcare systems. This latter aspect opens spaces for privatisation to accommodate patients who can pay for treatment, thus increasing inequalities. At the same time, the impact is not limited to the financial aspect, as the new therapeutic landscape is also altering the organisation of healthcare facilities and the everyday work of medical professionals. New ideas of medical progress are being assembled, particularly through the redefinition of what constitutes a successful cure, that is, extending the survival time through the continued use of several targeted treatments.

However, the linearity of biomedical models does not allow us to capture how the new therapeutic landscape changes the experiences of medical professionals and patients. In this case, the expectations of biomedicine and the concrete unfolding of individual experiences diverge significantly. The gap between what medical progress offers

– some extension of survival time for some patients – and what it is not yet able to offer – a significant extension of survival time for all patients, allowing them to lead a life similar to that pre-diagnosis – opens a space of unpredictability in their illness experiences that patients strive to fill as best they can. Patients find themselves redefining their expectations with regard to biomedical progress as they experience the difficulties and contradictions of the current treatments, and they do so by using material, experiential and moral assembly practices which illuminate the potentiality, but also the limits, of new therapeutic approaches. The redefinition of cancer further influences the relationship between patients, medical professionals and medical systems, creating more complex and sometimes conflictual relationships because of the need to frequently access medical treatments and facilities and the difficulties and the anxiety produced by the precarious success of new treatments. At the centre of these new assemblages is the patient's body, altered by cancer and its treatments, which is the subject of the next chapter.

Notes

1 The experiences of women using tamoxifen will be explored in Chapter 5.
2 Fluorouracil, developed in the 1950s, is an earlier example of a targeted drug, as it includes uracil in order to attach to cancerous cells more than to healthy ones (Timmermann, 2019). Tamoxifen, on the other hand, was the first to attach to a specific marker in cancerous cells, and is characterised by much lower toxicity.
3 This shows a contrast with the scepticism of some of the clinicians interviewed by Hedgecoe (2004) when the drug was introduced, with the linked controversies about costs and approval.
4 Viney and colleagues (2022) show further examples of this – how the introduction of oral chemotherapy can increase the pressure on blood testing services (as blood tests are needed before giving the treatment), or how follow-up services need to triage between symptoms to refer to oncologists and symptoms to refer back to the patient's GP.
5 See also Greco (2022a). The clinicians interviewed by Hedgecoe (2004) about Herceptin in particular were aware that the cost of the drug meant a possible reduction in resources for other treatments across the NHS. However, at the time, the impact was conceived at a larger scale,

well beyond breast cancer or even oncology, and therefore difficult to identify for the individual clinician.

6 I have dealt more in detail with chronicity, in particular in the case of metastatic breast cancer in the UK context, in a special issue edited with Nils Graber and published in *Anthropology & Medicine* (Greco and Graber, 2022) and an article included in the special issue (Greco, 2022a).

7 It is also worth noting that finding new indications for existing drugs, along with other strategies such as reformulating the drug to be administered in another way, is part of the 'life cycle management' through which companies try to maintain the market share, and often prolong the patent, of a drug – see e.g., Pantziarka et al. (2021).

8 The multidimensional nature of chronicity shows also how the measures of success of treatments for metastatic breast cancer capture only part of the possible aims of treatments (Greco, 2022a); indeed, the history of metastatic breast cancer research in the 1960s and 1970s shows several controversies about how to define success in relation to possible treatments (Toon, 2012).

9 This is one example of the different kinds of uncertainty linked to metastatic breast cancer – see Greco (2022c) for a broader discussion, and Chapter 5 in this book for a general discussion of uncertainty in breast cancer.

10 Kadcyla is still trastuzumab-based but adds a chemotherapeutic component in the same compound.

4

Assembling bodies: breast cancer and post-diagnosis metamorphoses

In her photography series *Intra-Venus*, Hannah Wilke shows her body profoundly altered by a lymphoma. The US artist, who located the female body at the centre of her artistic expression, exploring the interconnections between feminism, femininity and sexuality, presents in these pictures a vivid and honest portrait of a sick woman. The series title is a wordplay on a way of administering medical treatments, including chemotherapy, and Venus, the pagan goddess of beauty. Many of the photographs depict Wilke with no hair, and her semi-naked body traversed by tubes and patches. These powerful images encourage the observer to question beauty standards through the lens of illness. Can a woman with cancer still be beautiful? And does conventional beauty still have any relevance in the face of mortality?

Wilke illustrated an experience common to many women who, after a cancer diagnosis, find themselves redefining their position in relation to beauty norms. The changes brought on by illness and treatments can profoundly alter their body and the relationship women have established with it over the years. While some changes may be expected, such as hair loss due to chemotherapy, others, like weight gain and hot flashes from hormone therapy, can come as a surprise. Women often learn to recognise and appreciate their post-diagnosis body with all its changes. *Intra-Venus* suggests that, after cancer, women, rather than abandoning the dominant norms of beauty, reposition themselves in relation to them, redefining the meaning of attractiveness and seduction. However, the physical and emotional metamorphoses that come with cancer are complex and marked by ambiguities, ambivalence and sometimes grief for the body and life they had before the disease.

This chapter attempts to map the rich and nuanced strategies through which women come to terms with their new bodies, in particular through an exploration of the changes affecting the breast, understandably the most iconic of the body parts when it comes to breast cancer. The breast and its metamorphoses are explored, paying attention to how the medical system influences patients' individual perspectives. The objectives of medical professionals and patients only partially coincide, and their fulfilment is contingent on a medical system that can be rigid and offer only limited support.

In this chapter, I explore the multiple meanings and uses of the assemblages of post-mastectomy bodies. A breast reconstruction may include prostheses and the transplant of autologous tissue, but the reconstruction shows how bodies do not just 'end at the skin, or include at best other beings encapsulated by skin' (Haraway, 1985: 97). In the previous chapter, I focused on medical-bodily assemblages to indicate how changes in biomedicine, from the conceptualisation of a condition to innovations in treatment, are associated with the transformations of the disease itself and, consequently, with how patients experience the disease. Here, I focus more specifically on the bodily aspect of the medical-bodily assemblages that can be identified in the explicit reshaping of the body linked to breast cancer and its treatments. Body alterations, for example, through reconstructive surgery, make these assemblages tangible and visible. Moreover, when strong social norms, such as gender norms, target the body part concerned, bodily assemblages also reveal how these norms and expectations shape the body.[1]

The process of reconstruction involves negotiating with the medical system, grappling with the language of bodily integrity and exploring the practical uses of one's own body. By examining the different ways in which reconstructed bodies are assembled within their respective social and cultural contexts, we can go beyond the traditional feminist analyses of cosmetic and reconstructive practices, which often focus on resistance to or compliance with hegemonic ideas of normality and beauty.

What is gained and what is lost: or the aestheticisation of breast cancer

Breast cancer is strongly associated with the risk of losing the breast when a mastectomy, a surgical removal of the breast, is needed. The history of this operation is linked to the name of William Halsted, the US surgeon who, towards the end of the nineteenth century, implemented a meticulous technique known as radical mastectomy. Radical mastectomy involved the removal not only of the breasts but also of the pectoral muscles and the axillary contents (Lebovic, 2019). The surgery was highly debilitating, but removing a large part of the tissue around the tumour marginally reduced the risk of a local recurrence. For this reason, radical mastectomy remained in use until the 1960s (Lebovic, 2019). During the 1970s, a modified version of the radical mastectomy, in which the pectoral muscles are not removed, gradually replaced Halsted's surgery (Madden et al., 1972). Both radical mastectomy and modified mastectomy were based on the idea that breast cancer is a localised disease that, if left untreated, could extend to contiguous areas (Aronowitz, 2007). In the 1980s, in the US, modified mastectomy was the most widespread operation (Montini and Ruzek, 1989), but advances in surgery had meanwhile demonstrated the effectiveness of conservative surgery (lumpectomy, quadrantectomy), which does not include the total removal of the breast (Lerner, 2001 – who also notes how conservative surgeries gained acceptance among European surgeons at an earlier date than among those in the US). Canadian oncologist Vera Peters (1975) was the first to publish data from a retrospective study demonstrating the effectiveness of conservative surgery associated with radiotherapy (see Cowan, 2010). The clinical trials conducted by Bernard Fisher in the US (Fisher et al., 1985) and Umberto Veronesi in Italy (Veronesi et al., 1981) definitively demonstrated the validity of conservative surgery, which became the standard treatment for small tumours. According to Umberto Veronesi, the new surgical approach represents a paradigm shift in contemporary oncology, which, for the first time, commits to saving not only the patient's life but also her quality of life (Carlson, 2003). According to the Italian surgeon: '[T]he quadrantectomy caused an overturning in the history of cancer treatment, for it established at least three cornerstones on which modern oncology is founded: the importance of early diagnosis, the principle of minimum effective care, and the attention to the psychological dimension of the disease' (Veronesi, 2012: 25).

As mentioned in Chapter 3, conservative surgery and early diagnosis of breast cancer appear strongly intertwined, both because the operation is performed to remove small tumours and because the fact that small tumours can be treated with conservative surgery could encourage women to check their breasts and undergo screening. As we will see later, conservative surgery techniques have been developed to offer women the best possible aesthetic results.[2] However, before following the evolution of conservative oncological surgery, it is important to underline that mastectomy has not disappeared. On the contrary, there are indications of a resurgence of mastectomy. As we have seen in Chapter 3, it can be performed to treat *in situ* cancers and for genetically at-risk patients. A retrospective epidemiological study using data from the Kentucky Cancer Registry showed that mastectomy rates increased in the early 2000s after declining in the 1990s (Dragun et al., 2013). In the UK, mastectomy rates vary significantly from institution to institution. Research published in 2011 found that institutions reporting high mastectomy rates are associated with greater patient autonomy in decision making (Caldon et al., 2011). The centrality of mastectomy in the therapeutic landscape has led to the development of different breast reconstruction techniques, which can be divided into two groups. The first group includes techniques that use external materials to create the volume of the breast, such as a prosthesis filled with silicone or saline solution. The second group includes transplants of autologous tissue (fat or muscle) taken from the patient's back, abdomen or glutei.

Reconstruction is presented as the moment of restitution, when a woman regains, at least in part, what she lost to cancer: her breast. It has been historically contested among breast cancer activists (Lerner, 2006), with some, such as Rose Kushner, emphasising the importance of conservative surgery and access to reconstruction, and others, such as Audre Lorde (1980), criticising reconstruction as invisibilising the disease and its political implications. In France, in particular, I met both groups of patients promoting specific reconstructive techniques and others advocating non-reconstruction (Greco, 2016c). The post-mastectomy reconstruction, which generally follows the therapies, is considered the least stressful moment in the treatment pathway because the patient has completed the most difficult therapies, such as chemotherapy and radiotherapy. As Dr Gilles, a French plastic surgeon, stated: 'the reconstruction is almost a moment of happiness'. This assertion, however, seems at odds with the description of reconstruction as 'the obstacle course', as it has been defined by several patients (Greco, 2020b). These two definitions are formulated from two different positions, with surgeons often emphasising the benefits of reconstruction. For example, another French surgeon, Dr Françoise, told me that patients who have undergone reconstruction have better survival times. She explained these data by stating that undergoing a reconstruction shows 'a willingness to fight (*c'est un facteur battant*), [that is,] those who decide to have a reconstruction are also those who have the energy to do it, but they are also those who feel good because they have a reconstruction'. While some studies show a correlation between reconstruction and increased survival time, the main hypothesis is that the increased survival is attributable to patients undergoing reconstruction being more likely to have more economic resources (Bezhuly et al., 2009). Some of the surgeons whom I interviewed advanced another argument as an advantage of reconstructive surgery: the aesthetic improvement that can be obtained through the operation. The reconstruction becomes a moment when the norms underlying the canonical image of the female breast become explicit. In this regard, Dr Françoise said:

> One will never return back, and sometimes it's the occasion to do better than before, when you have a patient that is flat-chested, and you put a prosthesis on both sides, finally she gains something [...] well, she will not say it to you [that she gained something], but in any case [it was] at the cost of an unfortunate episode [such as] breast cancer.

Dr Françoise was therefore explicit that reconstruction can be a gain in relation to the pre-diagnosis breast, even though recognising that this happens as part of a negative event (and that patients themselves are not likely to describe it as a gain). Franca gave an account of the conversation she had with her plastic surgeon, which is along the same lines:

> [Before carrying out the reconstruction, the doctor told me:] 'You will see Madam, the ladies who have had this operation come back

afterwards, in consultation, with very low-cut clothes [*dei vestiti tutti scollacciati*] which show everything.' But I think that I would have preferred to do a liposuction of the buttocks, and my breast, I thought it fine as it was.

Franca did not appreciate this way of describing the operation: not only did she consider the tone unsuited to the context, but she also disagreed that her natural breast required any change. Other patients had a more favourable opinion of the changes produced by the reconstruction. As Angeline, a French woman in her forties, told me:

> At the very first appointment, when [the surgeon] told me about the operation, the first thing I asked was to have an augmentation, I asked if we could augment on the other side. I was determined [to have a breast augmentation], it was my carrot, as they say. I am very satisfied with the result, really. And I had seen three women who had shown me the fitting of prostheses, and I was very distressed because they had only done the [mastectomised] side, they had not had the other one redone and therefore they had a fifty-year-old woman's breast on one side and a twenty-year-old woman's on the other, and I didn't think that was pretty, and the fact that I did both at the same time, somehow I find myself with something that is almost prettier than before, I'm happy.

For Angeline, breast reconstruction was the 'carrot' that allowed her to find a positive element in a difficult situation. The woman was satisfied with the result and considered her breasts 'prettier than before'. She was among the patients who, in Dr Françoise's words, could gain something from reconstructive surgery. Angeline's experience demonstrates the importance that post-mastectomy reconstruction can have for many women and also shows the plurality of ways that they use to come to terms with and redefine their experience of illness (see also Chapter 6). Angeline's account reminds us that accessing surgical solutions that offer a good aesthetic result can improve the patient's quality of life.[3] Oncoplasty (see, e.g., Garrido et al., 2006) is an approach specifically aiming to apply cosmetic surgery techniques within an oncological context. The choice between mastectomy and conservative surgery depends on a number of factors, such as the size and location of the tumour and the size of the breast, which are also considered in relation to the anticipated aesthetic result (Cothier-Savey and Rimareix, 2008). Oncoplasty enhances the aesthetic results of a conservative approach making use of cosmetic surgery techniques. Garrido and colleagues (2006: 715) present it in these terms:

> Thus, even for a small tumour, it is possible to offer a breast reduction procedure to a patient with breast hypertrophy at the same time as the lumpectomy. In other words, any patient requiring treatment for breast cancer should be offered a detailed analysis of her breast and its possible defects.

This description shows how the objectives of cosmetic surgery have been introduced in the oncological context along with the techniques (Greco, 2016d). In particular, the authors discuss how purely aesthetic characteristics of patients' breasts should also be considered when they undergo breast cancer surgery, such as asymmetry, hypertrophy (excessively large breasts) and ptosis (sagging). This shows how deviations from a normative ideal of the breasts are medicalised along with cancer, aiming to bring both the cancerous breast and – often for reasons of symmetry – the contralateral healthy breast within this normative ideal. In recent years, a new approach called extreme oncoplasty (Silverstein et al., 2015) has been introduced to extend the conservative approach to cases that in the past would certainly have been treated with a mastectomy, that is, in patients with a tumour larger than five centimetres.

The institutional context of breast reconstruction

Surgical advances play a pivotal role in shaping breast cancer experiences; in this section, I focus on the institutional context in which these advances are implemented. In the UK, NICE guidelines suggest that, after a mastectomy, women should be offered both reconstruction options – immediate and delayed – 'whether or not they are available locally' (2018: 12), and they also emphasise the importance of informing women about the different surgical techniques available. However, the implementation of these guidelines may vary. A survey carried out in 2022 by Breast Cancer Now,[4] one of the leading British breast cancer charities, has shown that some patients are offered only one option, for example, a reconstruction with breast implants, because other types of intervention, such as free flap surgery, are not available locally. The report also highlights how, in some cases, the choices are restricted by the internal organisation of some medical institutions which, following a mastectomy, limit the time after which patients can request a reconstruction, or limit the number of operations that can be performed during a reconstruction, sometimes excluding the contralateral symmetrisation. As we will see in the next section, contralateral symmetrisation is an intervention on which women may have differing opinions. However, this operation can be experienced, as Angeline's case showed, as an integral part of the reconstruction process and necessary to obtain a whole image. Financial considerations are central to medical choices, however, and medical professionals are encouraged to analyse the financial impact of reconstruction in the medium term (see Atherton et al., 2011). Free flap surgeries are generally more expensive, as compared to the insertion of a prosthesis, but autologous reconstructions usually require less follow-up over the years, while in many cases the prostheses need to be replaced.

The financial question is also central in Italy, where a group of more than seventy breast surgeons discussed at the Italian Senate the difficulties that patients and medical professionals face in the case of breast reconstruction. In many Italian regions, immediate reconstruction is often not included among the surgical procedures that the regions reimburse to individual medical institutions. In some cases, the reconstruction operation is reimbursed only if performed after the mastectomy and identified as a separate surgical procedure (Moriconi, 2022). This can be difficult for women who would prefer immediate reconstruction, and it can be a financial issue for those institutions that decide to continue offering immediate reconstruction. Another factor to which the group of surgeons have drawn attention is that in several cases reconstruction operations carried out with microsurgical techniques, despite being longer and more complex, are reimbursed less than the insertion of prostheses. We have seen in Chapter 1 how the significant gap between the north and the south of the country marks the Italian institutional context. However, in the case of reimbursement practices for post-mastectomy reconstruction, we see an uneven situation with some regions, defined as virtuous, with more efficient reimbursement practices, and others less so, without any alignment across the traditional north–south axis.

In France, many of the patients whom I met told me they had undergone different treatments in different institutions, and many of the women with whom I spoke had reconstruction in private healthcare facilities and paid for it. The porous relationship between public and private healthcare that characterises France, and the fact that medical personnel, especially surgeons, often work in both public and private facilities, probably facilitate the movement of patients. For some patients, these operations carried out in the private sector are reimbursed through their medical insurance (see Chapter 1). Other women whom I met said they had paid for a procedure that should theoretically be guaranteed by the French health system (see Greco, 2015). Difficulties in accessing reconstruction increased during the COVID-19 pandemic, when elective surgeries[5] were paused in many European countries, including the three covered in this book. However, the pandemic highlighted an already existing phenomenon, as long waiting times often emerged as a problem in my fieldwork. Many patients in the UK, Italy and France have had to wait longer to access reconstructive surgery, which has often negatively impacted on their well-being and the ability to close a painful chapter in their lives. In France, during my fieldwork (and therefore before the pandemic), many patients mentioned long waiting times as one of the reasons for carrying out the reconstruction in a private facility. The concept of choice is dominant in the discourses surrounding breast reconstruction. However, this rapid excursus on the institutional context of post-mastectomy reconstruction shows how the surgical offer and the unequal distribution of such offers severely limit women's choices. In the three countries studied, only a minority of patients who undergo a mastectomy opt for surgical reconstruction.[6] Long waiting times, difficulty in accessing the technique deemed most appropriate, financial problems or communication difficulties with the medical staff are among the obstacles women face when they decide to pursue a breast reconstruction. The fieldwork also revealed women's different strategies to overcome these difficulties, mobilising a range of resources. From seeing multiple doctors and changing hospitals, to paying for the surgery, many of my interviewees overcame various obstacles to achieve a goal that was important to them.

The reasons why some women wish to undergo post-mastectomy reconstruction are complex and involve different aspects of their lives, as we will see in the following sections.

Negotiating surgery and its aims

The availability of several reconstructive techniques paves the way for further forms of negotiation and compromise for patients, who have to take into account both the limitations and risks that each option presents and what the medical staff can offer.[7] Dominant beauty standards emphasise the appearance of the breast over the sensations, emotions and experiences attached to it. Similarly, cosmetic surgeons tend to consider operations successful in which the resulting breast is similar to a normative one (Greco, 2016d). However, women's relationships with their bodies and normative beauty ideas are diverse, multifaceted and often under-explored. In this section, I focus on the processes of negotiation that women have to go through with the medical culture and the materiality of the body that can resist attempts to modify it and turn reconstructive surgery into a failure.

Analysing these aspects allows us to capture better the complexity and ambiguity of breast reconstruction, a phase of the therapeutic pathway that can increase the difficulties of the disease.[8] Florence was in this situation. In her late thirties, she had a mastectomy followed by a *latissimus dorsi* flap, using muscle and skin from her upper back to reconstruct a breast volume. During the interview, Florence said that doing a reconstruction was not crucial to her and that she felt she was somewhat pushed into it during the medical consultation. She recognised that the cosmetic result of the reconstruction was excellent, but after some time a recurrence of cancer in the reconstructed breast necessitated its removal. The second mastectomy was very difficult for Florence, as she was left with back pain caused by the removal of a muscle for a reconstruction that had not been a priority for her.

Régine, a French woman in her late fifties at the time of the interview, had a similar negative experience. Unlike Florence, Régine wanted a breast reconstruction, but she was sceptical about the prostheses the surgeon inserted in her contralateral breast to improve the aesthetic result. A subsequent infection in the contralateral breast exacerbated the difficulty of Régine's post-surgery phase. During the interview, she said that one of the factors that made that period more difficult was her awareness that most of the difficulties were caused by this contralateral symmetrisation, about which Régine had never been fully convinced and which she felt the surgeon had never discussed adequately with her. Régine wanted a reconstruction in order to find bodily integrity, which was very important for her, not to conform her breast and body to a normative idea of beauty. However, that symmetrisation ultimately interfered with her desire to regain her strength and to leave the experience of the disease behind.

Franca also had problems with the contralateral operation, which left her with constant pain in her nipple. While she had a strong desire for a breast reconstruction, she said that the operation was not enough to bring back a sense of bodily integrity; moreover, after the cancer and the surgery, even the healthy breast was no longer a part of her body capable of giving her the feeling and erotic pleasure she experienced before the diagnosis.

Amélie, a French woman in late fifties, told me she had refused contralateral symmetrisation because she did not want to undergo a second procedure and a second anaesthesia. She also told me that while she was pleased with the aesthetic result, her surgeon was not, as he thought a symmetrisation would have improved the outcome. Such divergences of opinion between doctors and patients on what constitutes a good aesthetic result emerged in several interviews. Clothilde's experience, for example, was similar to Amélie's, as she described in negative terms her first encounter with a plastic surgeon who had not wanted to use silicone prostheses that would have increased the size of Clothilde's breasts, also operating on the healthy breast. For Clothilde, this imposition of such a radical change was 'a lack of respect', and she decided not to undergo the surgery and to delay the reconstruction, even though she wanted to have one. Clothilde consulted other surgeons, some in the private sector, and eventually met a private surgeon who performed a breast reconstruction without inserting any contralateral prosthesis. She described this surgeon as someone who listened to her and respected her body and her desire not to alter her healthy breast. Clothilde was not the only patient to consult several surgeons, and was not the only one who paid to undergo a reconstruction (see Chapter 1). For Clothilde, having to move into the private sector was not a problem, but she was aware that for many patients it might well have been a problem. The interconnection between private and public structures, particularly strong in the case of breast reconstruction, allowed several women to consult more doctors, as they could move between the two. However, some women had to take out loans or use personal savings to pay for reconstruction in the private sector. In some cases, women had to pay several times, for the first surgery and for follow-up interventions needed years later (cf. Greco, 2015).

The story of Freya, a British woman in her forties, shows the role of another instance of negotiation that goes beyond the relationship between surgeon and patient, that of multidisciplinary teams (MDTs).[9] Freya and her surgeon agreed to perform an autologous reconstruction with fat harvesting and uplift on the other side. However, the MDT rejected this option as too invasive and proposed a dorsal flap instead. Freya disagreed with the MDT's decision and instead trusted her surgeon's judgement ('So when he came back to tell me that they didn't want to do it, I was really upset, I said "but to me, you are the person I chose, they're not the people that I know and I trust, and I believe in you"'). Ultimately Freya and her surgeon found a compromise by performing only one operation with a transplant of autologous fat tissue, which gave a satisfactory result.

The stories presented have a specific aspect of reconstruction in common, that is, contralateral symmetrisation, an operation involving a healthy breast, and for this reason its role raises several questions. In cosmetic surgery, conflicts between the aesthetic criteria of surgeons and those of patients are not uncommon.[10] It is, therefore, not surprising that episodes of negotiation and disagreement converge around this aspect, which, more than others, blurs the line between cosmetic and reconstructive surgery. The women whom I met did not always want a 'better' breast: often, they were trying to obtain a breast as close as possible to the one they had before the diagnosis. By refusing bigger implants or contralateral symmetrisation, they called into question the vision of the surgeons, which was often based on purely aesthetic criteria rather than on functional ones. The experiences of these women extended the semantic field of the term 'conservative'.

In medicine, 'conservative' is the surgery that, in opposition to mastectomy, makes it possible to preserve the breast. For some patients, preserving the body's integrity meant accepting the reconstruction, but refusing operations on the healthy breast, even if further surgeries could offer results closer to the aesthetic norm. Some patients also wanted to conserve their time and energy, avoiding the fatigue and stress of additional surgeries that they considered unnecessary. Complications related to contralateral symmetrisation were experienced as a further loss. At the same time, for some patients, like Angeline, contralateral symmetrisation was an indispensable part of finding themselves in their own bodies. As she pointed out, having better breasts is also a way to accept the experience of breast cancer.

The variety of experiences presented here shows that multiple factors can influence patients' decisions and redefine the centrality of the aesthetic result emphasised by cosmetic surgery. Furthermore, in exploring the reasons that pushed women to carry out reconstruction, we discover that, even when aesthetic reasons were present, they were also linked to other elements guiding the women's choices. Colette, a French woman diagnosed with breast cancer shortly before turning forty, said: 'The fact of having our breasts removed, in whole or in part, represents an attack on the mother and the woman, the [female] image seen through the eyes of others, seen through the eyes of the society.' This quote illustrates the complex relationship that, if not the totality, at least a significant portion of women have with the role that different social spheres attribute to the female breast (see also Manderson, 2011). However, it would be incorrect to consider reconstructive surgery only as a way to conform passively to normative beauty ideals.

The choice to undergo a reconstructive operation was, in many cases, the result of complex, contextual and provisional negotiations that women engaged between their own body, their desires and the expectations of their family, their children, their partners[11] and society more generally. As we have seen, the outcome of reconstructive surgery is not always positive, and the risk of complications is high. The women whom I interviewed were generally aware of the risks and limitations, but, for many, these were not enough to deter them from undergoing reconstructive surgery. The willingness to conform to normative aesthetic ideals, while occasionally present, was just a tile in the more complex mosaic of choices and factors guiding the actions of these patients. Among these was the need to do everything possible to stem the effects of the disease on their lives.

Sally, a British woman diagnosed in her thirties, told me that her surgeon did not give her an option for a reconstruction, which she felt was essential for her at that moment of her life. She added: 'As a thirty-seven-year-old woman, I felt that I wanted [a] choice for whatever reconstruction, and he said "mastectomy" and that was it. So he did not give me the choice of reconstruction and that's what I wanted at the time.'

Sally was not the only patient to emphasise the importance of reconstruction as a possibility that helps women to better face the prospect of a mastectomy. At the time of her diagnosis, Colette was a young woman with small children, a husband, a family and a job she liked. She told me that she was 'prepared for a certain number of things' at the moment of the diagnosis. Her words suggest that she had already considered the possibility of losing her breast, and also the possibility of undergoing a reconstruction. She had a reconstruction through the insertion of a silicone prosthesis, but while the reconstruction was initially successful, Colette had to have the prosthesis removed because complications appeared shortly after the surgery. She described the experience in these terms:

> When the prosthesis was removed, when there was a failure (*échec*), I was ready to stay with one breast. I am 38 years old, what do I want to do? I want to stay with only one breast? I would live well, too bad for my husband, do I still go for broke? (*j'essaie le tout pour tout*) I'm tired! ... There are not very many of us who want to be rebuilt ... We are only 30% on average, there is a study that has been done, we are the thirty out of a hundred women operated on the breast [who] choose reconstruction ... Gradually I said to myself 'ah bah! Maybe I'll do the dorsal flap and anyway, I can't do anything afterwards', so we did that, and then, voila, it's done.

Colette knew her options, and also that many women had decided against reconstruction. Immediately after her diagnosis, she was determined to undergo reconstruction; however, the failed surgery (*l'échec*) undermined her resolution, and she hesitated whether to attempt a second surgery or to remain asymmetrical. She told herself that she was 'ready to stay with one breast', but the choice was not simple. She felt too young to stay with only one breast, and the figure of her husband emerged implicitly in her narrative ('too bad for my husband'). We do not know whether the fact that she was in a heterosexual relationship might have steered her towards surgical reconstruction. During the interview, Colette often said that this second reconstruction was a way to 'go for broke' (*essayer le tout pour tout*) before giving up.

Béatrice's experience, although different, echoes Colette's complex pathway toward a second reconstruction. At the time of the interview, Béatrice, a French woman, was in her sixties and had been affected twice by breast cancer. The first time she was only thirty years old, and in that case it was possible to perform conservative surgery. A few years later, a recurrence in the same breast was diagnosed, and a mastectomy was necessary. For more than ten years, Béatrice lived in an asymmetrical body and was not interested in a reconstruction. However, with the passing of time, she changed her mind. Béatrice told me that cancer was not the only problem she had faced; she had had marital problems, resulting in a divorce. After the end of her marriage, a new partner entered Béatrice's life, and she described the new relationship as happy and fulfilling. After meeting her new partner, she decided to undergo a reconstruction. Unfortunately, an infection forced the surgeon to re-operate on Béatrice to remove the prosthesis a few days after the operation. When asked about this decision, Béatrice offered a lengthy answer which started by describing some details of her childhood. She told me about her complicated relationship with her parents, because of which she felt a need for appreciation and recognition. During childhood, Béatrice was a diligent student and sought, as she could, to make her parents proud of her. But she did not receive the appreciation she needed until several years later, as an adult. After talking at length about her parents, Béatrice added, 'when I met my [second partner], he did not ask me [to do a reconstruction] because he accepted me as I was. [I did it] for me and for him too, without him asking me ... [But] I wanted to have two breasts.'

When it comes to reconstruction, technique and aesthetic results are not the only important elements. For many women, the time and the context of the operation can be relevant, as Celeste, a southern Italian woman in her sixties, shows. She had undergone a mastectomy a few years before and told me that family members and medical personnel had tried to convince her to have a reconstruction. She thus decided to book an operation in Milan, a city far from her region of residence, but then cancelled it at the last minute because she was worried at the idea of having surgery far from home. However, Celeste did agree, sometime later, to have a reconstruction in a hospital near her home town.

For Sally, Colette, Béatrice and Celeste, the post-mastectomy reconstruction was an attempt to find a balance in their lives by attending to their bodies. The choice to perform a reconstruction can result from opposing forces, and the body materially produced by reconstructive surgery – often different from what is meant by a 'normal body' – incorporates the tensions and contradictions that women might be experiencing. Crompvoets defines reconstruction as 'the last bastion of hope' (Crompvoets, 2006: 90), the last hope that women have to regain a body conforming to the current standard of beauty. According to Crompvoets, it is only after the reconstruction that women begin to articulate a new self-image and accept the changes brought by the disease. The women whom I met had realistic expectations regarding the aesthetic outcome of their surgery, and they were aware that, from an aesthetic point of view, a reconstructed breast would be different from a real one, but often what women were trying to obtain was not just a two-breasted body but closure by doing everything in their power to limit the impact of the disease on their lives. However, the surgery can also be fraught with emotional tension, as it represents the last opportunity to take control of their changing bodies.

Uses of the post-reconstruction body

Élodie, a French woman who was almost sixty years old at the time of the interview, had discovered her first cancer at thirty-nine years old. At the time, she underwent a conservative intervention, followed by radiotherapy. Her surgeon advised her to contact a plastic surgeon to consider a partial reconstruction of the operated breast, but Élodie refused, as the altered image of her breast did not bother her or her husband. Several years later, Élodie discovered a recurrence on the same breast, and a mastectomy was necessary this time. About this second mastectomy, she said:

I had a tendency to consider that what is important is to take care of yourself, that afterwards you have a slightly bad conscience to attach too much importance to the image of your body or to things like that ... But indeed, when I found myself with a breast less it was really unbearable, it was really a body in which I no longer found myself. So there I didn't hesitate at all, I was really determined to do a reconstruction.

For Élodie, the aesthetic sequelae of the first operation were not significant enough to begin reconstruction, but the situation changed after a mastectomy. This operation broke her balance, and she could no longer recognise herself in her new body. What does it mean to no longer recognise yourself in your own body? In this expression, there is, of course, the idea of not recognising yourself in the image that the mirror reflects to you. However, the interviews show that this expression can also refer to the fact that a different body reduces the range of activities and experiences that women can have. Several interviewees highlighted that they were aware of the difference between a reconstructed breast and a natural one[12] and knew that a reconstructed breast does not replace the sensations of the natural breast (see also Manderson, 2011). Discussing a different surgery – oesophageal reconstruction – Mitchell and Snyder (2016) also point out that a surgical assemblage normally does not reconstitute the previous tissue, and therefore cannot really restore the 'before' state. But for many of the patients whom I met, the reconstruction was a pragmatic choice which made it possible to extend the range of uses of the body and give them greater freedom. As Clothilde told me: 'Even if it's totally fake, now I call it the "tit-toc" ... I think it's more pleasant for everyone, I tell myself there's no longer that side devastated, and then I can dress as I want, freedom too, so it's a social breast.' And the experience of Sandrine, a French woman in her forties, pointed in the same direction:

> [Without the prosthesis, I would be] completely crushed by the feeling of lack [...]. When I go to the swimming pool, I have a basic bathing suit, I put it on and nobody sees anything. I can wear normal bras. So that's great, I feel like I'm normal, whereas before I was abnormal. It was truly a gift. I can no longer wear very low-cut dresses, or go without a bra, but I find that [when] I'm dressed with a bra it's really good. [...] And, above all, I can play sports. I can't climb any more, same for all sports where there is tension, but [I can] swim [and] walk.

Sandrine did not question that her body was now different, but with the prosthesis, she could easily hide this difference and continue to play sports. For Sandrine, this was very important; in fact, immediately after the procedure she was 'completely obsessed' with the risk of developing lymphedema and thus losing the mobility of her arm. Fortunately, the recovery was perfect and she 'didn't feel at all that it affected [her] daily life'. Other women had a pragmatic vision of the reconstruction and have underlined how a reconstructed breast can make some everyday activities, such as attending a public gym class or going to the beach, more manageable than an external prosthesis would. As Clothilde reminds us, the reconstructed breast is a 'social breast', because it restores a socially accepted appearance to support the 'social gaze', that is, the normalising set of expectations that society puts upon women's bodies. Film theorist Laura Mulvey introduced the concept of male gaze (1975) to indicate how female characters in films are seen through the perspective of the men, who can be both male spectators and other male characters in the fiction. Since then, the male gaze has been used to indicate the pervasive expectations that men can have regarding women's bodies. However, the social gaze to which women refer is not just male; many women underline the role of female family members and friends in orienting their decision to pursue a normalised, two-breasted body, while others, like Sandrine, found comfort in female friendship. Reconstruction could also be a means to free oneself from this social gaze and the critiques that a nonconforming body can attract. In this sense, breast reconstruction can be simultaneously an exercise of agency on the woman's part and an acknowledgement of the oppression of aesthetic norms (Gagné and McGaughey, 2002). In this oscillation between agency and oppression, women can decide to select and assemble the functions that a reconstructed breast can have.

This allows us to understand why many women decided to reconstruct just the volume but not the nipple, or not to undergo symmetrisation, as they considered these details superfluous for the uses for which the new breast was intended. This can also help us to understand why many women could be simultaneously satisfied with their decision to undergo reconstructive surgery while considering the aesthetic result imperfect.

However, the partial aesthetic results was sometimes enough to limit the range of social uses of the reconstructed body. This was the case for Franca, who, during the interview, said that with her reconstructed breast she felt comfortable enough to wear a bathing suit but could not appear naked in front of other women when she was, for example, in the gym. If, for Sandrine, Clothilde and other women I encountered, reconstruction was sufficient to put into action a process of passing and gave them greater freedom than an external prosthesis, this was not the case for Franca. Reconstruction was not in itself sufficient for her to regain the full use of the body; what was needed was a negotiation on her part to find a balance between the pre-mastectomy body and the post-reconstruction body. However, negotiation processes do not happen in a vacuum but in different social settings. Several research projects have shown that, in Italy, women are exposed to sexualised messages (Valtorta et al., 2016) and may be more at risk of internalising the idea that their self-worth is linked to their image (Moscatelli et al., 2021). In this context, pressures to conform to unattainable and elusive beauty standards can make it more difficult for women with breast cancer to accept their post-diagnosis body.

While it is essential to acknowledge local variations in the pressure that normalising aesthetic norms have on women, it is also important to recognise that virtually every woman who receives a breast cancer diagnosis has to 'confront, in rapid succession, the dangers of the disease itself and […] subtle articulations of society's distaste for her "non-normalised" body […]. What resources are available for resisting the deep shame inscribed in this series of encounters?' (Fitts, 1999: 8). Among the individual and personal resources available, Sandrine, for example, in her journey of acceptance, found the support of other women, particularly other women with a different appearance. In the interview, she recalled: 'this summer, I went to Norway with my husband and other people I didn't know, and in the group, there was a girl who was badly burned, so my story was nothing compared to hers. And suddenly, we both found ourselves showering and laughing in a token-operated shower.' Meeting a disabled woman allowed her to put into perspective not only her own difference but also the strict norms limiting women's bodies. Sandrine had the opportunity to deconstruct and reject what Fitts calls 'society's distaste for [a] "non-normalised" body'. However, other women, such as Franca, for example, did not have the same opportunity and adapted to living in a body that they considered limited.

These experiences demonstrate the range of possibilities as well as the limits of the reconstructed body and the bodily assemblage achieved through surgery. They also emphasise the bodily assemblage work that women do with their bodies, the disease and the sociocultural context in which they live. Women negotiate the meaning of the reconstructed breast for themselves and for others.[13] This assemblage work produced a provisional and negotiated body, the acceptance of which is contextual and often needs further renegotiations when circumstances change. Moreover, this work is done not only by those who have undergone a post-mastectomy reconstruction but also by women who live in an asymmetric body, as we will see in the next section.

Living in an asymmetric body

A surgical reconstruction is not the only option, as women can decide not to carry out any reconstruction, and to live in an asymmetrical body.[14] And, as we have seen, most women who undergo a mastectomy do live in asymmetrical bodies. Many medical professionals whom I met said that women 'choose' not to undergo a reconstruction; however, in many cases, the rhetoric of choice is insufficient to capture the nuanced experiences of women living with an asymmetric body. In this regard, Marie, a French woman in her early fifties who lived with an asymmetrical body as a result of two breast cancer diagnoses, told me that she found the notion of choice inadequate to describe her situation. 'If I had a choice,' said Marie, 'I would have chosen not to have cancer.' But the rejection of the notion of choice goes beyond the understandable rejection of disease, and Marie detailed the stages through which she had accepted her asymmetrical body:

> I didn't choose to remain asymmetrical. A [surgical reconstruction] was not possible during the first two years, between surgery and chemo and radiotherapy my health conditions had to be stable [before considering a reconstruction], so it was technically not possible. I

would have loved, during these two years, to be able to look at myself in the mirror, because during those two years I hated myself, every day I hated the body in which I lived and in which I fought. Then it's okay, perhaps we can try [to undergo a reconstruction], but at that time I was starting to recover from chemo, I was working without too much difficulty, and I was not very keen [to have another operation], [I was thinking] 'why now? Why this rush now?' Even if I didn't love myself, I loved my son, I didn't want to tell him 'mum is going back to [the hospital]'. [So before it was] not possible [to undergo a reconstruction], now I don't want to. During that time, I continued to live, the love life continued, I went to the beach, I put on clothes ... well, after the reconstruction had become unnecessary. When did I make a choice between not possible [to undergo a reconstruction], not wanting [one] and not needing [one]? And the last phase is acceptance and a return to [a condition of] serenity and feeling good about yourself. So when did I make a choice? Never.

I decided to include this long excerpt from the interview with Marie in full because it perfectly illustrates the different and difficult phases she lived through, and through which she learned to accept her new body. But Marie was also extremely clear that living in an asymmetric body was not a choice but, rather, the result of a complex process of coming to terms with the disease at different stages of recovery. She did not reject a reconstruction based on an explicit opposition to female beauty norms. Indeed, she wanted to undergo a reconstruction, but the operation was postponed, first because it was medically not possible, then because of Marie's personal and professional commitments. Eventually, a reconstruction was simply no longer necessary, as she had learned to accept her new body and felt comfortable in it. Still, she was nonetheless explicit in rejecting the simplistic rhetoric of choice: Marie highlighted that, while waiting for the right moment to undergo a reconstruction, she did not put her social, professional and even sentimental life on hold, which continued in an asymmetric body, until she realised that she no longer 'needed' a reconstruction in order to feel whole again.

Analysing women's experiences through deconstruction of the rhetoric of choice allows us to capture the complexity of living in a one-breasted body, thus helping us to understand how women's bodies are (re)defined and (re)shaped in daily interactions. In many cases, the post-mastectomy asymmetric body is in transition, fluctuating among changes caused by the different treatments women undergo. As Marie mentioned, it is often not possible to do a reconstruction immediately after a mastectomy, because patients are receiving other treatments such as chemotherapy, and especially radiation therapy, which can alter the outcome of the reconstructive operation. But the asymmetric body can be fluid because women can decide whether and when they want to wear an external prosthesis simulating a two-breasted appearance.[15] An external prosthesis is an ambiguous object: it normalises the body without permanently erasing the signs of the disease. However, the normalisation that it offers, even if temporary, can be a problem. Brigitte decided to abandon the prosthesis so as to fully accept her asymmetric body: 'I gave up the prosthesis, and I started a work of acceptance of asymmetry. By giving up the prosthesis, I started to accept that I had an asymmetry, that my body was different and that I should start living with this different body.' For many women, the device offered the opportunity to keep away unwanted stares and comments. This was the case for Lucrèce, a French woman in her forties at the time of the interview who did not undergo reconstruction. She said: 'breast was not my thing (*le sein n'était pas mon truc*). I was not particularly attached to my breast, I put on a low-cut [dress], but that was it. I didn't spend all my time showcasing my breast.' Lucrèce highlighted how her breast had a limited role in defining herself and added that, after the mastectomy, she did not find it difficult to look at her new body in the mirror:

> When I woke up [from the operation] I looked at myself and didn't find it shocking. I didn't feel mutilated at all. I don't feel like I'm missing a part of me. On the other hand, in the eyes of others if I walk around and I haven't put on a prosthesis, I can clearly see that something is missing, but, in my head, nothing is missing ... I mean, at home I never put on the prosthesis, my children see me with one breast and they think it's normal. I don't feel mutilated at all. And I tell myself that if people weren't watching, I would go out without putting on a prosthesis.

The mastectomy did not alter the perception of her body as 'whole', and she used a prosthesis only to adapt her body to the gaze of strangers, because for her family the asymmetry was not a problem. Justine was another French woman, in her fifties at the time of the interview, living with an asymmetrical body. When I asked her if she had considered having a reconstruction, she told me that the medical staff had mentioned it but did not think she needed a breast reconstruction. When Lucrèce wore an external prosthesis, she did so for other people because she did not want to make them uncomfortable by showing a different body, but also for herself because the appearance of a conventional body could be a protection from the judgement of others. Lucrèce was not the only interviewee to reluctantly normalise her body. Justine told me that the prosthesis was uncomfortable and that she initially avoided wearing it. Her asymmetry was thus apparent, and she noticed that sometimes her colleagues cast critical glances at her body. She could tolerate the attitude of her colleagues; however, she told me that she did start to wear an external prosthesis after receiving a comment from her daughter, who invited her to hide the asymmetry.

Asymmetry distanced women from traditional standards of beauty and desirability and, in some cases, the interviewees tried to use this distance to their advantage, for example, to escape from explicit or implicit gender injunctions. This was the case for Apollonia, a woman from southern Italy who was seventy years old at the time of the interview and had undergone a mastectomy several years earlier. Apollonia hid her asymmetry by wearing a prosthesis, but from a personal point of view her asymmetry was not a problem. She told me that after her husband's death she had sometimes 'instrumentally' used the fact of having only one breast to fend off unwelcome suitors. Using her physical difference to deter the men around her allowed her to avoid unwelcome advances without necessarily being hostile. She could even pretend to protect men from her 'abnormal' body while actually aiming to protect her freedom as an adult woman who did not want to remarry.

While the experience of living in an asymmetrical body did not emerge in my British fieldwork, my results from France and Italy show interesting overlaps with previous research with younger cancer patients living in the UK. These studies have shown that women did not perceive their non-reconstructed bodies negatively and preferred not to undergo reconstruction so as to avoid unnecessary cosmetic surgery. Moreover, support from family and friends was central in the UK context as it was in the Italian and French ones (Holland et al., 2016; Archer et al., 2018). An important element emerging from the experiences of women who did not undergo a reconstruction is the lack of social awareness of asymmetric bodies. Many women, for example, have mentioned their difficulties in finding clothes that can adapt to an asymmetrical body. This is unfortunately not surprising, as the discrimination of the fashion industry against women whose body does not conform to stringent aesthetic norms is well known – for example, this has been explored in relation to women whose bodies are considered 'plus-sized' (e.g., Bishop et al., 2018). For women with one breast, it is possible to buy bras with a pocket to insert an external prosthesis, and charities and patient support groups can offer advice on how to adapt mainstream clothes to an asymmetric body,[16] but it is much more difficult to find clothes or bras designed for an asymmetric body. The assumption is that women with one breast do not want to make their difference visible to others. Some women adapt to this situation not only by combining clothes and fashion items, but by using their modified bodies as an opportunity to express and negotiate personal ideas of gender and femininity (cf. La et al., 2019). However, what emerges from women's experiences is society's lack of acceptance of the asymmetrical body. This can be another reason that makes the integration of asymmetry into women's lives an always partial process: it is easier to be asymmetrical in some situations than in others. But through these processes of assemblage, women stretch semantic and social boundaries to create new spaces for different bodies beyond the ideas of normality and beauty.

Conclusion

The experience of breast cancer can lead to significant changes in a woman's body, with the loss or alteration of the breast being one of the most challenging aspects of the disease. Reconstructing the breast involves combining different materials, such as silicone or autologous tissues. However, the process is often a negotiation between patients and the medical system, based on the resources available to the patient. In France, patients can use private healthcare, but this may exclude those with fewer resources. In the UK, reconstruction is generally done in the public sector, but intermediate regulatory instances (such as MDTs) may insert an additional level of negotiation in addition to the negotiation with the surgeons.

Moreover, the gradual process of aestheticisation of oncology seems to establish rhetorical and practical links between oncological and cosmetic surgery so as to justify the extension of cosmetic surgery techniques to the treatment of cancer. The patients whom I met shared only partially this emphasis on the aesthetic outcome of the surgery because, for them, the meanings and motivations of reconstruction were multiple and would go beyond just having a better breast.

The fact that beauty standards are not a priority for women does not mean they can dismiss them altogether, as women still need to navigate expectations to adhere to those standards. In daily life, women navigate these expectations by constructing different meanings and values for their bodies through their own bodily assemblage processes. Their homes, the doctor's surgery, the gym, the swimming pool or the beach are places where their bodies take on various roles and are perceived differently, contributing to different perceptions of wholeness and integrity. Through the reconstruction, women rearrange the uses of their bodies and individual and social values around the female body according to their personal hierarchies of what matters to them. Certainly, they have to take into account the materiality of their bodies, including the effects of disease and surgical transformations.

If surgeons wanted to reconstruct a beautiful breast, the women I met wanted to recreate not only a body that could be considered beautiful and natural but also a body in which to live a life as close as possible to their pre-cancer life. Some of my interviewees decided to undergo reconstruction after having lived in an asymmetrical body for a few months or a few years. For many women, a reconstruction had practical purposes: it was easier to find clothes that fit a double-breasted body, and if they went to the beach or the gym, a reconstructed breast, although different from a natural one, could hide their experience of the disease.

They did not want to draw attention at the seaside or in the street, while others mentioned that they did not want to shock or embarrass the people around them by disclosing their asymmetry.

The attention and care towards other's people reactions once again reveal the hegemony of the two-breasted image. However, hiding the asymmetry from others also means not having to reveal the pain and the trauma of breast cancer: a breast reconstruction can offer a sense of control over the narrative of the disease and therefore contribute to the patient's biographical assemblage. For this, a partial reconstruction may be sufficient. In particular, most of those whom I met and who did undergo a reconstruction have said they did not pursue a nipple reconstruction because this step was considered unnecessary. Creating a volume, which avoided the hassle of inserting the external prosthesis, was sufficient. The desire to find, through either surgery or prostheses, a life similar to the pre-illness one is also strongly influenced by ideas about how a female body should be. A double-breasted silhouette corresponds not only to dominant aesthetic standards but also to social and moral norms. It allows for immediate gender identification and reassures not only the patients, or at least some of them, but mainly those who move around them – family members, colleagues or perfect strangers. Breast reconstructive surgery re-establishes a gendered order that is still dominant today. And it is precisely this social reassurance inherent in the two-breasted image that some women want to undermine. This becomes more evident in the use of the asymmetric body.

The asymmetry is a fluid situation that can be hidden on some occasions – when women are with strangers – and revealed in others – with their partner. However, some women can use their dissident bodies to negotiate their place in society and reject normative female roles, as in the case of Apollonia. Women living in a post-diagnosis body replace one-dimensional beauty standards with visions that include the variety of uses of the body. These visions bring to the surface the flexible and nuanced relationship that women have with their bodies, which emphasis on the adherence to normative beauty standards cannot capture.

In her analysis of *Intra-Venus*, Julia Skelly (2007) underlines how the series of photographs is an example of fragmented femininity. The fragments of femininity that Wilke evokes are part of the everyday experiences of many women living in a post-mastectomy body. This chapter has been an attempt to show how women can use these fragments to recompose richer and deeper images of the self. In the next chapter, I will discuss another example of recomposition, examining how women seek balance amid the uncertainty of breast cancer.

Notes

1 While I will focus in this chapter on transformations regarding female breasts, these considerations can be extended to other body parts, especially to those that are socially tasked to carry information about gender, such as the genitals. For a discussion of genital normalising practices in the case of hypospadias surgery, see Kraus (2013).
2 I have previously discussed the aestheticisation of breast surgery in Greco, 2016d.
3 Wegenstein (2022) shows how the patients she interviewed in the US emphasised that reconstruction is very different in its aims from cosmetic breast surgery, but still gave high importance to the aesthetic outcome.
4 https://breastcancernow.org/delivering-real-choice-future-breast-reconstruction-in-england (accessed 8 August 2024).
5 This definition includes surgeries that are not urgent but can be extremely important to improve patients' quality of life.
6 See Héquet et al. (2013) for the French case. Data provided in 2020 by the Italian non-governmental organisation Beautiful after Breast Cancer Italia showed that around 30% of women undergo a mastectomy and that only half of them undergo reconstructive surgery following the mastectomy (Donna X Donna, 2020). For the UK, the report mentioned earlier, commissioned by Breast Cancer Now, states that only a minority of women who undergo a mastectomy opt for reconstruction.
7 I have explored the disagreements between patients and surgeons about the aesthetic outcomes of reconstructive surgery in more depth in Greco (2016d; 2020b).
8 The meanings of complications and multiple operations in breast reconstruction are also explored in Wegenstein's film vérité *The Good Breast* (2016).
9 For the role of multidisciplinary teams in cancer care in the UK see De Ieso et al. (2013).
10 Australian ethnographic data on cosmetic surgery show both surgeons disagreeing with patients who ask for larger implants (Jones, 2008) and patients who received larger implants than the ones they would have preferred (Parker, 2010). Aesthetic norms about the breast can be influenced, among other things, by class and race (Holliday and Sanchez Taylor, 2006). Sanchez Taylor (2012) in particular shows how some of the young working-class women she interviewed in the UK

preferred larger implants, aiming for the breast augmentation to be evident.
11 Fortier (2020) discusses breast reconstructions done for one's partner, and I discuss relationships more in detail in Chapter 6.
12 The aesthetic difference between natural and reconstructed breasts can be reduced with more complex reconstruction techniques, such as autologous transplants with fat tissue, but these kinds of surgery use microsurgical techniques, and not all medical facilities offer them. I have analysed this question more in detail in Greco (2016d; 2020b).
13 This work of bodily assemblage is not limited to 'permanent' surgical intervention – cf. Crowley's (2010) analysis of wearing hearing aids.
14 I have discussed the experiences of non-reconstruction, in particular when experienced as a form of resistance, in Greco (2016c.) In some cases, women can undergo a bilateral mastectomy, which results in a flat chest, a physical change that has different implications than an asymmetrical body. A prophylactic bilateral mastectomy can be performed to reduce the risk of developing cancer for patients with a genetic mutation; however, a bilateral mastectomy is performed less frequently than a single mastectomy. In this section, I explore the experiences of women who underwent a unilateral mastectomy, however, I have analysed the role of a flat chest in Greco, 2020c
15 Manderson's (2011) ethnography in Australia also discusses both the meaning of the missing breasts and the variable practices of when to hide and when to show the asymmetry.
16 See the brochure of the British charity Breast Cancer Now, 'Breast prostheses, bras and clothes after breast cancer', https://breastcancernow.org/sites/default/files/publications/pdf/bcc123_breast_prostheses_web_0.pdf (accessed 8 August 2024).

5

Breast cancer: an exercise in uncertainty

Audre Lorde documented her experience of breast cancer in *The Cancer Journals*, a powerful book published in 1980 that combines elements of memoir, journal writing, poetry and essay. The book substantially influenced the building of an alternative understanding of breast cancer. Lorde's autobiographic and political analysis pushes for the inclusion of the experiences of Black and queer women, calls attention to environmental causes of the disease and refuses the invisibilisation of breast cancer experiences. *The Cancer Journals* also addresses the fear that, even after the completion of therapies, any symptom might be a sign of a relapse (see also Gardner, 2009). Lorde describes the anxiety caused by breast cancer as 'an immobilizing yield to things that go bump in the night, a surrender to namelessness, formlessness, voicelessness, and silence' (1980: 8). Anxiety is closely connected to the deep state of uncertainty women find themselves in after receiving a breast cancer diagnosis. Patients adopt various strategies to give a name and shape to their anxieties in an effort to contain them, manage them and maintain a certain level of control over their lives. Attempts to retain control are inextricably linked to the resources that patients can mobilise and the spaces for action that the organisation of the local health systems allows.

One of the hallmarks of this uncertainty is its entanglement with the pharmacological, technological and biological changes that have characterised the approach to breast cancer in recent decades. As seen in Chapter 3, the very definition of breast cancer has been modified by descriptions of the disease that emphasise the role of biomarkers and individualised and stratified therapeutic approaches. In this context, not only the biomedical approach but also the meaning of the disease itself is in constant transformation. As we have seen, breast cancer has been divided into two different entities: 'curable' early-stage breast cancer and 'incurable but treatable' metastatic breast cancer. However, even in best-case scenarios, where treatments have obtained the best possible results (i.e., 'no evidence of disease'), the possibility of relapse extends the uncertainty of patients. In this context, some types of treatment – such as hormonal therapy, which is usually administered for five or ten years – have been extended or introduced to reduce the risk of relapse, creating a new normality (Trusson et al., 2016) in which patients live with the changes and the alterations caused by active treatments as well as by adjuvant therapies prescribed for several years.

For patients with metastatic breast cancer, there is an even more profound uncertainty: while dying from the condition becomes almost certain, current treatments have extended the survival times. However, at an individual level, patients do not know whether treatments will be effective for them, or for how long. Nor do they know the impact that a specific treatment will have on their quality of life. The relative improvements in metastatic breast cancer survival have opened up new spaces for uncertainty and instability in patients' lives. Women do not know how much time they have left or how they should organise it (Greco, 2022c). The uncertain and provisional nature of metastatic breast cancer has created a liminal space between a chronic and a terminal condition. Women inhabit this space uncomfortably. Some patients try to contain the uncertainty that marks their life by searching for different sources of information and becoming familiar with the biomedical world (Greco, 2020a). Others use the experience of the disease to redefine their expectations and their priorities. Previous theorisations of the impact of the disease were addressed using the concepts of biographic disruption and recomposition (Bury, 1982). However, these theorisations are less relevant in the context of the liminal lives of patients with metastatic breast cancer because their situation is altered by a sustained uncertainty that is difficult to recompose.

Patients find themselves living a provisional life and, in this context of instability, the solutions and approaches they establish must also be flexible and adaptable to a reality that can rapidly mutate.

Illness narratives have been a core methodological tool in the social studies of health and illness. In this book, while using this approach, I consider the limits and risks of the method, including the difficulties for patients in making sense of and expressing the illness; the provisional nature of narratives, which can change as patients elaborate further their understanding; the fact that the narrative is not only retrospective but also looks at the future, and the need to negotiate pre-existing dominant narratives (cf. Frank 1995). A way that I use to counterbalance the limitations of illness narratives is to look at them through the concept of biographical assemblage to push the analysis further, pointing out how patients need not only to understand their own experience but also to relate to biomedical knowledge and estimates and deal with the resulting uncertainty.

In this chapter, I explore the uncertainty and provisionality of the disease, and the approaches adopted to contain it, observing the ways that these elements constitute assemblages that are imperfect, unstable and changeable because breast cancer itself is unstable, not only as a biological reality but also as a biomedical and social phenomenon. New knowledge, redefinitions of previous approaches and the possibility (and hope) of new therapies and new drugs continuously reshape the meaning of the disease, another determinant that patients must manage as part of living with breast cancer. Patients need to rebuild a relation with their body that includes medical treatments and their side effects. Moreover, biomedical uncertainty around drug efficacy drives patients to engage in new ways with their present and future lives. In this sense, that the system of medical-bodily assemblages is open and ready for recombination is a necessity that begins at the moment of diagnosis, as the next section explores.

No longer healthy, not yet sick: the ambiguous space of the diagnosis

Breast cancer is a life-altering event. For many women, receiving such a diagnosis means crossing the border into what Susan Sontag (1978) has defined as the kingdom of the sickness. However, as with all borders, the one separating the sick from the healthy is the historically defined product of social and bureaucratic practices. For historian Ilana Löwy (2010), until the mid-twentieth century, one of the most significant traits of breast cancer was its visibility.

Before the introduction of modern diagnostic tools, cancers affecting internal organs could not be diagnosed. However, the unequivocal signs of late-stage cancer of the breast could not be missed by doctors. The widespread use of modern diagnostic technologies has overturned the situation. The aim now is to detect cancer as soon as possible, with current screening technologies promising to identify small lesions rapidly and with greater certainty. Accordingly, breast cancer screening programmes aimed at age groups considered more at risk are widespread in the countries I studied (see Chapter 3). However, in many cases women themselves initiate the diagnostic process because, thanks to numerous public health campaigns they know how to detect small changes in their breasts. Among my interviewees, the most common event was feeling a lump and seeking answers about its nature. In some cases, other signs were present, such as a change in the shape of the breast (a British patient told me that her breast had 'a funny shape') or a bloody discharge from a nipple. While all these changes can be linked to the presence of a tumour, none is in itself an unequivocal symptom of cancer. During our interview, a British radiologist, Dr Roger, underlined that most patients referred by their GP for a lump do not have a cancer but just 'a normal lumpiness in the breast'. The ambiguity of breast lumps means that many women have to insist with their GP for a referral for a mammogram.

The oncologists and radiologists whom I interviewed generally emphasised that screening appointments are organised to balance the need to offer an accurate diagnosis in a short time frame and avoid patient discomfort and anxiety. Dr Roger said that the aim is 'to get as much done as possible within that one visit'. In the countries where I have conducted fieldwork, this usually means that patients have a mammogram that is followed by a same-day ultrasound if the results of the mammogram are unclear. If the results remain ambiguous, a biopsy can also be performed that same day. However, in the latter case, patients have to wait one or two weeks for the results. Obtaining a breast cancer diagnosis is often neither straightforward nor rapid. In the suspended time during which women are no longer healthy and not yet sick, they try to make sense of an unexpected situation by interpreting contradictory signals. Sylviane, a French woman in her late fifties, described this as the most difficult period:

The most difficult period for me was not knowing. When you have exams, mammograms, ultrasounds etc., you can clearly see [from] the reaction of doctors, radiologists etc. that there is a problem, but they don't really tell you, because it's not their role to tell you, so I had to wait for my doctor to get the results ... and so it was that period for me that was the worst. They had not yet said the word cancer and so there was a question mark and that was difficult to live with, because you don't, don't know what you're going to fight against.

Some medical professionals conducting the tests are not allowed to formulate a diagnosis, but their suspicions transpire through their behaviour (Locock et al., 2016). Sylviane summarised perfectly this situation: the word cancer is not openly pronounced, it is replaced by a 'question mark' against which no action can be taken. This space of uncertainty can be particularly long for some women for whom reaching a conclusive answer about whether they have breast cancer is more complicated. When, at the beginning of our interview, I asked Clothilde, a French woman who was in her fifties when she received a diagnosis, how she discovered her cancer, she described her story as 'very complicated', almost difficult to believe. Like many women, Clothilde felt a lump in her breast and, following the advice of her family doctor, underwent mammography, followed by an ultrasound. The results were uncertain and, a few months later, she underwent magnetic resonance imaging (MRI) of the breast. All the diagnostic tests, including the MRI, were inconclusive, and medical professionals, including a radiologist and a surgeon, were unable to offer a clear answer about the nature of the lump. Repeated tests and medical appointments continued for almost two years in which Clothilde received contradictory information, with professionals reassuring her that there was nothing to worry about as they continued to conduct further tests. Eventually, a doctor decided to perform a micro-biopsy to dispel any doubt. Clothilde agreed to undergo this procedure, but, after two years of tests, she was starting to think that it was nothing serious. As such, she went alone to collect the test results:

> I went to pick up the results two weeks later: I was relaxed, my husband wanted to come with me, I had friends who also wanted to come with me, but I said 'Don't worry, they have done tests for a while now anyway, and they have found nothing. There is no reason

[to think] that they'll find [something] now.' And then there's the surgeon who says, 'It's cancer'.

After two years of inconclusive results, Clothilde was shocked to be told that she had cancer:

> I experienced it as a failure, women are told to have mammograms, get checked, so I was checked regularly by excellent people and so it was incomprehensible. The explanation is this: it was lobular cancer, and the lobular can't be seen on MRI or mammography [and] you have to do a biopsy, if you don't do a biopsy, it is not possible to detect it.

At the time of the interview – a few years after her diagnosis – Clothilde knew that her difficult diagnostic pathway was due to the nature of her cancer. She was also aware of her privileged situation: she had access to several tests and could be seen by several medical professionals. Nonetheless, she received a breast cancer diagnosis for which she was not emotionally prepared. The simplistic messages of many campaigns against breast cancer encourage women to get screened because mammograms can save lives. However, as Clothilde recognised, this ignores complex situations like hers. She is not the only woman whose experience was marked by contradictory information and a lack of clarity. Manon, another French woman who received a diagnosis shortly before turning fifty, told me that she went to her family doctor because she had a persistent pain under her mammary fold. Given the nature of this pain, Manon did not think that it could be cancer, but her doctor still referred her for a mammogram. During the interview, Manon recalled that the medical professional conducting the exam 'wasn't very clear'. In the end, they suggested that Manon's situation deserved further examination and advised her to go and see her doctor. According to Manon, the gynaecologist was also quite vague. Although she agreed that a biopsy might be needed, she did not give Manon any further insight. Recalling a colleague describing similar problems, Manon gave her a call. Unlike the doctors, the colleague urged Manon to book a biopsy appointment as soon as possible and gave her a list of places she could contact. Manon followed her colleague's advice, and also looked for information on the internet. The results of the biopsy – conducted at one of the specialised cancer centres suggested by her colleague, and in which Manon was able to secure an appointment only after insisting – showed what her online research had already led her to suspect: she had cancer. After the diagnosis, Manon was even more confused as to why the only person capable of giving her clear indications on a course of action was her colleague, who also urged her to speed up the process, while the medical professionals she encountered did not convey any sense of urgency. These initial encounters shaped Manon's experience and her relationship with medical professionals over the course of her journey.

Starting a diagnostic pathway often means stepping into a liminal zone in which the significance of minimal body changes is shaped by protocols, guidelines and the willingness and ability of medical professionals to conduct and interpret further tests. Historically determined, the diagnostic procedure and its results are an imperfect medical-bodily assemblage of the knowledge and resources available at both the individual and collective levels. Contemporary diagnostic pathways are processes that see different components dovetail to produce a cancer diagnosis. The patient's body is only one of these components. At the end of this process, many women found themselves in a very different position: when, to use Sylviane's words, the term cancer is mentioned, they become 'cancer patients'.

Attempting to contain uncertainty

The diagnosis closes a first moment of uncertainty, but opens up many other uncertainties: uncertainties regarding the subtype of cancer, the treatments available and the prognosis.

For many of these questions, the answer lies in the clinical examinations, biopsies and exploratory surgeries. Exam after exam, visit after visit, patients collect information about the type of tumour (HER2-positive, hormone-receptor-positive, triple-negative) and the type of treatment (radiotherapy, chemotherapy, hormone therapy) and prepare to adapt their lives to those treatments. In Chapter 1, we saw that, for many patients, moving between different regions and medical institutions and entering into contact with different medical professionals can be a way to maintain a certain control over their situation and assemble a more manageable personal situation. However, patients can use other different strategies to maintain an active role in a situation that often positions them as passively waiting. Among these strategies is searching for information, with online tools often representing the easiest way to do that (see Greco, 2020a). Some patients look for information about their individual situation. For example, Christelle, a French woman diagnosed with breast cancer shortly before turning forty and toward the end of her pregnancy, went online hoping in particular to read accounts of other women diagnosed while pregnant, because she felt 'very lonely in this situation'. Others had a selective approach to seeking information, deciding to only inquire about options for post-mastectomy reconstruction, but not for other types of treatments. This is because reconstruction, as we have already seen, is considered the moment in the sequence of treatments that offers greater margins of choice. Many of the medical professionals whom I interviewed expressed opposition to patients seeking information on the internet. In my fieldwork, I have found that patients were often dissuaded from researching online or redirected to sources deemed more reliable, such as institutional websites and the websites of national charities and associations. One reason that medical professionals often gave concerns the difficulty of understanding medical facts correctly without appropriate training. Moreover, some medical professionals interpreted patients searching for information as a sign of a lack of trust or as an attack on their expertise and skills. Although mistrust can sometimes be present, most of the women whom I interviewed used this form of autonomous inquiry as a compass to situate themselves within the confusing experience of living with breast cancer. The experience of Muriel clearly illustrates this:

> It was because I went to look on the internet that I refused axillary radiotherapy, because I went to see the website [of the institution where I was being treated]. [Doctors] do not have time to talk, so they say 'we have a very well done website, go see the internet', and so I came across a PowerPoint presentation by my oncologist explaining why, when you have removed more than ten lymphatic nodes, you do not need axillary radiotherapy [...] so when I saw the radiologist I told her that I didn't want the axillary radiation therapy, and when I said to her 'but look what I found', she asks me, 'where did you find it?' She says, 'I have to talk to my boss', and there too it was a nightmare! [I waited] more than three weeks to get answers and [I felt that there was a] problem with radiotherapy, because I had the

impression that it was up to me to decide whether or not I did it, and it's not okay either, because it's not the patient who has to decide, and so for three weeks I was very distraught.

This excerpt shows the contradictions inherent in the management of medical information, including how these contradictions shape the relationship women have with the medical system. In a system where doctors have many patients and little time, redirecting patients to institutional websites can be a way to reduce the length of consultations. However, doctors cannot always predict how patients will use this information or how it will impact on their therapeutic path. In the end, the radiologist agreed with Muriel that axillary radiotherapy was not necessary for her. It is worth noting that, as Muriel points out, patients want to better understand the role of treatments and what to expect, but often do not want the responsibility of deciding whether or not to pursue a treatment. They are aware that they do not have the tools (or even the energy) to make that decision. Furthermore, although information can become a negotiation tool that orients or rearranges patients' therapeutic pathways, seeking information does not mean not trusting doctors. For many women, it represents a way of reconfiguring trusting relationships to enable patients to better understand the actions and requests of medical staff, and select what information they can obtain on their own and what information it is critical to receive from doctors and nurses. During our interview, Manon often repeated '*je me suis renseignée*' ('I tried to find out'), and she started to do so when medical professionals were unable to give her information about her biopsy:

> During all these phases, I look for information, I read everything, I go to the websites, really I try to know as much as possible to understand. I understood that with the mammography and ultrasound report, everything [you need to know] is there. I just took the summary with the words in bold, typed them on the internet and from one site to another, I saw what everything means: ACR stands for American College of Radiology, and the images are graded from one to five, five means that there is probably a tumour and I go through all the text in this way.

This detailed description of how Manon searched for information on the internet shows how quickly and competently some patients can become familiar with medical information. Nonetheless, patients are aware that being seen to be too informed can backfire, requiring that they carefully manage their knowledge when interacting with medical professionals. In this sense, Manon's behaviour is illustrative. When he told Manon that her protocol included hormone therapy, the doctor asked whether she knew what that was. Manon told me that by then she had read everything she had found online about breast cancer treatments, that she knew what hormone therapy was and that she was, in fact, expecting it to be offered. However, she told the doctor simply that she had heard of it, understating her knowledge to avoid irritating (*agacer*) the professional by flaunting her knowledge. Communication between doctors and patients can be difficult, with lies and omissions from both sides not unusual (Fainzang, 2015). Although patients are aware of this and try to be careful, sometimes it can be difficult to strike the right balance, as Clothilde explained in her interview. Unlike Manon, Clothilde asked more questions, but could sense that this was occasionally perceived as a problem: 'I think I'm a pain in the neck (*que je suis une enquiquineuse*) for doctors, because I ask a lot of questions.' Other women considered gathering information to be more of a necessity than a choice. Camilla, after her metastatic breast cancer diagnosis, felt that she had 'to explore options yourself because people don't tell you things'. She underlined that oncologists are often very busy and medical appointments short, making gathering information important for making best use of the time with a medical professional. However, she added that patients with serious illnesses should not be put in the position of having to research and advocate for themselves, and that this behaviour is often a way to counterbalance the shortcomings of the medical system.

Not all the women interviewed looked for information, whether online or elsewhere, and many were satisfied by what medical professionals told them, agreeing with them that looking for information without a medical background could be misleading and distressing. However, many women saw developing a medical understanding of their condition as a sense-making activity and a way of managing uncertainty by demarcating small areas of agency within a disempowering situation. For example, Olivia, a British woman in her fifties, told me that she was satisfied with the information she received from the medical staff and that she was more interested in knowing why she had developed a cancer in the first place. After her diagnosis, she started to notice that numerous people at her workplace had similarly received a cancer diagnosis. Thinking this high number suspicious and possibly linked to work conditions, she insisted with others on an inquiry. The results showed that Olivia and her colleagues represented a 'natural cluster' of cancers because they all had different subtypes of cancer. During our interview, Olivia told me that knowing whether her cancer might be work related was important and that she was 'ready to fight' to obtain an answer. She was not the only patient I met who wanted to know the cause of her illness. Others connected the onset of the disease with traumatic or stressful life events. As we will see more in detail in Chapter 6, for many, a cancer diagnosis opened up a space for reflection, prompting them to revisit their past and present lives. In this way, the focus shifts from the biomedical aspect of the cancer to the broader and more complex biographical aspects of their life. Many women made apparent the importance of understanding the role of the disease in the economy of their lives, leading them to rearrange not only biomedical information but also personal and social information, values and experiences in a biographical assemblage. In this way, they could give new meaning to not only the disease but also their own lives. In the next section, I discuss how negotiating treatments and their meanings was a further way to maintain some control over one's life.

Complying with treatments: assembling the present and the future

Many of the patients whom I interviewed underwent different combinations of the treatments that historically characterise breast cancer's therapeutic pathway: surgery, radiotherapy and chemotherapy. At the end of this process, although no longer sick, the patients are not cured. According to Dr Jessica, a French psycho-oncologist who has worked for decades in services specialised in treating patients with breast cancer, one of the most difficult moments for women is not the phase of active treatments, but the end of that phase, because it represents 'the passage from being a sick person to being a not-cured person' (*'le passage d'un état de malade à l'état de non-guérie'*).

There is little certainty about what being cured means in the case of breast cancer. For Hortobagyi (2003), in the case of breast cancer, it might be appropriate to introduce the concept of 'personal cure', a situation achieved when a patient with breast cancer who has completed the treatments 'eventually dies from a different cause (e.g., cardiovascular disease, chronic obstructive lung disease, stroke, etc.) before a relapse from breast cancer can be documented' (Hortobagyi, 2003: 25). Hortobagyi suggests that, while this definition is inadequate because it does not give any useful information about survival times or the effectiveness of available treatments, for individual patients, 'this is a perfectly satisfactory definition of cure' (Hortobagyi, 2003: 25). However, this concept of personal cure offers no indication to patients of their status while they are still alive. The definition 'no evidence of disease' (and its acronym, NED), as we have seen, is used to indicate the situation of a patient who, after the initial course of treatments, no longer presents signs of cancer. NED does not guarantee that cancer cells are completely absent – it simply signals that cancer cells have not been detected through diagnostic tools. Following the active phase of treatments, hormone therapy is one way to increase the chances that patients with breast cancer remain in this non-sick state for as long as possible. As seen in Chapter 3, hormone therapy represents one of the best options for tackling breast cancer. Accordingly, it is often prescribed as adjuvant therapy to reduce the risk of relapse, especially local relapses on the contralateral breast. It is common knowledge that chemotherapy often has debilitating side effects: hair loss, nausea, fatigue. Compared to chemotherapy, hormone therapies are presented as easy-to-manage drugs that require patients to take just one tablet per day and have limited side effects. In reality, the list of side effects can be very long, including night sweats, weight gain, mood swings, vaginal dryness, joint pain, increased risk of thrombotic disease, thickening of the uterus and increased risk of endometrial cancer. Some patients also experience cognitive problems, including brain fog. Pre-menopausal patients undergoing hormone therapy can be prescribed an ovarian suppressor drug to stop ovarian activity. This means that many younger patients find themselves experiencing pharmacological menopause, which in some cases can be very debilitating and limit their quality of life.

In the UK, following NICE guidelines, hormone therapies are usually prescribed for at least five years after diagnosis, with some younger patients continuing therapy for ten years. Similar approaches are followed in France and Italy. Patients are told that completing this long course of treatment is important for reducing the risk of relapse. Trying to quantify the overall risk reduction can be complicated, but recent studies show that there is a 66% reduction in the relative risk of contralateral breast cancer with tamoxifen taken for four years or more (Gierach et al., 2017). Relative risk describes the proportion of patients who have experienced a contralateral relapse while using tamoxifen, compared with the proportion of patients who had a contralateral relapse and never used tamoxifen. It is more complicated to calculate the absolute risk and its reduction, because this depends on the stage of the disease and other biological characteristics of the tumour (Löwy, 2012). As the activist Barbara Brenner pointed out, '[o]ne of the major problems with the way that scientific studies are reported is that in most cases the figures provided represent the relative benefits of the intervention being studied instead of the absolute benefits that an individual woman might experience' (Brenner, 2016: 111). Understanding the extent of the benefits of hormone therapy is important because the completion of the five-year course is far from universal, with Hadji's (2010) review showing studies in which the completion rate was as low as 50%. The medical literature devotes ample space to what it defines as a non-adherence problem. While research concerning how to improve compliance affirms that it is crucial to make patients aware of the benefit of the treatment so as to reduce non-adherence, medical professionals tend to underestimate or even deny the impact of the side effects caused by hormone therapy (Sarradon-Eck and Pellegrini, 2012). In this context, what is defined as non-adherence to treatments is a more complex balancing and rearranging act by the patients. In his study of diabetes, Ferzacca (2000) suggests that compliance and non-compliance should be understood as '"idiosyncratic regimes" of both self-care and clinical practice' (Ferzacca, 2000: 29) that are defined by not only medical knowledge but also social and individual values, practices and experiences. My interviews illuminate the complex web of individual difficulties and considerations upon which women construct their 'idiosyncratic' approach to the therapies they have been prescribed.

Marie was well disposed to the idea of hormone therapy but suspended it after undergoing an operation to remove uterine polyps. At the time of the interview, she was waiting for the doctors to tell her whether therapy could be continued with another combination of drugs. Meanwhile, Clothilde told me she had experienced very serious side effects from tamoxifen: 'I had hot flashes. I was going crazy; I could have fifteen [episodes] during the day and every two hours at night. I woke up at night, everything was fine, and after three minutes, I was drowned up to my knees.' After trying to cope with the side effects for a year and a half, she asked her doctor to change the therapy, and she was prescribed an aromatase inhibitor.

The side effects of hormone treatment vary and are often assessed against the backdrop of the patient's situation. For example, patients with metastatic breast cancer who use tamoxifen frequently perceive the treatment differently, because in that case the drug is used not to reduce risk but to keep at bay the progression of the disease. For example, Holly, a British woman who received a diagnosis of metastatic breast cancer in her late thirties and at the time of the interview was taking tamoxifen with good results, said: 'I take a tablet at night, and I am pretty much fine. I feel so lucky. I live such a normal life.' In this case, the therapy did not alter the patient's everyday life, despite the side effects. On the contrary, it made it possible for Holly to keep living a 'normal life'. Many patients confronting more complex clinical situations often find themselves having to weigh the benefits and risks of hormone therapy, which often leaves room for doubts and uncertainties. This has been the case for Muriel, who had recently experienced thrombosis caused by chemotherapy, which required her to undergo six months of anticoagulant therapy. Muriel had also started hormone therapy for her hormone-dependent cancer, and her main concern was not the side effects – which she nonetheless described as unpleasant – but the fact that hormone therapy increases the risk of thrombosis. Accordingly, she pondered whether to stop hormone therapy:

> I admit that I don't know what to do. The American [websites] say that [hormone therapy] is great, that many have benefited from it, that it's statistically better when you can benefit from it. I also see how tiring it is, it's frightening, but I try to tell myself that it's to protect myself. But if I don't have to take any more anticoagulants afterwards, we'll see, but if I have to take anticoagulants for life I'd

be really angry, but I can't decide to stop, I don't want to have another cancer.

Muriel searched for information in both French and English, a language she knows very well, and knew that hormone therapy could offer her a statistical benefit. However, she had to weigh this possible benefit against the problems that the therapy could cause.

Morgana, diagnosed shortly before turning forty, was taking tamoxifen at the time of the interview but told me that she planned to stop the therapy in a few months because she aimed to take the drug for a total of three years. The many side effects ranged from joint pain to weight gain and cellulite, making it difficult for her to be comfortable in her own body. Morgana told me that she had tried to talk about these problems with her oncologist, who, however, minimised the side effects of the drug and scolded her for her lack of compliance. Morgana was also finding it difficult to deal with hot flashes and menopausal symptoms, effects accentuated by the fact that she was also taking an ovarian suppressant. She described her physical and emotional response as follows:

> [I have] a sort of anger for this thing, for the artificial menopause [caused by] tamoxifen. For the joint pain in my knuckles, [before that,] I didn't even know I had knuckles. (*Laughter*) At night I wake up, I feel the pain and listen to it, I accept it and let it go away. And getting up from chairs takes so much effort.

Morgana was also experiencing cognitive problems, to the extent that the brain fog caused by the drug required her to interrupt her studies. This made her further determined in her decision to stop therapy after three years. The protection that tamoxifen offers is proportional to the number of years that it is taken, something Morgana was well aware of. As such, she refused to consider stopping the therapy a failure, instead presenting it as a success, and praising her own efforts, commenting, 'I guaranteed myself three years, I held up for three years, I did well'. What in the eyes of her oncologist was inadequate and a sign of non-compliance took on a completely different meaning for Morgana. For her, the three years of therapy were years of physical pain and sacrifices and the result of a negotiation between the instructions established by the medical protocols and the need to continue to live an active life. Morgana is not the only patient who had difficulty in discussing the side effects of hormone therapy with her doctor. Medical professionals tend to consider hormonal therapy an effective and safe treatment (Sarradon-Eck and Pellegrini, 2012). This opposition between the pharmacological experience constructed by biomedicine and the embodied experience of patients is certainly due to the different perspectives through which side effects are evaluated. As mentioned in the previous chapter, tamoxifen is considered a tolerable drug with limited side effects, and this opinion is in part due to the comparison between hormonal therapy and chemotherapy. However, in the experience of Morgana and many other patients, there remains a trace of the distrust, attenuated but not eradicated, that the medical system shows towards women who express their physical pain.[1] The reduction in the years of therapy decided by Morgana is a response, albeit implicit, to this mistrust. It represents a way to put at the centre not the construction of the experience of the medical system but her own embodied perception of side effects. In this sense, her self-congratulations ('I did well') are a way to resist the trivialisation of side effects by presenting enduring them for three years as an achievement.

Morgana was not the only patient who had not fully followed the doctors' instructions. Brigitte told me that she had stopped chemotherapy when her doctor announced that she had to change the type of drugs:

> I have to switch to Taxotere chemo and so I found out on the internet that it is an extremely irritating product that gives tingling to the fingertips, that numbs the fingers [and toes] too. In some people the sensitivity of the fingers and feet never comes back ... when you handle an object like that, you don't know what your fingers are touching and for me that's inconceivable because since I was very little, since the age of ten, I knit, I crochet, I do manual work, and I love to use my hands, I also learned to massage and it's out of the question for me to never feel my hands again.

Brigitte was firm in her decision. She inquired about the therapy and the side effects and decided that, in her case, they were not acceptable. The peripheral neuropathy that chemotherapy would have caused was unacceptable for her because it would have meant giving up an activity that had defined her since childhood – *tricoter* – and giving up a tactile way of experiencing the world that she considered fundamental. Gagnon and Holmes (2016) use the concept of assemblage to rethink the side effects of antiretroviral drugs and how these can be seen as the product of the relationship between bodies, technologies and social and medical systems. Their analysis represents an invitation to approach side effects in a more open-ended way, to make space for different experiences of the interactions between patients' bodies, the technology represented by the drug and the social organisation of illness and healthcare. The stories of Morgana and Brigitte feature attempts to keep the relationship between their own body and the treatments fluid and open by valuing other aspects of life over survival times in order to make the therapies more acceptable. In these negotiations, patients consider not only the impact that therapies have on survival times, but also their impact on quality of life. While measures of survival time are oriented toward the future, patients want to preserve their present life as well. In this sense, the refusal to undergo chemotherapy with Taxotere and the disinclination to take tamoxifen for five years cannot be dismissed as non-compliance but should be understood as attempts to keep the relationship with therapies open and as ways of negotiating the repercussions of the disease on their life.

The radical uncertainty of metastatic breast cancer

As more and more efficient therapies become available for cancer patients, extending survival time, the fear that cancer may return increasingly characterises the lives of many recovering from cancer (Skowronski et al., 2019). For patients with metastatic breast cancer, this fear is not hypothetical: the rift of uncertainty that the diagnosis opens swallows a significant portion of the previous life and identity of patients who are no longer simply ill, but terminally ill.[2] Several of the patients whom I met defined the diagnosis of metastatic breast cancer as a devastating experience that profoundly altered the present and forced them to redefine their plans and expectations for the future. Among the most difficult aspects was the impossibility of knowing how much time they had left to live. As mentioned, even though median survival times for patients with metastatic breast cancer are increasing, only one third survive five years after the diagnosis, with some patients living longer depending on the biological characteristics of the tumour and their response to treatments (see Sundquist et al., 2017). At the time of diagnosis, it is not possible to foresee, for an individual patient, how the disease will develop, how effective treatments will be and what their life expectancy will be. This uncertainty takes over the lives of these women, profoundly altering also their present. Medical professionals can help patients to navigate this difficult moment. Dr Mark, a British oncologist, described trying to alleviate patients' fears by explaining that while metastatic breast cancer is a terminal condition and they will most probably die because of it, they are not currently dying from breast cancer but, rather, living with it: 'I say to my patients "you are not going to wake up dead anytime soon"'. Some patients find this approach helpful. For example, Mary, a British woman in her fifties whose cancer had spread to her bones, was told by her consultant that there is 'a range of stage four'. She found this explanation useful because it helped her to understand her situation and what she might expect in the future. However, the ambiguous nature of metastatic breast cancer and the changes that the condition undergoes – increasingly being defined as a chronic condition (cf. Greco, 2022a; and Chapter 3) – can increase the difficulties that women face. The uncertainty and difficulty associated with predicting the course of the disease characterise the experience of metastatic breast cancer. Kathy, a British woman diagnosed in her fifties with breast cancer with metastases already spread to several organs, described the information and advice she received from medical professionals as contradictory. She was told that the treatment could keep the disease at bay for a few years, and simultaneously that she should make contact with palliative services. Several patients with metastatic breast cancer, especially in the UK, had received this advice, and one of the oncologists I interviewed in the UK, Dr Yasmine, said that the advice can be confusing. Palliative care and hospice services can offer support with pain management, but they are also strongly linked to end-of-life care. It is difficult for patients to reconcile this idea with the information that their condition is manageable. The mere fact that these services are mentioned amplifies the uncertainty of the situation. The limited time that medical professionals often have to discuss matters with patients represents another challenge.

Several patients whom I met had consulted more than one oncologist. Some did so because they wanted to change medical professionals.

Others just needed more or different information so they could decide how to proceed with their life. Nicole, a French woman who was fifty years old when she was told that her cancer had returned and that she had lesions in her bones, told me that 'It's impossible to have statistics'. Nicole would have liked more information regarding the life expectancy for her subtype of cancer, the likelihood of being able to return to work and whether she should remain in her apartment on the third floor of a building without an elevator. Receiving unsatisfying responses to her precise questions, Nicole, frustrated by the evasiveness of the medical staff, booked an appointment with another oncologist in another hospital in Île-de-France. This second oncologist was able to give her the information she needed. As we saw in Chapter 1, the organisation of the French and Italian healthcare systems allows patients to approach doctors more flexibly than in the UK. Many of the patients who consulted several doctors, including Nicole, were satisfied with their decision and said that this was a good strategy not only for obtaining new information but also for checking the quality and reliability of the information already obtained. However, even patients with the most resources face the inherent difficulty of predicting the evolution of the situation. The impossibility of anticipating the development of the disease means that moments of stability, in which the patient might live with a limiting but stable condition, become elusive. A study conducted in Italy (Alfieri et al., 2022) shows how even patients with oligometastatic situations feel that a rapid deterioration is always possible, and mentions the wide range of health-preserving practices that patients need to take. This unstable situation makes it impossible for patients to plan for the future, significantly impacting on the present and making it difficult for many women to make decisions on how to orient their lives. Furthermore, recent years have seen growing attention on the financial impact cancer can have on patients, even those residing in countries with universal healthcare (see, among others, Flaum et al., 2020). Out-of-pocket payments are often costly, and a debilitating disease like cancer negatively affects the professional lives of many patients. The story of Robyn, a British woman in her forties, illustrates the financial stress caused by uncertainty. At the time of the interview, Robyn was about to start a new treatment, but it was impossible to know whether it would work. She said that if the treatment did not work she could be 'on [a] very short-time lifespan', but also expressed hope that she could be one of the patients who, as her consultant told her, have good results with capecitabine. This uncertainty about the future affected her present because she did not know whether to continue working – because the new treatment could significantly extend her survival time – or whether it might be better to retire early and enjoy her last years living on her savings. These experiences suggest that a deep uncertainty about the future characterises even the best moments, influencing patients' psychological well-being and their views on their future and their personal relationships.

Considering the impact of scarce and ambiguous information on patient lives, some expressed a negative opinion about having too much information. Olivia, a British woman in her fifties, told me that a few years after the end of treatments for an HER2-positive tumour, the cancer returned, this time with brain metastases. After the diagnosis of the recurrence, doctors told her that her tumour subtype can return even after five years, with patients diagnosed with HER2-positive breast cancer exposed to an increased risk of developing brain metastases. After the treatment for early-stage breast cancer ended she was happy to be able to put the disease aside; she remembered the doctors mentioning the word remission and thinking: 'they treated me, I am done'. Now that she was receiving treatment for metastatic cancer, she added: 'I am glad I didn't know that [as] I enjoyed the five years.' Olivia told me that even if she had known about the risk of relapse, she could not have done anything about it, and that not knowing allowed her to live the period between the end of treatments and the diagnosis of metastases more peacefully. Even at the time of the interview, aware of the incurability of metastatic breast cancer and that the treatment would eventually stop working, she felt that she did not need to know everything:

> I know that the treatment I am on today will stop working eventually, and I just said to [the oncologist] 'Have you got something else in your back pocket?' and she said 'Oh yes', and that's all I need to know, I don't need to know what, [what is important is] the fact that she reassured me.

The uncertainty about the disease's trajectory and the efficacy of available therapies significantly impacts on patient lives, even when the condition is momentarily under control. In a context that sees patients struggle to control the repercussions of the disease for their present and future life, knowledge might not always be useful, because, as Olivia noted, they cannot do anything. As we have seen in Chapter 3, many patients might not agree with Olivia's position, and, in this oscillation, we can see reflected the changes that metastatic breast cancer is undergoing in its slow redefinition from a terminal condition to a chronic one (see also Chapter 3; and Greco, 2022a). However, while the definition of 'chronic' can capture some of the changes in the treatment approach, it remains unsatisfying (Greco, 2022a).

In Chapter 2, I discussed how the rhetorical shifts in discourses around breast cancer influence the social script underpinning the disease. More than early-stage breast cancer, metastatic breast cancer disrupts the dominant expectations: redefining a terminal disease as an opportunity for moral growth is indeed difficult. With no or little support, women with metastatic breast cancer find themselves having to do emotional and practical work to adapt to the new condition so as to maintain an acceptable quality of life. The volatile condition of metastatic breast cancer is often exacerbated by the social context in which women live. Difficulty in obtaining satisfactory answers from medical personnel and financial and professional difficulties represent barriers that intensify the uncertainty and isolation of patients. In this situation, the assemblage processes that patients use to navigate the difficulties (e.g., consulting different doctors to triangulate information and planning for the future) are kept open so as to include both the inevitable and unpredictable changes related to the disease.

Conclusion

For patients with breast cancer, the diagnosis represents an alteration of their lives that introduces uncertainties and ambiguities. Even in *The Cancer Journals*, a book about strength and empowerment, fear is a term that occurs often: 'I was also afraid that I was not really in control, that it might already be too late to halt the spread of cancer, that there was simply too much to do that I might not get done, that the pain would be just too great' (Lorde, 1980: 27), writes Lorde a few pages after the passage quoted at the beginning of this chapter. One of the main causes of uncertainty and loss of control is the risk of a recurrence, especially if the cancer spreads to other organs, and most therapies aim to reduce this risk of the disease returning in its metastatic form. This objective is central to oncology, and the focus on it often means minimising the side effects of therapies – as in the case of hormone therapy, which is prescribed for five years and, in some cases, even ten. Side effects are a consequence of the encounter between not only the drug and the patient's body but also the drug and the other aspects of their life (their aspirations, their plans for the future, the type of life they live and the aspects of it that they want to preserve) and the changes produced (neuropathy, early menopause, fatigue and brain fog) that are located in these contexts and that can be intensified by the entanglement with the treatment. Post-diagnosis bodies are the results of imperfect medical-bodily assemblages between the materiality of the disease and the limits of biomedicine. Patients respond to this with other forms of provisional and imperfect bricolage-assemblage. This can involve the decision to not undertake certain therapies or to interrupt therapies earlier than prescribed. Although choices of this type are viewed negatively and defined in the medical literature as examples of non-compliance, they are the result of reflections that consider the different needs that patients have and attempt to preserve important elements of their present while trying to extend their future life through therapy. By searching for information and deciding to only partially follow medical indications, patients recombine the medical indications using forms of biographical and bricolage-assemblages. Women try to maintain some control over their lives by limiting the uncertainty of the disease and deciding to value not only the need to extend survival time but also their quality of life. These assemblages are equally imperfect, but also temporary and elastic. A major change that alters the precarious balance built by women is the diagnosis of metastatic breast cancer. As we have seen, this phase – which oscillates between a terminal and a chronic condition – introduces greater uncertainty into the life of patients. The near certainty that breast cancer will be a patient's cause of death overlaps and conflicts with the impossibility of knowing when this will happen. In addition, frequent changes in therapies to keep the disease at bay often force patients to readjust to new side effects. The uncertainty that marks women's experience forces them to implement forms of recombination and assembly that are open, provisional and in need of readjustment and redefinition. The illness experiences of women faced with death, an invasive presence for many and especially for those with metastatic cancer, becomes difficult to grasp and describe. The individuality of the illness experience emerges forcefully, as does its ineffability. The illness narratives collected here represent an effort against this ineffability of illness and death. Moreover, although partial, these stories show how the uncertainty caused by breast cancer is also defined by elements such as gender or class. The processes of biographical assemblage, which also include silence about one's pain, both moral and physical, are forms of effort and work that are frequently neither recognised nor supported. Additionally, women must also undertake the invisible work of relational (re)assemblage, of their personal and professional lives post-diagnosis, which I will discuss further in the next chapter.

Notes

1 There is extensive scholarship discussing the scepticism with which the medical system looks at women's pain, from the difficulties in obtaining a diagnosis of endometriosis (Lamvu et al., 2020) to the spectre of hysteria resurfacing in the case of women with chronic pain (see, among others, Åsbring and Närvänen, 2002; Werner et al., 2004; Löwy, 2021).
2 I have analysed the uncertainty and the 'crisis of the presence' in metastatic breast cancer in Greco (2022c).

6

Between disruptions and recompositions: the post-diagnosis life

In *L'usage de la photo*, a book published in 2005 and written by the French writer Annie Ernaux and her then-lover Marc Marie, we can read that Ernaux has always wanted to keep a visual trace of what remains after an intimate encounter. This desire gave rise to the idea of photographing the clothes and the misplaced domestic objects left behind by the couple after their intimate encounters, and these pictures are the starting point of the reflections in the book. However, on the following page, immediately after the description of the genesis of the project, another fundamental piece of information, very different from the previous one, is offered to the reader: in 2002, Ernaux was diagnosed with breast cancer. Her reaction to the diagnosis is described as a mixture of astonishment – no other woman in her family has ever had breast cancer – and resignation, since breast cancer is another of those things that happen to women. In the portrayal of the relationship, breast cancer is sometimes at the centre, more often in the background. Still, the reader knows that Ernaux's love story and her cancer treatments are unfolding together. The overlapping of these two fundamental aspects of life – love and illness – that the book vividly presents, reflects how breast cancer creeps in and alters, without erasing, the romantic, social and professional life of the women I interviewed.

In this chapter, I explore the ramifications that a breast cancer diagnosis can have, offering further an overview of the strategies women use to reconfigure their lives. The consequences of breast cancer bring women to reassemble social and sentimental experiences (see Lahti and Kolehmainen, 2020) as well as professional pathways (cf. Bend and Priola, 2023). This dimension can be understood through the concept of relational assemblage – while all assemblages are based on relations between humans and other components, here I use the concept to describe what are usually understood as interpersonal relationships, while emphasising that the formation, transformation *and* decline or interruption of different relationships can be understood as specific assemblages (Lahti and Kolehmainen, 2020). In this sense, the assemblages go beyond the interaction between patients' bodies, treatments and biomedical tools, extending to social roles and relations. Breast cancer can profoundly alter the relationship that women have with their partners, but also with their children (if they are mothers) and with other family members. Cancer does not erase traditional gender roles within the family. They continue to define the kind of support women can receive while they are still expected to provide care and fulfil their duties as wives and mothers. Women's efforts in managing their illness, planning their treatments and continuing to take care of their family are often invisibilised and undervalued (Pritlove et al., 2019). Professional identities and careers are also reshaped: breast cancer can disrupt career progressions but can also bring patients to rethink their priorities, reducing their engagement with jobs while they explore other options and opportunities. And it is not just the family and professional life: cancer alters women's social identities and social lives, and old friendships may not withstand the brunt of the disease. In the friendships that do persist, the roles are reconfigured, as sometimes friends become part of the support available to patients. New forms of biosociality (Rabinow, 1996), that is, social relations created around patients' groups, advocacy or simply around everyday experiences linked to the same diagnosis can be created and replace the disrupted network. However, the post-diagnosis reconfiguration of romantic, professional and social life requires essential work from women. The support available for rebuilding fundamental aspects of life is often limited, and those who cannot rely on personal resources struggle the most. Building on the analysis presented in Chapter 5 of the uncertainties brought by the disease and of patients' partial biographical assemblages to deal with their possible futures, in this chapter, I explore the processes of assembling social roles, relationships, working experiences and emotions. I show how patients use these new assemblages to find a necessary, albeit often precarious, balance after the diagnosis.

The couple in the aftermath: heterosexuality and breast cancer

The impact of the diagnosis on couples (especially heterosexual couples) has been the subject of various research projects, with contradictory results. Several studies support the idea that a cancer diagnosis can have negative repercussions on relationships (Kirchhoff et al., 2012), while others suggest that cancer is not in itself a reason for divorce (Carlsen et al., 2007) but it might accelerate the separation of partners with difficulties pre-existing the diagnosis (Taylor-Brown et al., 2000). The variability in the experiences of women can explain these discrepant analyses. Further, the attention to the ramifications of breast cancer within heterosexual couples is linked to the image of breast cancer as a highly sexualised disease (see, e.g., Lupton, 1994) that is often considered an attack on womanhood (Ericksen, 2008), with medical professionals in some instances reinforcing the perception of breast cancer as a threat to femininity and the heterosexual norms (see Greco, 2016d).

The philosopher Sandra Lee Bartky introduced the concept of fashion-beauty complex, defining it as 'a major articulation of capitalist patriarchy' (Bartky, 1982: 135), the goal of which is to emphasise how adherence to beauty norms is an indispensable requirement for women in many spheres of life, from the romantic to the social and professional. At the same time, love relationships are increasingly becoming commodities hinged on the neoliberal system (see Illouz, 2007). In this context, the aesthetic and emotional changes produced by the disease can profoundly affect the sentimental life of women. Dr Frédéric, a French cosmetic surgeon specialised in breast reconstruction, for example, told me during the interview that if the patient is in a relationship, he prefers to discuss the details of reconstructive surgery with her partner (whom he always referred to as 'the husband') present. This is because, according to him, the outcome of a breast reconstruction operation concerns the couple and not just the woman. This idea was expressed in different ways by other medical professionals. Dr Véronique, an oncologist who worked in the Paris region, discussed the importance of undergoing breast reconstruction, in particular for younger patients:

> When I see young patients … I think of a patient [in particular], when she had her cancer, she was under 40, she had a mastectomy and she

never wanted a reconstruction … I see her with this breast, this scar, and I think of her husband who sees her under the shower, on vacation, and I think that she is really mutilated.

The oncologist could not understand the patient's decision to live in an asymmetrical body, and her attention went to the patient's husband, who might have been suffering from living with a woman with an asymmetric body. In this vision, the centrality of the man in the couple emerges as an element that should orient patients' behaviour, pushing them to a stricter adherence to gender norms by undergoing a breast reconstruction so as to normalise the body.

The complexities of how different factors can redefine or interrupt a relationship have led Lahti and Kolehmainen (2020) to approach breakups as assemblages. Some of the women whom I interviewed had seen their relationships brought to an end by the disease and/or by different aspects of their post-diagnosis lives. Josiane, a French woman in her fifties, whose breast reconstruction proved problematic, requiring several interventions, told me that her husband had reacted badly to the disruption brought by the cancer. Josiane agreed to go to couples therapy to try to resolve the situation, but, unfortunately, the efforts were in vain and her husband left her. The bodily changes seemed to have been one of the main reasons for the break: 'my husband left me because of this. He took it very badly that I had breast cancer, he couldn't touch me anymore. He met someone else and left.' Josiane's situation was not unusual, and this probably partly explains the emphasis that some medical professionals put on breast reconstruction: their approach, while reinforcing oppressive body norms, can be grounded in their everyday experience with women with breast cancer and their partners. The impact of the disease on married life goes beyond the physical changes and includes a different way of relating to the world which can create a rift in the relationship, pushing partners in opposite directions. Other women have discussed how breast cancer has exacerbated incompatibilities and accelerated a breakup. Letitia, a British woman in her early seventies with metastatic breast cancer, thought that her divorce was partially linked with her diagnosis because, as she said, 'my husband was always one for making plans, always going for new things, and [after the diagnosis] I became more hesitant about long-term planning'. Some doctors and representatives of patient organizations whom I interviewed have said that separations are sometimes also initiated by patients, who, following the disease, see their relationship through a new lens. Béatrice told me that her ex-husband had always had a negative attitude, but that it was only after her diagnosis that she found the courage to leave him, saying that, after having gone through the experience of breast cancer, she could not tolerate the pessimism that he was bringing into her life.

However, breast cancer can also reveal the richness and capacity for containment (see Greco, 2023; and Chapter 2) of romantic relationships. Stéphanie, a French woman in her sixties, told me how difficult it was to cope with her relapse, living alone and with her children abroad. At the time of the diagnosis, she already knew her partner, but she thought the relationship could not withstand the shock of breast cancer. However, her prediction turned out to be wrong, and Stéphanie and her partner married at the end of the treatments:

> I felt the shock because I was alone, the children were far away and [I was] all alone to cope with such an illness. That wasn't easy. I already knew my husband and he was wonderful, [but] I thought we were going to break up, but not at all, as soon as I finished chemo we got married.

Stéphanie was not the only patient in a happy relationship with a supportive husband. Sandrine said:

> My husband was very nice, I am lucky to have an adorable husband. In relation to that [breast cancer] he was brilliant. Sometimes when I said to myself 'I'm ugly, I can't look at myself in the mirror', he would say to me 'but no, you're beautiful'. [And that] is really important, in my opinion it's fifty per cent of the thing. [However], despite this prosthesis, I still have the feeling that it's not like it was before and [I ask myself], would I be naked in front of another man? I do not think so.

Annarita, an Italian woman in her fifties who received a diagnosis at thirty-eight, said that her mastectomy was 'a tragedy', but that her husband, despite not being a perfect partner, had never considered her post-surgical body a problem:

> With my husband, it was different. We were both young, he did other stupid things, but at this level, he never made me feel bad [about the mastectomy], but with someone else ... I already have trouble in front

of the doctors when I go to do the check-ups. It's me who feels ... mutilated; I'm missing something.

Annarita and Sandrine acknowledged their husbands' support in dealing with the mastectomy; however, both claimed they could not have a new relationship with another man. For Sandrine, this was a hypothetical thought, but for Annarita, who was divorced and not in a relationship at the time of the interview, this choice had an impact on her life. Annarita felt she was missing something, making it impossible for her to think of having a man in her life. Sandrine and Annarita's experiences illustrate the powerful interplay between cancer and the socio-cultural context of the disease. Both women were grateful to their partners for accepting their bodies, but, in a society that values women for their appearance, neither would feel comfortable with another man. It is also not by chance that Annarita is the most insecure, considering that, as I discussed in Chapter 4, the Italian context reinforces the perception that a woman's worth depends on her appearance.

However, structural aspects of healthcare systems can also contribute to reshaping the relationship. For example, in situations of scarce resources, partners often find themselves cast in the role of supporters and advocates. Mary's experience can illustrate this aspect: she told me that a few years after the end of the treatments, she began to have severe back pain that did not subside with the painkillers prescribed by the GP. One afternoon the pain was so unbearable that she was forced to go to the emergency room with her husband. When she arrived, the staff on duty tried to persuade Mary to go home and keep taking the painkillers, but her husband intervened and insisted that further tests be carried out. Unfortunately, the tests revealed that the cancer had returned and that Mary's pain was caused by bone metastases. She said that without her husband's intervention, she would have been too tired to advocate for herself.

Mary was not the only one who talked about her husband's support in dealing with treatments and mediating with medical staff. Other women expressed gratitude to their husbands and partners and discussed the importance of the material, financial and emotional support their partners gave. Franca, for example, said that her husband had always been a source of support for her: 'My husband has always been very close to me, he has helped me a lot, he has always been a very pragmatic man and I think that in some ways he has helped me more than the psychologist.' These flexible reconfigurations of partners' roles can help a couple resist the shock caused by the disease. However, for women with metastatic breast cancer the reconfigurations are more precarious and need to take into consideration what will happen to their partner after they are gone. This was expressed by Olivia, who said:

> I got a very supportive husband ... Me and my husband, we have sort of organised ... he watches me cook because he can't cook, but he can fix everything ... we have our separate roles, but if I go first he is going to be stuck on the management of money, so I'm trying to have him looking at how I do that, but I do all at the computer but he looks at the computer and it goes huuuu, but he is getting there and I think he'd handle [things] a lot better if I go first than if I did because I haven't got a clue.

This tender description of the daily life of Olivia and her husband shows how the disease disrupts the balance and the strategies that couples, especially those in long-term relationships, put in place, and forces them to revise them. In Olivia's story, we can see yet another example of how breast cancer alters the present and the future of women's lives. For Olivia, the primary concern is ensuring her partner's well-being after her departure, and ensuring that the division of roles that worked so well for them does not hurt her husband.

Reassembling the family: between motherhood and patienthood

The sentimental and couple's life is not the only aspect that breast cancer disrupts. The gendered nature of the disease extends to how care is redefined within one of the most gendered of contemporary institutions: the family. The contradictions within the family have been at the centre of feminist analysis at least since the 1970s. The abolition of the family has been a dominant feature of many feminist reflections (see, among others, Lewis, 2019 and Weeks, 2023), and while this institution is far from having been abolished, significant cultural, financial and legislative transformations taking place since the late 1960s have changed its functioning, and the roles and expectations of its members. However, modernising tendencies coexist with a more traditional organisation, making the family a place where genuine love and affection intersect with the need to perform unequal care work and emotional labour. Family relations can be a form of support for women with cancer while, at the same time, entailing demands that they keep caring for other people – children, partners, older relatives – even while unwell. Women try to balance their need for self-care brought on by the disease and the need to care for others. This balancing act (Sulik, 2007) is essential and often expected, as the domestic work and emotional labour that women perform do not simply support their household but are also crucial to the survival of capitalistic and neoliberal systems (Federici, 2014). While wealthier women can outsource a portion of care work to other people, usually women from a lower social class, many others cannot do that. Moreover, regardless of their class position, most women must continue to perform at least part of that work, even when living with breast cancer (Mackenzie, 2014). The diagnosis does not erase traditional roles and relations, but they may be altered and eventually recomposed according to new balances. Emotions and affections are essential in shaping and influencing women's role in their family – which we can consider as a specific kind of relational assemblage. As Price-Robertson and Duff remind us, 'family assemblages […] do not depend on human capacities exclusively, and must be understood in terms of complex associations between human and nonhuman entities' (2019: 1039 – in this case, one of the nonhuman entities is cancer itself). In this section, I trace the contours of these new family assemblages and new reconfigurations brought on by a cancer diagnosis. Women are often extremely worried about both the disease and the impact it might have on their children. Annarita, who was diagnosed when her children were younger, told me that the only thing she wanted was to live long enough to raise them: 'I would pray every day [saying] "Dear God just give me the possibility to raise my children" and now [I am relieved] as they are adults.' For women with small children, there is little practical support available to help them fulfil their parental role while trying to take care of themselves. For example, Kelly, a British woman in her early forties, said that during the months of chemotherapy, when she was unemployed, one of the greatest difficulties was not feeling well enough to look after her two children and, at the same time, not being entitled to any financial help to subsidise childcare. The young woman said that she had to ask her parents for financial help to pay for external childcare. Kelly's story exemplifies how existing ideologies and political approaches shape family assemblages. The UK has been historically characterised by a reluctance to establish a universal offer of public childcare and continues to fund such services at lower levels than other Western European countries (Saxonberg, 2013). More generally, childcare has always been seen as a provision the main aim of which is to encourage low-income parents – especially women – to work in order to decrease their dependence on the welfare state. In this context, a situation such as that of Kelly's, an unemployed mother too sick to take care of her children while undergoing debilitating treatments, was simply not taken into account. Kelly and her family were left alone in a moment of vulnerability because, in a neoliberal system, the scarce forms of support are there not to protect individuals, but to assure the protection of the neoliberal economic system itself. The ambivalent feelings of gratitude and guilt that Kelly expressed toward the financial support received from her parents are also a powerful illustration of the role of the traditional family. With the retreat of the state and the reinforcement of traditional roles, the family simultaneously offers protections that the state has stopped supplying, and legitimates the neoliberal ideology of self-reliance while emphasising traditional gender roles.

The welfare state and childcare support are historically more developed in France, and although many of the women whom I met there expressed concern about the impact that the disease could have on their children, none discussed difficulties similar to those Kelly had encountered. In Italy, the childcare support provided by the welfare state is slightly better than that in the UK (cf. Saxonberg, 2013), but situations like Kelly's, in which the family offsets the lack of state support, seem to be common, often producing the same feelings of ambivalent gratitude towards family members, especially parents and in-laws.

Financial uncertainty is often compounded with the biomedical uncertainty explored in Chapter 3, and this puts increased pressure on mothers with breast cancer. As Annarita's story shows, women do not know how much time they have left, and they feel the need to maintain a normal life for their children, limiting the upheaval that their illness can bring into their life while trying to share as many good moments as possible with them because they know that there may not be other opportunities in the future (see Bell and Ristovski-Slijepcevic, 2011; Mackenzie, 2014). Kathy had similar concerns, which were amplified by the fact that her metastatic diagnosis made it much more difficult to determine how much time she had left, and how to share this with her children. During the interview, she said that after her diagnosis, she began to put together memory boxes and write letters for her children in order to be there for them after her death. While disruptions are exacerbated for women with small children, women with older or young adult children also need to rethink the relationship with them, and how their role as parents might need to change in the time that remains. Many of the women whom I interviewed were worried that they might not be around to guide their teenage children toward adulthood, and were sad at the idea of not witnessing them reaching important milestones in their life. Moreover, mothers of older children were also struggling to make the most of the time they had left. For example, Daisy told me she was uncertain about how to use her money. She first thought of leaving it as an inheritance for her daughters, but then eventually decided to use it to travel with them and build good memories for the future. Another example of how women want to create a link with their children's future is the story of Sylviane. During her interview, she said that, despite being in remission, the diagnosis made her realise it was time for some important conversations. So Sylviane asked her daughter whether she would prefer her mother to be cremated or buried. Sylviane's own mother had been cremated, following her wishes. Sylviane said that her mother's ceremony had been very touching, but added that the absence of a physical place where she could gather herself (*se recueillir*) to honour her mother's memory weighed heavily on her. On the other hand, her father had been buried, and, although she was not religious, going to her father's tomb helped Sylviane remember him and the good times they had spent together. Sylviane said that she asked her daughter about her preferences in this matter because preparing for a good death – in her words – meant thinking not only about oneself but also about the needs of the people who would remain afterwards (*le gens qui sont la après vous*).

While greater attention was given to how to communicate the diagnosis to younger children, several women whose children were teenagers or young adults also described difficulties in discussing the diagnosis with them. In some cases, women choose to manage the impact of the disease by hiding it, or at least some aspects of it, from their adult children, in particular from sons. Adeline, a French woman who was in her sixties at the time of the interview, and had had two mastectomies due to cancer in her forties, said that she did not reveal the real nature of her illness to her teenage children, and as a way to protect them tried to wear an external breast prosthesis to hide her flat chest. Adeline was one of the many patients I met who tried to normalise their body to keep the disease hidden. However, this practice has its limits, as Franca's experience shows. She told me that it was extremely difficult to explain her health problems to her children, who were upset to see their mother tired and without hair, and how, even several years later, she felt the effects of the disease on the relationship: 'I have two children, before there was a [different] relationship with them, now I find it difficult even to hug them, because I have this breast as hard as a rock.' For Franca, the physical alterations of the disease were a stark reminder that the relationship with her children had been altered.

For some women, however, the changes caused by the disease were alleviated by the acceptance that family members showed (see Greco, 2023). Annamaria, a southern Italian woman in her sixties, was moved as she described an episode in which her daughter helped her to overcome the hair loss caused by chemotherapy by offering to cut her hair: 'my daughter once picked me up and said "come here, come here, [I'll cut your hair]" 'cause I was gonna wash my hair. I'm pretty strong, I try to take things in a good spirit let's say, but it's a trauma to see this hair that has fallen out.' Ida, another southern Italian woman in her sixties, was grateful to her sons, who, in a short time, learned to take care of themselves and help her while she went through treatments. Ida was particularly proud of her sons as in southern Italy is less common for men to do domestic and care work, and the fact that they were willing and able to do that to support their mother was interpreted as a clear sign of love and affection.

These different cases illustrate how the disease simultaneously extends and disrupts the structure of the traditional family. The difficulties women face show the fragility of the family institution in neoliberal societies and expose the lack of social protection, especially for women with younger children who require more support. However, the strategies that women implemented seemed to reinforce the importance of the family, not only as a place of affection but also as a support system. Breast cancer and, more generally, the experience of illness does not seem to have the potential to contribute to the abolition of the family, but it is certainly an experience that reveals its cracks and contradictions. And, as we will see in the following sections, the disruption a cancer diagnosis brings can also extend to social and professional life.

The social life after cancer: friendship and new forms of support

After a diagnosis, the social life of patients can be reassembled according to new balances and needs. As seen in Chapter 2, the disease pushes many women to engage in activism. Meetings, conversations and participation in various initiatives are often also a way to meet people with similar difficulties and create more informal forms of support. Many of the patients whom I interviewed described positively the connections resulting from activism. Some women found it difficult to talk about their experiences with friends unfamiliar with cancer. They were afraid of being boring or burdening others with the weight of their difficulties,[1] or that their interlocutors might not fully understand them. On the contrary, talking about their experiences with someone who was going or had gone through a similar path could be easier, as in many cases there were similar experiences and a shared vocabulary that facilitated the conversation.

However, even this form of sharing had its drawbacks, and some patients told me they preferred not to participate in associative activities and meetings. Poppy, who, as we saw in Chapter 2, did not find support groups helpful, preferred to cultivate relationships with friends and family. She often mentioned that friends were available to accompany her to radiotherapy or chemotherapy or to visit her and spend time with her, whenever she decided not to go out due to fatigue and the risks of infections caused by chemotherapy. Franca was another interviewee for whom friendship had been a source of support, and she said that among her friends there were those 'who accompanied me to have chemotherapy, who accompanied me to buy a wig. Maybe I preferred to involve them rather than my mother or my husband, who was at work.'

Other patients, especially those with school-age children, said they had little time and energy and wanted to dedicate what they had to the care of their children, and that for this reason they preferred to limit contact with other patients and their involvement in patients' activities. For example, when I asked Josiane if she had the opportunity to share her experience with other patients, she replied:

> No, because I didn't want to stay immersed in this sick world. I wanted to stay as normal as possible. I had children to take care of, and even when I was in chemo, I went to pick them up at school. I wanted at all costs to remain completely normal, and to talk all the time with people who, like me, were sick, it was to label [myself] as sick.

This excerpt shows, on the one hand, the need to continue taking care of one's children even during treatments, and, on the other hand, the desire to refuse the sick role and maintain a 'normal life' as much as possible. Women negotiate their role as patients with caution, as external factors can intervene to influence how much they can push back and hide their status as cancer patients. One of these factors is the effects of the treatments on the body. Abby, a British woman in her fifties with metastatic breast cancer, said that, prior to her diagnosis, she had an active and rich life. She used to be self-employed, but the disease and the side effects of the treatment significantly reduced her ability to work. She had difficulties walking, and, while describing the impact of the disease in her life, she said: 'I feel like [my life] has shrunk, it was very expansive before and now, I mean, it's just tiny, I barely walk up the road, and I have to get a taxi for almost everywhere I go.' Abby was not the only patient who thought her life was drastically changed. Daisy, for example, when I asked how her life had changed with the diagnosis of metastatic breast cancer, replied: 'I try to get up every day even if it is just for a walk, having said that the first four or five days after chemotherapy I cannot do anything.' The pain and fatigue caused by both the disease and the treatments severely limit the activities that patients can do, and daily actions such as taking public transport or driving, even when possible, were now only undertaken when necessary, as many patients had limited energy. In this context, having a support network was essential. As we saw in the previous section, for many women, this network was the family, but friendships played this role in many cases. Lucrezia, an Italian woman in her forties, underlined how friends were particularly important in the post-operative phase: 'My [female and male] friends have been extremely close to me, also because when I left the hospital and went home I wasn't good for anything [she laughs]. [They helped me] with everything …'. Other interviewees, especially those with a metastatic diagnosis, needed more long-term support. When I asked Daisy if there was anyone who could help her, she said:

> I have very good friends. I can pick up the phone and say 'I need shopping' or 'can you come and we can have a cup of coffee?' [With] two of my best friends we go for lunch or for dinner once a month, it is something we decided we would do.

This extract shows how Daisy was surrounded by friends she could count on, but, as I discuss below, friendships and the capacity to maintain specific forms of sociality do not always withstand the impact of the disease. Furthermore, in particularly complex situations, when there are multiple needs, women can find themselves carefully assessing when asking for help is necessary and when it is better to try to get by on their own, albeit with difficulty. This was the case for Muriel, whose diagnosis of breast cancer followed that of lymphoma by a few years:

> It's not so simple when you have cancer … [when I had the lymphoma] I couldn't do nothing, I had chemo every five days: it was devastating. After the sterile room, I couldn't do anything, I needed help all the time, so I asked for help all the time. I did the planning, one [friend would] do the shopping for me and another would prepare the meals. But when it started again two years later [with breast cancer] it was almost easier to be alone than to ask for help. I asked for help when I couldn't do otherwise. I asked to be picked up from chemo if I felt tired, they would cook something to eat. If I couldn't do otherwise, I would call a friend to do some shopping for me, but it [was] not the same essential daily support system. I didn't go out anymore, I spent a lot of time on this couch with a book.

For Muriel, talking about her experience with lymphoma was more painful than talking about breast cancer. The former was a period of extreme difficulty in which she was forced to ask for constant help, and the people around her provided a 'daily support system'. During the active phase of the treatments for breast cancer, Muriel felt it was not possible to ask for the same support and tried to get by on her own as much as possible, asking for help only when absolutely necessary. From Muriel's words, we can see not only the gratitude for the help received but also the awareness that support from friends might be a limited resource, to be drawn on when strictly necessary. For her, this meant spending most of the time alone.

Muriel was not the only one who worried about the impact that the disease can have on the people close to her. Camilla stated repeatedly during the interview that she had a solid network of friends and family with whom she could talk. However, she was careful not to burden them, and felt guilty that her diagnosis could negatively affect those close to her. In the same way, Clothilde discussed towards the end of the interview how some dear friends had never reached out to her after the diagnosis, not even through a phone call. She was saddened by this behaviour, but at the same time she understood that underlying it there might have been a fear of illness and death, which in some cases could be difficult to manage. The experiences of the women interviewed show how the disease affects not only their professional and sentimental life but also their social life. Friendships were altered, and friends often became indispensable caregivers. The help of friends, like that of family members, contributed to making up for the lack of institutional support networks and represented a necessary emotional and practical help for many women.

The working life and the life beyond work of women with breast cancer

The difficulties that women face in professional life are well documented (see, e.g., Jenson, 2018). Gender biases, asymmetries of power and the difficulty in balancing professional duties with family responsibilities are just some of the obstacles women encounter (see, e.g., Maruani, 2018). In this already complex situation, a breast cancer diagnosis introduces further obstacles. Several aspects of professional life are reconfigured by the disease (see O'Brien, 2005 for a general overview on disability and working life; Rolland et al., 2023 for the situation in France; and van Maarschalkerweerd et al., 2020 for the situation of patients with breast cancer), and this section explores these reconfigurations. The new, rearranged, post-diagnosis professional lives and identities are influenced by the organisation of different welfare systems, the availability or absence of protective measures in case of illness and the values that each woman attached to their working self before the diagnosis. In this sense, the working lives of patients are a further kind of relational assemblage, involving at least the patient, their skills and needs; the employment context, with its demands and accommodation; and the broader components of state regulation of work and welfare, public attitudes to disability and other elements (cf. Bend and Priola, 2023).

Several patients told me that they continued working during the active treatment phase, and in most cases by choice, because maintaining the pre-diagnosis routine was helpful. However, these women also recognised that continuing to work was possible because the working environment offered them the support and flexibility – part time, shorter hours, understanding line managers and colleagues – that allowed them to adapt their schedules and tasks to the new needs introduced by the diagnosis.

Several women in their late fifties and sixties among those interviewed told me that they were offered the opportunity to take early retirement, and often they had accepted it with enthusiasm, as the disease had shifted their priorities and needs. Clothilde, for example, when I asked for how long she had to take her hormonal treatment, replied: 'I'm finishing in a month and I've just retired, and I hope everything will be fine now and I'll be able to move on.' In her answer, the end of treatments and the end of work are joint, to mark a turning point and the beginning of a new chapter in her life. Mireille, a French woman in her late fifties, said during the interview that she tried to return to work but that the sequelae of the treatments made resuming her professional activity difficult, to the point that the occupational therapist who was following her case advised her to ask for early retirement on health grounds. Although this move reduced her monthly income, Mireille described it as the best possible option and said that, in the end, she was satisfied with this opportunity because not working allowed her to use her energy for other, more fulfilling activities, including the initiatives she was carrying out as a patient-activist.

Émilie, another French woman in her fifties, had also been on medical leave (*arrêt maladie*) for two years at the time of the interview, and she told me that she was unsure whether to return to work. Before her illness, she worked in accounting, and she described her job as one 'where you cannot make mistakes'. At the time of the interview she was unsure whether she could return to that level of responsibility, as she felt weakened by the disease and the treatments. During the interview, she told me that as the end of the period of leave approached she was uncertain whether to retire early or return to part-time work. In the meantime, Émilie kept herself busy by participating in the initiatives of an association of cancer patients and by engaging in new activities, such as painting and sculpture, and she told me that she was happy trying new things.

Early retirement was a prospect that produced contradictory reactions. On the one hand, there was the frustration of having to face further limitations related to the disease; on the other, there was the relief of having more time to recover and the pleasure of discovering new interests, including forms of patient activism. The situation can, however, assume different meanings for women with metastatic breast cancer: the terminal diagnosis changed how they viewed the future, as the possibility of enjoying a new turn in life seemed reduced, and the changes were seen more as a sacrifice than an opportunity. Nicole, describing her life shortly after being told that her cancer had spread to various parts of the body, told me: 'I do a weekly chemo since August. I stopped working [...] and it's probable that I will not work anymore, my life has been seriously shaken (*bouleversée*). Here you see me on my feet; I manage to do some things, but still it's not a normal life.' Nicole did not choose to quit her job; she loved it, but it was too demanding, and her physical condition did not allow her to cope with its rhythms. Mary also had to leave her job and struggled to adapt to post-diagnosis life. She said quitting her job had altered her role in society and added: 'I feel now that I just look at the world. I watch others rather than participate.' Camilla also expressed similar feelings:

> I felt that my job was my identity, and when I lost it I felt very depressed, because your life changes overnight, and I feel that not only your life has changed significantly, but I felt that I was ruining everybody's else life, my family, because it's such a stressful thing for everybody to live with.

While Camilla was aware that she could no longer continue to work, as her job was very demanding, she also emphasised how her identity was tied to her professional role. Further, she added that the difficulties she was experiencing in coping with these changes impacted on the people close to her. For women with metastatic breast cancer, stopping work meant giving up an essential part of their existence and having to reconfigure their role in life without the opportunity to seek out new experiences (see also Alfieri et al., 2022). The experiences of Mary and Camilla reflect the suffering and struggle to live when some element anchoring one's identity has vanished. Their comments show the significance of employment in creating one's identity and social life. For women with metastatic breast cancer, it is possible to slow the course of the disease, and many people alternate challenging times with periods of improvement. However, it is highly improbable that they can return to their pre-diagnosis health condition. This implies a significant change in the lifestyles of many women. This sense of irreparability intensified the disorientation expressed by Mary and Camilla.

Another important aspect is the age at which the diagnosis is received. The effects of a gradual worsening of labour conditions have been experienced especially by younger workers, and the vulnerability deriving from the fact that younger women are more likely to be in temporary and more precarious positions (see Jenson, 2018) is emphasised further by a cancer diagnosis. Older women were likely to have had less experience with fixed-term contracts, and to have spent more years in the same workplace. For many younger women whom I met, continuing to work was a necessity and not a choice. Morgana, for example, told me that after the diagnosis she returned to work with a part-time schedule because the side effects of her treatments (discussed in Chapter 5) made it impossible for her to resume her role full time. The fatigue of working while coping with the debilitating effects of hormone therapy, combined with the significant reduction in salary, made Morgana question whether she should continue. However, given her age, she hoped that at the end of the treatment her personal and professional life could resume at a fuller pace. Younger women can indeed have their professional lives altered in multiple ways, with ripple effects, the impact of which is visible even after years, as Kelly's experience shows. Diagnosed with breast cancer in her early thirties, shortly before the diagnosis Kelly had left the company where she had worked for fifteen years to embark on a new career path, which unfortunately had not been successful. Kelly was therefore unemployed while undergoing active treatments. The young woman returned to work a few years later, but the time spent unemployed, combined with the fatigue of the treatments, pushed her to accept a position below her qualifications. Kelly said that, on the one hand, it was necessary, from both a personal and a financial point of view, to return to work, while on the other hand she felt that she did not want 'to go back to work to that level of responsibility' (the one she had before the diagnosis). For several years Kelly was satisfied with her job, the flexible hours of which fitted in well with her family commitments, but closer to the time of the interview she had started to view her professional life differently:

> now the whole breast cancer is eight years ago, and I would like to step up [professionally], but now it is a bit difficult because I have not been in that role, and this [cancer] changed me, because [after the diagnosis] I didn't want to go back to what I was doing.

Kelly's experience shows that the disease can not only limit opportunities but also change the relationship with work in ways incompatible with the rigid organisation of working life in most sectors.

Kelly was not the only woman to reconsider her priorities after a diagnosis. A French woman, Louise, had a similar and perhaps more radical experience. When I met Louise, she had just turned fifty, had three children and was in remission from a breast cancer diagnosed a few years earlier. A few months before her diagnosis, she had been fired by the company where she had worked for several years as an executive. The loss of her professional status and her diagnosis suddenly plunged her into the precarious world of the unemployed and the sick. However, the disruption of her previous identity opened up new opportunities for Louise, as she said that the disease had allowed her to reassemble her life and 'go towards other centres of interest'. Before the diagnosis, for example, Louise had already started to look for another job, but the disease had altered her job search in several ways, as she explained:

> I lived as if I was thirty years old when I was no longer thirty years old. My job search, for example, I no longer see it the same way. Because before [the diagnosis] I was looking for a job as if I still had thirty years of career ahead of me. Today I say to myself 'but why are you looking for a job?' […] I no longer want to work forty hours a week to put money aside for later, the later is no longer there […]. There are more important things to do, things with my kids, that are more important than working eight hours a day for a guy who is going to kick you out at the first redundancy plan.

Many younger women felt that a diagnosis of breast cancer and the side effects of treatment, often resulting in early menopause, had pushed them towards physical and emotional changes usually experienced later in life. However, Louise's interview shows another facet of these transitions, as she felt that the diagnosis had realigned her life with her actual age. Louise used the illness to reorient her life and reposition her priorities, and she concluded that the precariousness of the existence she had experienced through her cancer diagnosis was incompatible with the demands of the professional life she had led before the disease. For Louise, however, this realisation was not brought about just by the disease but by the combination of illness and unemployment. Louise underwent a mastectomy, but no surgical reconstruction. The question I asked before she started discussing her working life was whether she was thinking of undergoing a breast reconstruction. Interestingly, toward the end of the interview, she said: 'So we are moving away from mastectomy, but I think that my reconstruction is there first. I think I need to rebuild myself, but it doesn't go through the physical.' Louise thought that a reconstruction after the disease was needed, but, for her, reconstructing just a breast was not enough and probably was not even necessary. Instead, she stretched the boundaries of the term and, in the same way, stretched the boundaries of her experience with the disease, using it as an opportunity to rebuild her life, priorities and place in the world in a new way. The will to use breast cancer as a catalyst for change was also mentioned by Sylviane, who was relatively young when she was diagnosed: '[cancer] helped me to avoid postponing things to the next day… to [avoid saying]: "I want to do that and I'll see when I retire". Now I tell myself, "it's not when I retire, it's today". And that helped me a lot.' For Sylviane, cancer was an invitation to live more fully in the present, not to postpone experiences and activities for a future time – her retirement – that may not exist. The idea of wanting the disease to be a way to improve their life was expressed in different ways by other women whom I interviewed. For some women, cancer has been a way to understand who the important people in their lives are – and this for both friendships and relationships – while others have said that the diagnosis had prompted them to rebuild the relationships with loved ones – partners or adult children. In Chapter 2, I have discussed the new rhetoric that is constructing cancer as an opportunity for moral growth and self-improvement and how the expectations that cancer can lead to a better life can be a form of cruel optimism for some patients. However, there is a substantial difference in how Sylviane and Louise used their cancer experiences to change their lives, as they, especially Louise, show what can be defined as a form of political and critical growth. Louise and Sylviane were challenging in different ways the strong link in capitalist society between professional identity and personal value, reclaiming the importance of a life not entirely dominated by work. This approach, in a way, contrasts with the simplistic idea that cancer can make people appreciate more the life that they have, as it shows how, on an individual level, the disease can bring significant changes in the social and political perspectives of patients and trigger a willingness for changes that challenge the neoliberal work ethos.

Conclusion

In this chapter, I have presented the different forms of disruption of the women's sentimental, social and professional lives and further explored their strategies of recomposition as processes of relational assemblage. I consider relational assemblages as attempts to define new relations and social roles in response to both the disruption introduced by cancer and the transformation of social roles that the status of cancer patient entails. A fundamental element of these reconfigurations is cancer. Marc Marie defines the relationship with Ernaux as 'un ménage à trois' (Ernaux and Marie, 2005: 103), as cancer is constantly present, altering their plans and dictating what the couple can and cannot do. Women living with cancer know well how the disease recomposes family roles, alters the balance with their partners and children.

The family is an ambiguous terrain: in a neoliberal system that offers limited state support, for many women the main or only source of help was that offered by partners, parents, siblings or adult children. But this help can come at a price, as it was often emotionally and practically difficult for women to ask for and accept it, as they were used to seeing themselves as the ones providing support (and often found themselves still doing so after the diagnosis).

In many cases, marital relations were redefined. Partners found themselves providing material and moral support; new roles and new balances emerged and coalesced around the disease. In still other cases, older children provided support. Despite the contradictory role of this institution, women who could not count on the support of the family found themselves in an even more fragile situation. For some of them, their network of friends turned into a support system. The changes linked to the illness also affected the professional sphere, where the problems induced by the disease added to job insecurity and uncertainty. In some cases this led to a change of approach towards professional roles – what I have defined as political growth.

The concept of biosociality allows us to capture the new connections and relations that emerge around the shared biomedical identity. However, a disease also breaks down and transforms existing relations, for example, with friends who stop calling or partners who leave. The resulting absences leave traces that become part of the recomposed family and social landscape in which women with cancer find themselves living. Women's experiences are heavily influenced by the position assigned to them in society. It is, for example, well known that even nowadays women still find themselves with more care responsibilities than men. The roles of mother, partner and worker intersect, often limit each other and are strongly reshaped by the disease. In this case as well, the experiences of illness, although strictly individual, cannot be separated from the context in which women live and the social roles assigned to them. The disease disrupts a balance that is already very precarious for many, especially for mothers and workers. In this sense, breast cancer is a female disease not only because it involves a strongly gendered part of the body but also because it forcefully resurfaces the precariousness of the female condition. And it is precisely this precariousness of the pre-illness experience that makes the attempts at recomposition described here necessary.

Reading the recomposition after the disruptions caused by the disease through processes of assemblage allows us to grasp the contingent and dynamic nature of these rearrangements that women used to create new affective and pragmatic configurations in which they located themselves as wives, mothers, friends, workers *and* breast cancer patients. This new piece of identity alters how women perceive their place in these spheres of their lives. These new practical and emotional reconfigurations were necessary to recompose and continue their life after a breast cancer diagnosis.

Note

1 Arteaga Pérez in her research on colorectal cancer (2022b) shows how even within a family there can be an extensive work on the part of both patients and relatives to limit showing negative emotions.

Conclusion: the meaning of assemblages and assemblages of meanings in breast cancer

> Disease is a subspecies of information malfunction or communications pathology; disease is a process of misrecognition or transgression of the boundaries of a strategic assemblage called self. (Donna Haraway)

Illness shatters the boundaries of our body, identity and life. A breast cancer diagnosis throws women into a state of deep confusion as they face an imminent risk. Cancer infiltrates and transgresses (in the etymological sense of 'going beyond') what Donna Haraway (1989: 15) defines as the 'strategic assemblage' of the self. In this book, I have explored how women respond to breast cancer's transgression using the concept of assemblage. I have explored three levels of assemblages: bodily, institutional and cultural, and socio-relational, and shown how assemblages can be understood through different articulations of the concept. By considering these different types of assemblages, we gain a deeper understanding of the different aspects of breast cancer experiences.

The assemblages informing women's experiences begin with their bodies, the first element to be altered by the disease; the medical-bodily assemblages expressed through the surgical and pharmacological treatments linked to the disease alter even more the tissues and the biological processes of patients' bodies. Moreover, breast cancer is not only one of the most gendered diseases but also one strongly linked to women's appearance. If we turn our attention from pharmaceutical to surgical interventions, as in the case of reconstruction, the technical possibilities to maintain a traditional female image play a fundamental role in reassembling the body. The alterations go beyond treatments and include redefinitions of the ill body through the stages of cancer and the presence of specific biomarkers and genes. Biomedical tools, including survival curves, standardised medical pathways and protocols, and the regime of personalisation, constituting what I have defined as medical-bodily assemblages, define how patients' bodies are altered by different treatments. These tools also determine how long patients spend in treatment and the choice of treatments themselves, contributing to transforming the body and the sense of self. The preference for one type of reconstructive technique over another is also linked to the uses that women intend to make of their bodies, which constitute a first aspect of the biographical assemblage. This is because physical changes seep through the body and influence patients' social, professional and emotional lives, affecting the relational assemblages linked to the disease. Furthermore, for many women, reconstruction is not necessary. They find themselves living in asymmetric bodies, which redraws the boundaries of the self and allows women to negotiate new relations with the dominant ideas of beauty and normality. In doing so, breast cancer patients advance the deconstruction of the normative ideas that constrict the bodies of all women, regardless of whether or not they have received a cancer diagnosis. The changes brought about by the disease often continue for years: scans are repeated annually, hormone therapies are prescribed for five or sometimes ten years, prostheses need to be changed and, for younger women, breast cancer often means an early entry into the changes of menopause. At the same time, the risk of a relapse is always present, even several years after the initial diagnosis. The post-diagnosis body is a precarious and unstable entity, and managing its instability requires specific biographic assemblages.

If, as Collier and Ong (2007) argue, biomedicine is a global assemblage that adapts to local contexts in a universal healthcare context, new therapies introduced into public healthcare systems need to be not only effective but also economically sustainable. New therapies need to be integrated into local systems through specific organisational assemblages, which can lead to friction with how these local systems are organised (as in the case of metastatic breast cancer therapies in the UK and France). Even when this global assemblage is completed and the therapies are introduced in the protocols and formal pathways, patients still have to navigate the system to ensure their therapeutic pathway is correctly assembled and negotiate access to (or avoidance of) specific treatments, conducting their own bricolage-assemblages. The treatments that patients access, in turn, are based on specific medical-bodily assemblages that define links between biomedical concepts and the organs and tissues of patients. Such medical-bodily assemblages also guide specific bodily assemblages through which surgery and other physical transformations shape patients' bodies.

Standardised protocols can only partly predict the impact of the disease and the therapies. The variability of both efficacy and side effects, and a range of possible complications, mean that medical-bodily assemblages change from case to case. Women respond by constructing their own biographical assemblages of meaning and practice. Searching for information, consulting more than one doctor and asking for second opinions, learning how to navigate health systems, switching between public and private healthcare and deciding which treatments to undergo while interrupting others: all these actions represent attempts at finding meaning and solutions that are not in opposition to those proposed by biomedicine, but complementary to them, in an effort to strike a balance between biomedical injunctions and patient needs.

Alongside the modifications introduced by biomedicine, other changes are linked to the social and cultural context. As we have seen, although the rhetoric of the pink ribbon is also present in Europe, it is often manipulated in a utilitarian way by associations that use a known aesthetic to locate themselves in the associative panorama, establishing new forms of cultural-political assemblage. There is now some degree of criticism of the rhetoric of the pink ribbon and the type of activism – based on glamorisation and cause-related marketing – that the Komen Foundation (among others) exemplifies. As we have seen, a hallmark of breast cancer is its individualisation. From the injunction to avoid dangerous lifestyles, to emphasising personalised therapies, breast cancer is presented as an individual problem. Different forms of associationism developed around the disease amplify these messages, from informational websites and patient meetings organised by local groups, to end-of-treatment workshops. The goal is to construct the ideal patient, a patient capable of taking care of her own health. However, assemblages and changes occur at not only a bodily but also a moral level of the cultural-political assemblages, with the pervasive message that cancer can be an opportunity for moral growth. Patients are asked to follow medical pathways and social and moral scripts, and they find themselves navigating messages that can contradict their experiences. In some cases, they can diverge from these social scripts and assemble new values, usages and meanings. In doing so, they build more personal biographical assemblages from negotiations between different elements, including aspects of their pre-diagnosis life and their own expectations and hopes for their post-diagnosis future. Some patients also adopt a more critical approach to the messages they receive, leading them to what I have defined as political growth rather than a moral one. Both cultural-political assemblages and biographical assemblages involve a 'montage of dissimilars' (see Saldivar, 1979) that sees individual aims and goals intersect with external cultural discourses and patients orient themselves among contradictory messages and instructions.

We have also seen that many patients renegotiate the role of the disease in their lives by negotiating treatments. Some patients rearrange and negotiate the therapies, adapting them both to their present and future life, trying to preserve essential functions of their bodies. In these cases, patients know they are contravening biomedical prescriptions and the social script urging them to adapt their behaviour so as to avoid a possible relapse. Selective and negotiated adherence to treatments is part of the bricolage-assemblage and another way of managing the relationship with biomedicine and the ways that biomedicine shapes the body. An individual's prospective biography is partial, contextual, provisional and more open. It requires specific biographical assemblages by collecting information on the possible evolutions of the disease, finding a personal place in relation to the organisation of healthcare, the treatments and the public discourses about breast cancer, and attempting to find meaning in these complex entanglements. Social roles reshaped around the disease do not always coalesce around forms of biosociality linked to breast cancer and its subtypes. Furthermore, personal and emotional relationships often fall apart as a consequence of the disease. Relational assemblages are frequently reconfigurations that include absences in a woman's present life as part of the negotiations required of her.

As mentioned in the Introduction, while I have covered three countries and collected rich materials, the pervasive nature of breast cancer means that there are experiences that I could not include in my analysis. However, other researchers have touched on them. Projects have covered the experiences of cis and trans men with breast cancer (Sledge, 2021) and LGBT+ people with cancers (e.g., Meidani and Alessandrin, 2017; Meidani, 2020; Bryson et al., 2020). Other studies have covered in more detail the intersections between international migration and access to cancer treatments (e.g., Pian, 2015; Kotobi and Sargent, 2023; Ludet et al., 2023) and racial specificities of cancer experiences (e.g., Gibbon, 2016; Madlock Gatison, 2016; Wright, 2023). Incorporating these and further complexities in future studies would expand our understanding of the provisional assemblages of cancer.

Experiences of cancer and experiences of gender

The assemblage processes that have been explored in this book are strongly connected to how illness can be socially interpreted. One of the aims of, and a common thread that runs through, this book has been to explore intimate, embodied events that profoundly altered the lives of the women encountered and to try to understand how a private and complex experience like breast cancer is shaped, defined and influenced by social and cultural aspects. In this book I have illustrated how patients can partly reappropriate, reshuffle and redefine the sense of the illness. The social and cultural elements defying the experiences of disease can be rearranged but not eliminated (or at least, not all of them). Among the aspects that remain, there is undoubtedly the impact of gender. As was seen in the Introduction, breast cancer is a prism for gender. Social constructions, definitions and ideas of femininity and of what is intrinsic and inherent in being a woman are inseparable from the experience of illness. As we have seen, this does not mean that women adhere to these definitions of gender. Medical-bodily, biographical and relational assemblages are, in fact, ways to deal with ideas of gender.

The body is the most visible element in which gender norms are made and unmade. My analysis of surgical practices shows how the female body is the terrain of multiple assemblages – medical-bodily, cultural-political and biographical. However, it also shows how reconstructive surgery is not simply a (re)construction of the canonical image of femininity but also a way to question it. Women who desire a specific reconstructive technique, those who stop at the reconstruction of a volume through the insertion of a prosthesis and decide that they do not need the reconstruction of the nipple or other surgeries, or those who use an external prosthesis illustrate the multiplicity of ways in which normative femininity is realised, and, ultimately, its ephemeral character.

McCann (2018) analysed the adherence to norms of femme femininity in terms of assemblages. One element she emphasises is how this adherence is a way of feeling connected with other women. This approach 'helps to refigure the core issue of femme as one of belonging rather than visibility' and 'offers a way of reconceptualizing the feelings and attachments of at-home-ness that are invoked by femme' (McCann, 2018: 285). McCann suggests extending this approach to norms of femininity more generally. We have seen how reconstruction is not simply a way to re-establish conformity and compliance with dominant ideas of femininity but also an attempt to regain a sense of 'at-home-ness' (to borrow McCann's term) in one's body and life post-diagnosis. For other women, as we have seen, illness becomes an opportunity to escape precise norms of self-presentation and find new spaces for action and individual growth through dissident forms of embodiment.

However, it is not only the body that is made and unmade but also the social roles linked to femininity. Sulik (2007) emphasised how, for many women, illness represents the moment in which they are forced to abandon caring roles and start to receive care, both from the medical system and from their entourage. The stories of the women I met show how the two roles often coincide and are reassembled. Some women turn to their partners and family for support, but they continue to provide support and reassurance. Furthermore, the disease introduces a new temporal dimension in care, the future. Many women find themselves negotiating care practices that can be effective not only in the present but also in a future of which they will not be part. Building memories that will comfort children, partners and friends is indeed an act that responds to a gendered vision of the female role and the organisation of the family. At the same time, other women try to 'use' their experience of illness as a way to extend the space assigned to them by gender roles. They try to rebuild the life that breast cancer has shattered in new ways that include empowerment and reappropriation of one's life.

Experiences of gender and illness experiences are strongly intertwined, and opposite tendencies intersect. From reconstructive surgery to the rhetorics of resilience and courage, illness is constructed as an adjuvant of normative femininity. As we have seen, most women do not entirely reject these indications; they are instead subjected to partial, creative and sometimes subversive forms of integration. Analysing these processes through the concept of assemblage is what has made it possible to observe this redefinition of gender norms in breast cancer experiences.

Comparing healthcare systems in transition

The organisation of breast cancer treatments is characterised by rapid, fragmented and costly innovation. In this book, I have focused on the experiences of illness in three European countries (the UK, France and Italy) with healthcare systems that can be described as universal. However, different approaches fall under the definition of universalism. A marked integration of the public and private sectors and significant forms of co-payment characterise Italy. Although none of the patients I interviewed in Italy paid for mastectomies or chemotherapy, it is not uncommon for Italian women to have diagnostic tests and specialist follow-up consultations in the private sector. At the same time, many French women have paid for reconstruction, with the social insurance system and the possibility of it partly covering the costs of private healthcare facilitating the public/private blend. In the UK, the NHS represents the last bastion of public service remaining after the wave of privatisation that swept the country in the 1980s and 1990s. This gives the NHS a symbolic role absent in the French and Italian healthcare systems. Despite this, even in the NHS, as we have seen, several forms of privatisation are creeping in, including in cancer care.

Among the heuristic advantages of comparing similar contexts, there exists the possibility of seeing not only differences but also similarities. In this case, the comparison has highlighted similarities that show how European healthcare systems deal with medical innovations for cancer.

Jain (2013) observes how the for-profit insurance-based US system is characterised by the distorting principle that the funding (and profit) of cancer research depends on maximising the treatments and payments for insured patients with cancer. Beyond the explosion in the cost of cancer drugs, and the speculation on life expectancies that characterises the whole insurance system, it also means that uninsured patients are largely excluded from several kinds of treatments, with even insured patients sometimes driven to bankruptcy by co-payments. This means extracting value from patients who are insured and well positioned on survival curves, while categorising uninsured patients as a low-value, surplus population.

The cost-benefit analysis in universal healthcare systems is not about calculating the life expectancy of each individual patient but, rather, the cost of treatment for the overall group of patients.[1] In Chapter 3, I have shown an example of this calculation concerning the introduction of trastuzumab. Even in a social insurance system such as the French one, and more so in single-payer systems such as those of the UK and Italy, the assumption is that every drug approved for use in the public sector will be available to anyone. Public discourse focuses on the collective cost of cancer treatments and, in some instances, on the idea that this cost is bound to increase progressively with the ageing of the population.[2] The positive aspect is that no patient in any of the three countries is excluded from treatment because they are uninsured, and any co-payment[3] is unlikely to drive them into bankruptcy. The negative aspect is that universal systems cannot curb the rise in cancer drug costs, which sometimes means not covering the costs of newly introduced drugs when their effectiveness and cost-benefit relation are not clearly defined.

Private health insurance presents some of the same issues in the refusal to refund costs for drugs that await full approval. However, in universal healthcare systems, one of the main limits is their (at least partial) obligation to follow the logic of systems built on private insurance-focused systems, asking patients to resort to complementary insurance or pay out-of-pocket to cover the additional, if not the entire, cost of specific treatments.

Consequently, in the three countries I have discussed, some of the social inequalities present, for example, in the US context, are substituted, to a degree, by inequalities linked to the subtype and stage of cancer. Most treatments are provided (almost) for free to all patients, especially if they develop only early-stage breast cancer and do not require any experimental treatment. However, patients who could benefit from experimental treatments, especially if they develop metastatic breast cancer, can find that public healthcare systems do not cover such treatments. The extent to which this coverage may be less comprehensive than that offered by certain private healthcare insurance policies is linked to the local authorisation of new drugs.

Personalised cancer medicine has high costs attached and most often extends life by a few months rather than years, yet it alters the nature of universal healthcare and the principle of solidarity on which those systems are based (see Fleck, 2022). The intersection between policies of retrenchment and the cost of many cancer drugs, with breast cancer at the forefront, is accelerating the privatisation of healthcare systems by creating spaces for patients who can afford to pay for treatment. Some patients, especially in the case of metastatic breast cancer, turn to private services for treatment, which significantly impacts on women who decide to go down this path and women who do not. The presence of a private route is perceived as an element that destabilises a system based on equality. In addition to inequalities between patients who either have or lack additional health insurance and inequalities between patients who can and cannot pay out-of-pocket, there are further inequalities in the cultural and social capital necessary to navigate the system and assemble one's own access to specific treatments, even before needing to pay for them.

Although the healthcare systems in the UK, France and Italy each have their own historical development, which continues to influence local organisational assemblages of biomedicine, they are not stable entities. The partial privatisations, wider political changes and transformations linked to medical innovations are changing the nature of each system. These tensions were particularly apparent during the COVID-19 pandemic, but they also manifest in recurring crises that see healthcare systems described as overwhelmed. Generally speaking, each healthcare system is in transition, holding to its universalism and national history while contending with external global pressures.

Livingston (2012) has analysed the mediation between sophisticated biomedical knowledge and the scarcity of means in a cancer ward in Botswana in terms of improvisation. However, improvisation is not a term that we would immediately associate with cancer care in the Global North, where policy makers and professionals endeavour to improve the organisation of healthcare. The role of scientific language in stabilising and objectifying the reality that scientists study is known (see Wolfgram, 2016), and biomedical language is no exception. Terms such as pathways, protocols and personalised medicine reinforce the idea that not only biomedical knowledge but also biomedical practices are stable, objective and linear. They present treatment pathways that stand in semantic opposition to the improvisation described in the Global South. However, my ethnographic research questions this linearity and shows that tinkering and improvisation also play an essential role in cancer care in the European countries I have studied. Rather than being due to a lack of tools and instruments, the tinkering processes can be traced to gaps in a generally functional system, to complexities introduced by innovations and to the irreducibility of individual patients to the standard. In this sense, the concept of assemblage, and in particular the distance between the organisational assemblages of healthcare institutions and the bricolage-assemblages of individual patients, enables us to capture the heterogeneous, provisional and non-linear aspect of cancer care in Europe, which counters ideas of linearity and objectivity in not only cancer care but also biomedicine more generally.

Breast cancer and disease–society assemblages

My analysis of socio-relational assemblages follows a long-standing notion within medical anthropology, that health problems and social vulnerability are intimately interwoven (see Singer, 2009). We have theorisations of how social and health problems interact dynamically and feed back into each other via the concepts of recursive cascades and recursive debilities (Manderson and Warren, 2016; Rogers, 2022). What we lack is a way to understand how these multiple difficulties are provisionally reassembled without ever being fully resolved.

In this book, I have explored how biomedical and social context elements influence patient experiences. Despite claims that early-stage breast cancer is curable and personalised therapies can turn metastatic breast cancer into a chronic disease, both stages introduce uncertainty into patient lives. The fear of a relapse, the side effects of treatments and the impact of the disease on the social life of the patients are elements that women must consider as they navigate their post-diagnosis life. A relevant factor is age, with younger patients finding themselves suffering the effects of an increasingly precarious world of work amid the dismantling of welfare state guarantees.

As discussed in this book, breast cancer is a highly gendered disease, in terms not only of its bodily changes and public discourse but also of how it impacts on women's place in society, including their work and their relations of care. If, for the women interviewed in France, the welfare state guarantees still offer some forms of protection and support (for example, in the case of childcare), personal support networks play a more central role in the UK and Italy. Breast cancer can disrupt an already fragile balance.

Women use cultural and social frameworks, along with the support of family and social networks, to contain the impact of illness. These containment methods are a negotiation between the resources that are available and those that would be necessary to deal with the disease. By interpreting these methods as relational assemblages, we can see how they are adaptable and temporary.

Women face not only the uncertain outcome of treatments but also financial, social and professional instability, which the disease can amplify. This could also explain why the cultural script is sometimes adjusted to accommodate political growth rather than moral growth.

The literature often considers disruptions introduced by a disease as part of a linear trajectory that can be recomposed in a new equilibrium that incorporates the limitations of the disease (for a critique of this assumption, particularly regarding metastatic breast cancer, see Greco, 2022c). Although this might be the case for many women, analysing these new situations as biographical assemblages allows us to highlight their provisional and dynamic nature and the work necessary to maintain them. The post-diagnosis equilibrium is not a stable endpoint but demands continuous renegotiation, with the effects of the disease often continuing to be felt many years later. This is even more true for patients with metastatic breast cancer, whose life is constantly dominated by the disease. The new positions in the world that the women whom I met have achieved were never concluded processes. Instead, they remained open, due to the need to include the changes associated with the social context and the breast cancer itself. Here, it is also important to underline that, while the stage of the disease (early-stage or metastatic, as well as the location of the metastases) significantly influences the experience of the disease, other biological elements – such as the tumour subtype – have a limited role in shaping patients' experiences. In this sense, the segmentation of patients according to biomarkers does not produce 'personalised' medicine in the sense of offering different approaches for each individual, nor does it seem to capture patient experiences, remaining confined to the more strictly biomedical domain.

My comparative study has shown, on the one hand, a continuity of patient experiences across different biological profiles of their cancers. On the other hand, it has shown how those experiences can be understood as assemblages that are far more complex than the different attempts to standardise and simplify not only therapies but also the whole illness trajectories of patients.

Beyond specific aspects of breast cancer (for example, its gendered nature, the relative visibility of the surgical consequences), many of the points raised here apply well beyond the specific case, not only because of the breast-cancer-ization (Bell, 2014) of other cancers but also because assemblages of biomedical tools and patient bodies, biographies and social roles are essential to most diseases. In this sense, the provisionality of assemblages can illuminate both illness experiences and the uncertainties central to contemporary societies.

Notes

1 As discussed in Chapter 1, the approach to the costing and approval of new drugs differs between the three countries, with the UK intervening less in setting the cost per unit but acting more restrictively in terms of approving drugs for use in the public healthcare sector. Despite these internal differences, the general implications of the model are shared across the three countries.
2 The same ageing of the population is often invoked to justify cuts under the fiction that the economic resources available for healthcare are the only non-flexible factor.
3 These can include the 'ticket' costs for most healthcare interventions in Italy, fees above those covered by public insurance in France, and top-up payments in the UK.

References

Aggarwal, Ajay, Fojo, Tito, Chamberlain, Charlotte, Davis, Courtney and Sullivan, Richard (2017) 'Do patient access schemes for high-cost cancer drugs deliver value to society? lessons from the NHS Cancer Drugs Fund', *Annals of Oncology* 28:8, 1738–50.

Alfieri, Sara, Brunelli, Cinzia, Capri, Giuseppe, Caraceni, Augusto, Bianchi, Giulia V. and Borreani, Claudia (2022) 'A qualitative study on the needs of women with metastatic breast cancer', *Journal of Cancer Education* 37, 1322–31.

Allsop, Judith and May, Annabelle (1993) 'Between the devil and the deep blue sea: managing the NHS in the wake of the 1990 Act', *Critical Social Policy* 13:38, 5–22.

Allsop, Judith, Jones, Kathryn and Baggott, Rob (2004) 'Health consumer groups in the UK: a new social movement?', *Sociology of Health & Illness* 26:6, 737–56.

Alonzo, Angelo A. (1979) 'Everyday illness behavior: a situational approach to health status deviations', *Social Science & Medicine Part A: Medical Psychology & Medical Sociology* 13, 397–404.

Amironsei, Razvan and Bialecki, Jon (2017) 'Assemblages: (pre)political, ethical and ontological perspectives', *SubStance* 46:1, 3–20.

Andersen, Rikke Sand (2023) 'Introduction: Crafting Cancer Anticipations', in Rikke Sand Andersen and Marie Louise Tørring (eds), *Cancer Entangled: Anticipation, Acceleration, and the Danish State*. New Brunswick, NJ: Rutgers University Press, 1–22.

Andersen, Rikke Sand and Tørring, Marie Louise (eds) (2023) *Cancer Entangled: Anticipation, Acceleration, and the Danish State*. New Brunswick, NJ: Rutgers University Press.

Andria, Barbara, Auriemma, Luigia, Attanasio, Chiara, Cozzolino, Santolo, Cristinziano, Adriano, Zeuli, Laura and Mancini, Antonio (2013) 'The impact of innovation for biotech drugs: an Italian analysis of products licensed in Europe between 2004 and 2011', *European Journal of Hospital Pharmacy* 20:6, 328–35.

Archer, Stephanie, Holland, Fiona G. and Montague, Jane (2018) '"Do you mean I'm not whole?" Exploring the role of support in women's experiences of mastectomy without reconstruction', *Journal of Health Psychology* 23:12, 1598–609.

Arliaud, Michel and Robelet, Magali (2000) 'Réformes du système de santé et devenir du "corps médical"', *Sociologie du Travail* 42:1, 91–112.

Aronowitz, Robert A. (2007) *Unnatural History: Breast Cancer and American Society*. Cambridge: Cambridge University Press.

Arteaga Pérez, Ignacia (2022a) 'Game-changing? When biomarker discovery and novel forms of patient work meet', *Medical Anthropology* 41:2, 156–68.

Arteaga Pérez, Ignacia (2022b) 'Emotion work during colorectal cancer treatments', *Medical Anthropology* 41:2, 197–209.

Åsbring, Pia and Närvänen, Anna-Liisa (2002) 'Women's experiences of stigma in relation to chronic fatigue syndrome and fibromyalgia', *Qualitative Health Research* 12:2, 148–60.

Atherton, Duncan D., Hills, Alexander J., Moradi, Pouria, Muirhead, Nina and Wood, Simon H. (2011) 'The economic viability of breast reconstruction in the UK: comparison of a single surgeon's experience of implant; LD; TRAM and DIEP based reconstructions in 274 patients', *Journal of Plastic, Reconstructive & Aesthetic Surgery* 64:6, 710–15.

Banerjee, Dwaipayan (2020) *Enduring Cancer: Life, Death, and Diagnosis in Delhi*. Durham, NC: Duke University Press.

Bardazzi, Rossella (2009) 'Is health care demand rationed by income and other determinants? An empirical assessment for Italy', *Studi economici* 97:1, 111–43.

Barrett, Ann, Roques, Tom, Small, Matthew and Smith, Richard D. (2006) 'How much will Herceptin really cost?', *BMJ* 333: 1118.

Bartky, Sandra Lee (1982) 'Narcissism, femininity and alienation', *Social Theory and Practice* 8:2, 127–43.

Bartlett, John M.S. and Parelukar, Wendy (2017) 'Breast cancers are rare diseases – and must be treated as such', *npj Breast Cancer*, 3: 11.

Batt, Sharon (2017) *Health Advocacy Inc.: How Pharmaceutical Funding Changed the Breast Cancer Movement*. Vancouver: UBC Press.

Baum, Michael (2015) '"Catch it early, save a life and save a breast": this misleading mantra of mammography', *Journal of the Royal Society of Medicine* 108:9, 338–9.

Bayliss, Kate (2022) 'Can England's national health system reforms overcome the neoliberal legacy?', *International Journal of Social Determinants of Health and Health Services* 52:4, 480–91.

Bell, Kirsten (2012) 'Remaking the self: trauma, teachable moments, and the biopolitics of cancer survivorship', *Culture, Medicine, and Psychiatry* 36:4, 584–600.

Bell, Kirsten (2014) 'The breast-cancer-ization of cancer survivorship: implications for experiences of the disease', *Social Science & Medicine* 110, 56–63.

Bell, Kirsten and Ristovski-Slijepcevic, Svetlana (2011) 'Metastatic cancer and mothering: being a mother in the face of a contracted future', *Medical Anthropology* 30:6, 629–49.

Bell, Kirsten and Ristovski-Slijepcevic, Svetlana (2015) 'Communicating "evidence": lifestyle, cancer, and the promise of a disease-free future', *Medical Anthropology Quarterly* 29:2, 216–36.

Bend, Gemma L. and Priola, Vincenza (2023) '"There is nothing wrong with me": the materialisation of disability in sheltered employment', *Work, Employment and Society* 37:3, 645–64.

Benjamin, Laure, Buthion, Valérie, Vidal-Trécan, Gwenaëlle and Briot, Pascal (2014) 'Impact of the healthcare payment system on patient access to oral anticancer drugs: an illustration from the French and United States contexts', *BMC Health Services Research* 14, 274.

Berlant, Lauren (2011) *Cruel Optimism*. Durham, NC: Duke University Press.

Besle, Sylvain and Sarradon-Eck, Aline (2022) 'Chronicity and the patient's decision-making work. The case of an advanced cancer patient', *Anthropology & Medicine* 29:1, 76–91.

Bezhuly, Michael, Temple, Claire, Sigurdson, Leif J., Davis, Roger B., Flowerdew, Gordon and Cook Jr., E. Francis (2009) 'Immediate postmastectomy reconstruction is associated with improved breast cancer-specific survival. Evidence and new challenges from the surveillance, epidemiology, and end results database', *Cancer* 115:20, 4648–54.

Bishop, Katelynn, Gruys, Kjerstin and Evans, Maddie (2018) 'Sized out: women, clothing size, and inequality', *Gender & Society* 32:2, 180–203.

Böhm, Katharina, Schmid, Achim, Götze, Ralf, Landwehr, Claudia and Rothgang, Heinz (2013) 'Five types of OECD healthcare systems: empirical results of a deductive classification', *Health Policy* 113:3, 258–69.

Bouvenot, Gilles (2018) 'Modalités et déterminants de la fixation des prix des médicaments des cancers en France', *Bulletin de l'Académie Nationale de Médecine* 202:5–6, 977–88.

Boyd, Phoebe-Jane (2017) 'Race for Life's branding is cliched and infantile. It's time to sink the pink', *The Guardian*, 3 April, www.theguardian.com/commentisfree/2017/apr/03/race-for-life-branding-pink-cancer-research-uk-gender-stereotypes (accessed 19 August 2023).

Braun, Susan (2003) 'The history of breast cancer advocacy', *The Breast Journal* 9:s2, S101–3.

Brenner, Barbara A. (2008) 'Breast cancer is recurrent, not chronic, and the distinction matters', *Our Bodies Ourselves*, www.ourbodiesourselves.org/2008/11/breast-cancer-is-recurrent-not-chronic-and-the-distinction-matters/ (accessed 28 July 2023).

Brenner, Barbara (2016) *So Much to Be Done: The Writings of Breast Cancer Activist Barbara Brenner*. Minneapolis: Minnesota University Press.

Brown, Phil (2007) *Toxic Exposures: Contested Illnesses and the Environmental Health Movement*. New York: Columbia University Press.

Bryson, Mary K., Taylor, Evan T., Boschman, Lorna, Gahagan, Jacqueline, Rail, Genevieve and Ristock, Janice (2020) 'Awkward choreographies from cancer's margins: incommensurabilities of biographical and biomedical knowledge in sexual and/or gender minority cancer patients' treatment', *Journal of Medical Humanities* 41, 341–61.

Buchanan, Mary, O'Connell, Deirdre and Mosconi, Paola (2004) 'Europa DONNA, the European breast cancer coalition lobbying at European and local levels', *Journal of Ambulatory Care Management* 27:2, 146–53.

Bungay, Hilary (2005) 'Cancer and health policy: the postcode lottery of care', *Social Policy and Administration* 39:1, 35–48.

Burawoy, Michael (2000) 'Introduction: Reaching for the Global', in Michael Burawoy, Joseph A. Blum, Sheba George, Zsuzsa Gille, Teresa Gowan, Lynne Haley, Maren Klawiter, et al., *Global Ethnography: Forces, Connections, and Imaginations in a Postmodern World*. Berkeley, CA: University of California Press, 1–40.

Burawoy, Michael (2009) *The Extended Case Method: Four Countries, Four Decades, Four Great Transformations, and One Theoretical Tradition*. Berkeley, CA: University of California Press.

Burki, Talha Khan (2019) 'UK health tourism for private cancer care', *The Lancet Oncology* 20:3, 334.

Bury, Michael (1982) 'Chronic illness as biographical disruption', *Sociology of Health & Illness* 4:2, 167–82.

Caldon, Lisa J.M., Collins, Karen A., Wilde, David J., Ahmedzai, Sam H., Noble, Thomas W., Stotter, Anne, Sibbering, D. Mark et al. (2011) 'Why do hospital mastectomy rates vary? Differences in the decision-making experiences of women with breast cancer', *British Journal of Cancer* 104:10, 1551–7.

Carlsen, Kathrine, Oksbjerg Dalton, Susanne, Frederiksen, Kirsten, Diderichsen, Finn and Johansen, Christoffer (2007) 'Are cancer survivors at an increased risk for divorce? A Danish cohort study', *European Journal of Cancer* 43:14, 2093–9.

Carlson, Robert H. (2003) 'Drs Veronesi and Fisher on scientific evidence and paradigm shifts', *Oncology Times* 25:11, 28–30.

Cartabellotta, Nino, Cottafava, Elena, Luceri, Roberto and Mosti, Marco (2022) *5° Rapporto GIMBE sul Servizio Sanitario Nazionale*, Fondazione GIMBE.

Carter, Meg (2015) 'Backlash against "pinkwashing" of breast cancer awareness campaigns', *BMJ* 351, h5399.

Castel, Patrick and Friedberg, Erhard (2010) 'Institutional change as an interactive process: the case of the modernization of the French cancer centers', *Organization Science* 21:2, 311–30.

Checkland, Kath, Allen, Pauline, Coleman, Anne, Segar, Julia, McDermott, Imelda, Harrison, Stephen, Petsoulas, Christina et al. (2013) 'Accountable to whom, for what? An exploration of the early development of Clinical Commissioning Groups in the English NHS', *BMJ Open* 3, e003769.

Chee, Heng Leng, Whittaker, Andrea and Por, Heong Hong (2017) 'Medical travel facilitators, private hospitals and international medical travel in assemblage', *Asia Pacific Viewpoint* 58:2, 242–54.

Chenhall, Richard D. and Senior, Kate (2018) 'Living the social determinants of health: assemblages in a remote Aboriginal community', *Medical Anthropology Quarterly* 32:2, 177–95.

Coleman, Anna, Segar, Julia and Checkland, Kath (2015) 'The devolution project in Greater Manchester: Introduction to the special issue', *Representation* 51:4, 377–84.

Collier, Stephen J. and Ong, Aihwa (2007) 'Global Assemblages Anthropological Problems', in Aihwa Ong and Stephen J. Collier (eds), *Global Assemblages: Technology, Politics, and Ethics as Anthropological Problems*. Malden, MA: Blackwell, 3–21.

Cothier-Savey, Isabelle and Rimareix, Françoise (2008) 'Principes généraux de la chirurgie oncoplastique du sein', *Annales de chirurgie plastique esthétique* 53:2, 102–11.

Cowan, Donald H. (2010) 'Vera Peters and the conservative management of early-stage breast cancer', *Current Oncology* 17:2, 50–4.

C.R.E.A. Sanità (2017) 'Osservatorio sui tempi di attesa e sui costi delle prestazioni sanitarie nei Sistemi Sanitari Regionali: I Report', report.

Crompvoets, Samantha (2006) 'Comfort, control, or conformity: women who choose breast reconstruction following mastectomy', *Health Care for Women International* 27:1, 75–93.

Crowley, Vicki (2010) 'A rhizomatics of hearing: becoming deaf in the workplace and other affective spaces of hearing', *Discourse* 31:4, 543–58.

Currier, Dianne (2003) 'Feminist technological futures: Deleuze and body/technology assemblages', *Feminist Theory* 4:3, 321–38.

Dalstrom, Matthew (2013) 'Medical travel facilitators: connecting patients and providers in a globalized world', *Anthropology & Medicine* 20:1, 24–35.

Dao, Amy and Mulligan, Jessica (2016) 'Toward an anthropology of insurance and health reform: an introduction to the special issue', *Medical Anthropology Quarterly* 30:1, 5–17.

Davis, Elizabeth M. (2016) 'Pink is for (Survivor) Girls: Late-Stage Breast Cancer, Silence, and Pink Ribbon Culture', in Ainette Madlock Gatison (ed), *Communicating Women's Health: Social and Cultural Norms That Influence Health Decisions*, New York: Routledge, 31–46.

de Belvis, Antonio Giulio, Ferrè, Francesca, Specchia, Maria Lucia, Valerio, Luca, Fattore, Giovanni and Ricciardi, Walter (2012) 'The financial crisis in Italy: implications for the healthcare sector', *Health Policy* 106:1, 10–6.

De Certeau, Michel (1980) *L'invention du quotidien, 1: Arts de faire*. Paris: Union générale d'éditions.

De Ieso, Paul B., Coward, Jermaine I., Letsa, Ioanna, Schick, Ulrike, Nandhabalan, Meera, Frentzas, Sophia and Gore, Martin E. (2013) 'A study of the decision outcomes and financial costs of multidisciplinary team meetings (MDMs) in oncology', *British Journal of Cancer* 109, 2295–300.

Deleuze, Gilles (1989) 'Qu'est-ce qu'un dispositif?', in Various authors, *Michel Foucault philosophe. Rencontre international. Paris, 9, 10, 11 Janvier 1988*. Paris: Seuil, 185–95.

Deleuze, Gilles and Félix Guattari (1980) *Mille plateaux: Capitalisme et schizophrénie*. Paris: Minuit.

Del Vecchio Good, Mary-Jo, Good, Byron J., Schaffer, Cynthia and Lind, Stuart E. (1990) 'American oncology and the discourse on hope', *Culture, Medicine and Psychiatry* 14:1, 59–79.

De Martino, Ernesto (1961) *La terra del rimorso: Contributo a una storia religiosa del Sud*. Milan: Il Saggiatore.

De Michele, Grazia (2016) 'Radical objects: "Cancer Sucks"', *History Workshop*, https://www.historyworkshop.org.uk/material-culture/radical-objects-cancer-sucks/ (accessed 22 July 2024).

Domenighetti, Gianfranco, Vineis, Paolo, De Pietro, Carlo and Tomada, Angelo (2010) 'Ability to pay and equity in access to Italian and British national health services', *European Journal of Public Health* 20:5, 500–3.

Donna X Donna (2020) 'La ricostruzione mammaria dopo il tumore al seno', Beautiful After Breast Cancer ONLUS.

Dragun, Anthony E., Pan, Jianmin, Riley, Elizabeth C., Kruse, Barbara, Wilson, Mary R., Rai, Shesh and Jain, Dharamvir (2013) 'Increasing use of elective mastectomy and contralateral prophylactic surgery among breast conservation candidates: a 14-year report from a comprehensive cancer center', *American Journal of Clinical Oncology* 36:4, 375–80.

Drummond, Michael, de Pouvourville, Gerard, Jones, Elizabeth, Haig, Jennifer, Saba, Grece and Cawston, Hélène (2014) 'A comparative analysis of two contrasting European approaches for rewarding the value added by drugs for cancer: England versus France', *PharmacoEconomics* 32:5, 509–20.

Duff, Cameron (2014) *Assemblages of Health: Deleuze's Empiricism and the Ethology of Life*. Dodrecht: Springer.

Duff, Cameron (2023) 'The ends of an assemblage of health', *Social Science & Medicine* 317, 115636.
Dunn, Phoebe, Fraser, Caroline, Williamson, Skeena and Alderwick, Hugh (2022) 'Integrated care systems: what do they look like?' The Health Foundation, www.health.org.uk/publications/long-reads/integrated-care-systems-what-do-they-look-like (accessed 28 July 2023).
Edmiston, E. Kale (2018) 'Community-led Peer Advocacy for Transgender Healthcare Access in the Southeastern United States: The Trans Buddy Program', in Cecilia Vindrola-Padros, Ginger A. Johnson and Anne E. Pfister (eds), *Healthcare in Motion: Immobilities in Health Service Delivery and Access*. New York: Berghahn, 185–201.
Ehrenreich, Barbara (2001) 'Welcome to Cancerland: a mammogram leads to a cult of pink kitsch', *Harper's Magazine*, November, 43–53.
Eisenstein, Zillah (2001) *Manmade Breast Cancers*. Ithaca, NY: Cornell University Press.
Engelberg, Miriam (2006) *Cancer Made Me a Shallower Person: A Memoir in Comics*. New York: HarperCollins.
Eraso, Yolanda (2020) 'Oestrogen receptors and breast cancer: are we prepared to move forward? A critical review', *BioSocieties* 15, 627–49.
Ericksen, Julia A. (2008) *Taking Charge of Breast Cancer*. Berkeley, CA: University of California Press.
Ernaux, Annie and Marie, Marc (2005) *L'usage de la photo*. Paris: Gallimard.
Esserman, Laura J., Thompson, Ian M. and Reid, Brian, Nelson, Peter, Ranshoff, David F., Welch, H. Gilbert, Hwang, Shelley et al. (2014) 'Addressing overdiagnosis and overtreatment in cancer: a prescription for change', *The Lancet Oncology* 15:6, e234-2242.
Exworthy, Mark and Lafond, Sarah (2021) 'New development: commercialization of the English National Health Service: a necessity in times of financial austerity?', *Public Money & Management* 41:1, 81–4.
Fagan Robinson, Kelly and Arteaga Pérez, Ignacia (2023) '"Hard-to-Reach"? Meanings at the Margins of Care and Risk in Cancer Research', in Linda Rae Bennett, Lenore Manderson and Belinda Spagnoletti (eds), *Cancer and the Politics of Care: Inequalities and Interventions in Global Perspective*. London: UCL Press, 210–31.
Fainzang, Sylvie (2015) *An Anthropology of Lying: Information in the Doctor–Patient Relationship*. Farnham: Ashgate.
Federici, Silvia (2014) 'The Reproduction of Labour Power in the Global Economy and the Unfinished Feminist Revolution', in Maurizio Atzeni (ed), *Workers and Labour in a Globalised Capitalism: Contemporary Themes and Theoretical Issues*. Basingstoke: Palgrave Macmillan, 85–110.
Ferzacca, Steve (2000) '"Actually, I don't feel that bad": managing diabetes and the clinical encounter', *Medical Anthropology Quarterly* 14:1, 28–50.

Figueroa-Magalhães, Maria Cristina, Jelovac, Danijela, Connolly, Roisin and Wolff, Antonio C. (2014) 'Treatment of HER2-positive breast cancer', *Breast* 23:2, 128–36.

Fisher, Bernard, Bauer, Madeline, Margolese, Richard, Poisson, Roger, Pilch, Yosef, Redmond, Carol, Fisher, Edwin et al. (1985) 'Five-year results of a randomized clinical trial comparing total mastectomy and segmental mastectomy with or without radiation in the treatment of breast cancer', *New England Journal of Medicine* 312:11, 665–73.

Fitts, Karen (1999) 'The pathology and erotics of breast cancer', *Discourse* 21:2, 3–20.

Flaum, Nicola, Papaxoinis, George, Hockenhull, Kimberley, Barrusio, Jorge, Backen, Alison, Cunningham, David and Mansoor, Wasat (2020) 'Financial burden and financial toxicity in patients with colorectal, gastro-oesophageal, and pancreatobiliary cancers: a UK study', *Journal of Cancer Policy* 25, 100236.

Fleck, Leonard M. (2022) 'Precision medicine and the fragmentation of solidarity (and justice)', *Medicine, Health Care and Philosophy* 25, 191–206.

Forrest, Christopher B. (2003) 'Primary care gatekeeping and referrals: effective filter or failed experiment?', *BMJ* 326, 692.

Fortier, Corinne (2020) 'Seins, reconstruction, et féminité. Quand les Amazones s'exposent', *Droit et Cultures* 80, https://doi.org/10.4000/droitcultures.6721

Foucault, Michel (1994) 'Le jeu de Michel Foucault', in idem, *Dits et écrits (1954–1988)*. Paris: Gallimard, 298–329.

Fox, Nick J. (2011) 'The ill-health assemblage: beyond the body-with-organs', *Health Sociology Review* 20:4, 359–71.

Frank, Arthur W. (1995) *The Wounded Storyteller: Body, Illness, and Ethics*. Chicago, IL: University of Chicago Press.

Frisina Doetter, Lorraine and Neri, Stefano (2018) 'Redefining the state in health care policy in Italy and the United States', *European Policy Analysis* 4:2, 234–54.

Gabriele, Stefania (2015) 'Crisi, austerità, sistemi sanitari e salute nei Paesi dell'Europa meridionale', *Meridiana* 83, 63–90.

Gagné, Patricia and McGaughey, Deanna (2002) 'Designing women: cultural hegemony and the exercise of power among women who have undergone elective mammoplasty', *Gender & Society* 16:6, 814–38.

Gagnon, Marilou and Holmes, Dave (2016) 'Body–drug assemblages: theorizing the experience of side effects in the context of HIV treatment', *Nursing Philosophy* 17:4, 250–61.

Garattini, Livio, Nobili, Alessandro, Badinella Martini, Marco and Manucci, Pier Manuccio (2023) 'The role of general practitioners in the EU: time to draw lessons from a too wide range?', *Internal and Emergency Medicine* 18, 343–6.

Gardner, Kirsten E. (2006) *Early Detection: Women, Cancer, and Awareness Campaigns in the Twentieth-Century United States*. Chapel Hill, NC: University of North Carolina Press.

Gardner, Kirsten E. (2009) 'Disruption and cancer narratives: from awareness to advocacy', *Literature and Medicine* 28:2, 333–50.

Garrido, Ignacio, Gangloff, Dimitri, Trocard, Pierre, Wagner, Aude, Rafii, Arash, Chopin, Nicolas and Ferron, Gwenael (2006) 'Les bonnes indications de l'oncoplastie', *Oncologie* 8:8, 714–23.

Geertz, Clifford (1986) 'Making Experience, Authoring Selves', in Victor W. Turner and Edward M. Bruner (eds), *The Anthropology of Experience*. Urbana, IL: University of Chicago Press, 373–80.

Getrich, Christina M., García, Jacqueline M., Solares, Angélica and Kano, Miria (2018) 'Buffering the uneven impact of the Affordable Care Act: immigrant-serving safety-net providers in New Mexico', *Medical Anthropology Quarterly* 32:2, 233–53.

Gibbon, Sahra (2007) *Breast Cancer Genes and the Gendering of Knowledge: Science and Citizenship in the Cultural Context of the 'New' Genetics*. Basingstoke: Palgrave Macmillan.

Gibbon, Sahra (2016) 'Translating population difference: the use and re-use of genetic ancestry in Brazilian cancer genetics', *Medical Anthropology* 35:1, 58–72.

Gibbon, Sahra, Joseph, Galen, Mozersky, Jessica, zur Nieden, Andrea and Palfner, Sonja (eds) (2014) *Breast Cancer Gene Research and Medical Practices: Transnational Perspectives in the Time of BRCA*. Abingdon: Routledge.

Gibson, Rebecca E., Upshur, Ross E.G., Young, Nancy L. and McKeever, Patricia (2007) 'Disability, technology, and place: social and ethical implications of long-term dependency on medical devices', *Ethics, Place & Environment* 10:1, 7–28.

Gierach, Gretchen L., Curtis, Rochelle E., Pfeiffer, Ruth M., Mullooly, Maeve, Ntowe, Estelle A., Hoover, Robert N., Nyante, Sarah J. et al. (2017) 'Adjuvant endocrine therapy and risk of contralateral breast cancer among US women with breast cancer', *JAMA Oncology* 3:2, 186–93.

Giordano, Livia and Giorgi, Daniela (2011) 'I programmi di screening in Italia', in Eugenio Paci and Donella Puliti (eds), *Come cambia l'epidemiologia del tumore della mammella in Italia: I risultati del progetto IMPATTO dei programmi di screening mammografico*. Pisa: Pacini, 27–36.

Gordon, Deborah R. and Paci, Eugenio (1997) 'Disclosure practices and cultural narratives: understanding concealment and silence around cancer in Tuscany, Italy', *Social Science & Medicine* 44:10, 1433–52.

Greco, Cinzia (2015) 'The *Poly Implant Prothèse* breast prostheses scandal: embodied risk and social suffering', *Social Science & Medicine* 147, 150–7.

Greco, Cinzia (2016a) 'Blaming the southern victim: cancer and the Italian "Southern Question" in *Terra dei fuochi* and Taranto', *Anthropology Today* 32:3, 16–19.

Greco, Cinzia (2016b) 'Taking sides: a reflection on "partisan anthropology"', *Medicine Anthropology Theory* 3:3, https://doi.org/10.17157/mat.3.3.447

Greco, Cinzia (2016c) 'Vivre avec un corps asymétrique. Mastectomie, résistances et réappropriation', *Cahiers du Genre* 60, 81–99.

Greco, Cinzia (2016d) 'Shining a light on the grey zones of gender construction: breast surgery in France and Italy', *Journal of Gender Studies* 25:3, 303–17.

Greco, Cinzia (2019) 'Moving for cures: breast cancer and mobility in Italy', *Medical Anthropology* 38:4, 384–98.

Greco, Cinzia (2020a) 'Too much information, too little power: the persistence of asymmetries in doctor–patient relationships', *Anthropology Now* 12:2, 53–60.

Greco, Cinzia (2020b) 'Quête, combat ou négociation? Raconter les marges d'action dans le cas de la reconstruction post-mastectomie', *Corps* 18:1, 225–34.

Greco, Cinzia (2020c) '"À quel sein se vouer?" Analyser le rôle du sein à travers les traitements chirurgicaux pour le cancer du sein', in Anastasia Meidani (ed.), *Masculinités et féminités face au cancer: Expériences cancéreuses et interactions soignantes*. Toulouse: Érès, 41–56.

Greco, Cinzia (2021) 'Care, Choice, and Cure: Exploring the Logics of Mobility of Patients with Breast Cancer in Italy and France', in Cecilia Vindrola-Padros (ed.), *Care Work and Medical Travel: Exploring the Emotional Dimensions of Caring on the Move*. Lanham, MD: Lexington, 51–68.

Greco, Cinzia (2022a) 'The nebula of chronicity: dealing with metastatic breast cancer in the UK', *Anthropology & Medicine* 29:1, 107–21.

Greco, Cinzia (2022b) 'Divergent ethnography: conducting fieldwork as an autistic anthropologist', Member Voices, *Fieldsights*, 26 May, https://culanth.org/fieldsights/divergent-ethnography-conducting-fieldwork-as-an-autistic-anthropologist (accessed 22 July 2022).

Greco, Cinzia (2022c) 'The uncertain presence: experiences of living with metastatic breast cancer', *Medical Anthropology* 41:2, 129–40.

Greco, Cinzia (2023) 'Practices of containment in the "south-within-the-north": women with breast cancer in southern Italy', in Linda Rae Bennett, Lenore Manderson and Belinda Spagnoletti (eds), *Cancer and the Politics of Care: Inequalities and Interventions in GLOBAL PERSPECTIVE*. London: UCL Press, 171–89.

Greco, Cinzia (2024) 'Coexisting cancer regimes: transformations of breast and lung cancer in the United Kingdom', *Health* 28:4, 615–32.

Greco, Cinzia and Graber, Nils (2022) 'Anthropology of new chronicities: illness experiences under the promise of medical innovation as long-term treatment', *Anthropology & Medicine* 29:1, 1–13.

Greene, Jeremy A. (2018) 'The disappointment of the biosimilar', *Journal of Law, Medicine & Ethics* 46:3, 791–3.

Greene, Jeremy A. and Riggs, Kevin R. (2015) 'Why is there no generic insulin? Historical origins of a modern problem', *New England Journal of Medicine* 372:12, 1171–5.

Grosz, Elizabeth A. (1994) *Volatile Bodies: Towards a Corporeal Feminism*. Bloomington, IN: Indiana University Press.

Gubar, Susan (2012) *Memoir of a Debulked Woman: Enduring Ovarian Cancer*. New York: WW Norton & Company.

Guerrera, Antonello (2019) 'Colm Tóibín: "Il cancro non è maestro di vita"', *La Repubblica*, 22 May, www.repubblica.it/robinson/2019/05/22/news/colm_to_ibi_n_il_cancro_non_e_maestro_di_vita_-300788888/ (accessed 19 August 2023).

Guillot, Bernard (2017) 'Le prix des médicaments anticancéreux est-il justifié?', *Oncologie* 19:11–12, 381–5.

Hadji, Peyton (2010) 'Improving compliance and persistence to adjuvant tamoxifen and aromatase inhibitor therapy', *Critical Reviews in Oncology/Hematology* 73:2, 156–66.

Hamarat, Natasia (2020) '(Se) Mobiliser autour des transformations du corps suite à la maladie grave. Le cas des associations de femmes atteintes de cancer du sein', *Droits et Cultures* 80, https://doi.org/10.4000/droitcultures.6422

Hanefeld, Johanna, Horsfall, Daniel, Lunt, Neil and Smith, Richard (2013) 'Medical tourism: a cost or benefit to the NHS?', *PLoS ONE* 8:10, e70406.

Haraway, Donna (1985) 'A manifesto for cyborgs: science, technology and socialist feminism in the 1980s', *Socialist Review* 80, 65–108.

Haraway, Donna (1989) 'The biopolitics of postmodern bodies: determinations of self in immune system discourse', *differences* 1:1, 3–43.

Harbeck, Nadia, and Rody, Achim (2012) 'Lost in translation? Estrogen receptor status and endocrine responsiveness in breast cancer', *Journal of Clinical Oncology* 30:7, 686–9.

Heberle, Renee (2015) 'The Personal is Political', in Lisa Disch and Mary Hawkesworth (eds), *The Oxford Handbook of Feminist Theory*. Oxford: Oxford University Press, 593–609.

Hecketsweiler, Philippe, Guillard, Jean-François and Czernichow, Pierre (2001) 'Le système de santé français', in Pierre Barbier and Serge Bonfils (eds), *Diversité des systèmes de santé occidentaux: l'harmonisation impossible?* Montrouge: Libbey Eurotext, 51–72.

Hedgecoe, Adam (2004) *The Politics of Personalised Medicine: Pharmacogenetics in the Clinic*. Cambridge: Cambridge University Press.

Hedgecoe, Adam (2006) 'It's money that matters: the financial context of ethical decision-making in modern biomedicine', *Sociology of Health & Illness* 28:6, 768–84.

Héquet, Delphine, Zarca, Kevin, Dolbeault, Sylvie, Couturaud, Benoît, Ngô, Charlotte, Fourchotte, Virginie, De La Rochefordière, Anne et al. (2013) 'Reasons of not having breast reconstruction: a historical cohort of 1937 breast cancer patients undergoing mastectomy', *SpringerPlus* 2, 325.

Holland, Fiona, Archer, Stephanie and Montague, Jane (2016) 'Younger women's experiences of deciding against delayed breast reconstruction post-mastectomy following breast cancer: an interpretative phenomenological analysis', *Journal of Health Psychology* 21:8, 1688–99.

Holliday, Ruth and Sanchez Taylor, Jacqueline (2006) 'Aesthetic surgery as false beauty', *Feminist Theory* 7:2, 179–95.

Hortobagyi, Gabriel N. (2003) 'The curability of breast cancer: present and future', *European Journal of Cancer Supplements* 1:1, 24–34.

Hunleth, Jean and Steinmetz, Emily (2022) 'Navigating breast cancer screening in rural Missouri: from patient navigation to social navigation', *Medical Anthropology* 41:2, 228–42.

Illouz, Eva (2007) *Cold Intimacies: The Making of Emotional Capitalism*. Cambridge: Polity Press.

Issa, Amalia M. (2007) 'Personalized medicine and the practice of medicine in the 21st century', *McGill Journal of Medicine* 10:1, 53–7.

Jackson, Emily (2010) 'Top-up payments for expensive cancer drugs: rationing, fairness and the NHS', *Modern Law Review* 73:3, 399–427.

Jain, S. Lochlann (2013) *Malignant. How Cancer Becomes Us*. Berkeley, CA: University of California Press.

Jay, David (2012) 'The SCAR project', *Social Semiotics* 22:1, 39–46.

Jenson, Jane (2018) 'A Comparative Perspective on Work and Gender', in Jane Jenson, Jacqueline Laufer and Margaret Maruani (eds), *The Gendering of Inequalities: Women, Men and Work*. London: Routledge, 1–16.

Johnson, Ericka (2018) 'Anatomical Assemblages: Medical Technologies, Bodies and their Entangled Practices', in Cecilia Åsberg and Rosi Braidotti (eds), *A Feminist Companion to the Posthumanities*. Cham: Springer, 189–97.

Jommi, Claudio (2015) 'Innovation and drugs price and reimbursement: a comparison between Italy and the other major EU countries', *Global & Regional Health Technology Assessment: Italian; Northern Europe and Spanish* 2:3, https://doi.org/10.33393/grhta.2015.336

Jones, Meredith (2008) *Skintight: An Anatomy of Cosmetic Surgery*. Oxford: Berg.

Jordan, V. Craig (2003) 'Tamoxifen: a most unlikely pioneering medicine', *Nature Reviews Drug Discovery* 2:3, 205–13.

Jordan, V. Craig (2006) 'Tamoxifen (ICI46,474) as a targeted therapy to treat and prevent breast cancer', *British Journal of Pharmacology* 147:S1, S269–76.

Jusot, Florence (2014) 'La complémentaire santé: une source d'inégalités face à la santé?', *Les Tribunes de la santé* 43:2, 69–78.

Kangas, Beth (2002) 'Therapeutic itineraries in a global world: Yemenis and their search for biomedical treatment abroad', *Medical Anthropology* 21:1, 35–78.

Keating, Peter, Cambrosio, Alberto and Nelson, Nicole C. (2016) '"Triple negative breast cancer": translational research and the (re)assembling of diseases in post-genomic medicine', *Studies in History and Philosophy of Science Part C* 59, 20–34.

Kellaway, Kate (2017) 'Victoria Derbyshire: "After cancer, I'm squeezing life out of every second"', *The Observer*, 17 September, www.theguardian.com/tv-and-radio/2017/sep/17/victoria-derbyshire-after-cancer-squeezing-life-every-second-dear-cancer-love-victoria (accessed 28 July 2023).

Kelly, Michael, Morgan, Anthony, Ellis, Simon, Younger, Tricia, Huntley, Jane and Swann, Catherine (2010) 'Evidence based public health: a review of the experience of the National Institute of Health and Clinical Excellence (NICE) of developing public health guidance in England', *Social Science & Medicine* 71:6, 1056–62.

Kendrick, Karen (2008) '"Normalizing" female cancer patients: *Look good, feel better* and other image programs', *Disability & Society* 23:3, 259–69.

Kerr, Anne, Chekar, Choon Kee, Ross, Emily, Swallow, Julia and Cunningham-Burley, Sarah (2021) *Personalised Cancer Medicine: Future Crafting in the Genomic Era*. Manchester: Manchester University Press.

King, Samantha (2006) *Pink Ribbons, Inc. Breast Cancer and the Politics of Philanthropy*. Minneapolis: Minnesota University Press.

Kirchhoff, Anne C., Yi, Jaehee, Wright, Jennifer, Warner, Echo L. and Smith, Ken R. (2012) 'Marriage and divorce among young adult cancer survivors', *Journal of Cancer Survivorship* 6:4, 441–50.

Klawiter, Maren (2008) *The Biopolitics of Breast Cancer. Changing Cultures of Disease and Activism*. Minneapolis: Minnesota University Press.

Kleinman, Arthur M. (1973) 'Medicine's symbolic reality: on a central problem in the philosophy of medicine', *Inquiry* 16:1–4, 206–13.

Kleinman, Arthur M. (1997) 'Suffering and Its Professional Transformation: Toward an Ethnography of Interpersonal Experience', in idem, *Writing at the Margin: Discourse Between Anthropology and Medicine*. Berkeley, CA: University of California Press, 95–119.

Knobé, Sandrine (2009) 'Engagement associatif et cancer. Résultats d'une enquête sociologique', *Bulletin du Cancer* 96:5, 511–17.
Kosofsky Sedgwick, Eve (1993) *Tendencies*. Durham, NC: Duke University Press.
Kotobi, Laurence and Sargent, Carolyn (2023) 'Precarity and Cancer among Low-income Populations in France: Intractable Inequalities', in Linda Rae Bennett, Lenore Manderson and Belinda Spagnoletti (eds), *Cancer and the Politics of Care: Inequalities and Interventions in Global Perspective*. London: UCL Press, 232–53.
Kraus, Cynthia (2013) 'Hypospadias surgery in a West African context: The surgical (re-)construction of what?', *Feminist Theory* 14:1, 83–103.
La, Jessica, Jackson, Sue and Shaw, Rhonda (2019) '"Flat and fabulous": women's breast reconstruction refusals post-mastectomy and the negotiation of normative femininity', *Journal of Gender Studies* 28:5, 603–16.
Lahti, Annukka and Kolehmainen, Marjo (2020) 'LGBTIQ+ break-up assemblages: at the end of the rainbow', *Journal of Sociology* 56:4, 608–28.
Lamvu, Georgine, Antunez-Flores, Oscar, Orady, Mona and Schneider, Beth (2020) 'Path to diagnosis and women's perspectives on the impact of endometriosis pain', *Journal of Endometriosis and Pelvic Pain Disorders* 12:1, 16–25.
Lancet Oncology (2023) 'Access to cancer medicines in the UK', *The Lancet Oncology* 24:5, 415.
Larchanché, Stéphanie (2012) 'Intangible obstacles: health implications of stigmatization, structural violence, and fear among undocumented immigrants in France', *Social Science & Medicine* 74:6, 858–63.
Lebovic, Gail S. (2019) 'Oncoplastic Surgery: The Renaissance for Breast Surgery', in Cicero Urban, Mario Rietjens, Mahmoud El-Tamer and Virgilio S. Sacchini (eds), *Oncoplastic and Reconstructive Breast Surgery*. Cham: Springer, 3–12.
Lerner, Barron H. (2001) *The Breast Cancer Wars: Hope, Fear, and the Pursuit of Cure in Twentieth-century America*. Oxford: Oxford University Press.
Lerner, Barron H. (2006) 'Power, Gender and Pizzazz: The Early Years of Breast Cancer Activism', in Mary C. Rawlinson and Shannon Lundeen (eds), *The Voice of Breast Cancer in Medicine and Bioethics*. Dodrecht: Springer, 21–30.
Lewis, Sophie (2019) *Full Surrogacy Now: Feminism against Family*. London: Verso.
Ley, Barbara L. (2009) *From Pink to Green: Disease Prevention and the Environmental Breast Cancer Movement*. New Brunswick, NJ: Rutgers University Press.
Littlejohns, Peter, Chalkidou, Kalipso, Culyer, Anthony J., Weale, Albert, Rid, Annette, Kieslich, Katharina, Coultas, Clare et al. (2019) 'National

Institute for Health and Care Excellence, social values and healthcare priority setting', *Journal of the Royal Society of Medicine* 112:5, 173–9.

Livingston, Julie (2012) *Improvising Medicine: An African Oncology Ward in an Emerging Cancer Epidemic*. Durham, NC: Duke University Press.

Llewellyn, Henry (2022) 'Emerging tissue economies: personalized immunotherapies and therapeutic value in cancer', *Medical Anthropology* 41:2, 169–82.

Llewellyn, Henry, Higgs, Paul, Sampson, Elizabeth L., Jones, Louise and Thorne, Lewis (2018) 'Topographies of "care pathways" and "healthscapes": reconsidering the multiple journeys of people with a brain tumour', *Sociology of Health & Illness* 40:3, 410–25.

Lock, Margaret (2001) 'The tempering of medical anthropology: troubling natural categories', *Medical Anthropology Quarterly* 15:4, 478–92.

Lock, Margaret (2017) 'Recovering the body', *Annual Review of Anthropology* 46, 1–14.

Locock, Louise, Nettleton, Sarah, Kirkpatrick, Susan, Ryan, Sara and Ziebland, Sue (2016) '"I knew before I was told': breaches, cues and clues in the diagnostic assemblage", *Social Science & Medicine* 154, 85–92.

Lorde, Audre (1980) *The Cancer Journals*. Argyle, NY: Spinsters, Ink.

Love, Richard R. and Philips, John (2002) 'Oophorectomy for breast cancer: history revisited'. *Journal of the National Cancer Institute* 94(19): 1433–4.

Löwy, Ilana (2010) *Preventive Strikes. Women, Precancer, and Prophylactic Surgery*. Baltimore, MD: Johns Hopkins University Press.

Löwy, Ilana (2012) 'Cancer du sein et tamoxifène: la gestion d'une incertitude thérapeutique', *Science Sociales & Santé* 30:1, 73–83.

Löwy, Ilana (2021) 'Long Covid, chronic fatigue syndrome and women: the shadow of hysteria', *Somatosphere*, https://somatosphere.com/2021/long-covid.html/

Ludet, Louise, Teixeira, Luis, des Guetz, Gaëtan and Schantz, Clémence (2023) 'Therapeutic mobility and breast cancer in France: experiences of African women', *SSM – Qualitative Research in Health* 4, 100314.

Lupton, Deborah (1994) 'Femininity, responsibility, and the technological imperative: discourses on breast cancer in the Australian press', *International Journal of Health Services* 24:1, 73–89.

Lyons, Tomas G. (2019) 'Targeted therapies for triple-negative breast cancer', *Current Treatment Options in Oncology* 20, 82.

Mackenzie, Catherine Ruth (2014) '"It is hard for mums to put themselves first": how mothers diagnosed with breast cancer manage the sociological boundaries between paid work, family and caring for the self', *Social Science & Medicine* 117, 96–106.

Madden, John L., Kandalaft, Souheil and Bourque, Roche-Andre (1972) 'Modified radical mastectomy', *Annals of Surgery* 175:5, 624–34.

Madlock Gatison, Annette D. (2016) *Health Communication and Breast Cancer among Black Women: Culture, Identity, Spirituality, and Strength*. Lanham, MD: Lexington.

Maietti, Elisa, Sanmarchi, Francesco, Toth, Federico, de Pietro, Carlo, Fantini, Maria Pia and Golinelli, Davide (2023) 'Changes in private health service utilisation and access to the Italian national health service between 2006 and 2019: a cross-sectional comparative study', *BMJ Open* 13:5, e070975.

Manderson, Lenore (2011) *Surface Tensions: Surgery, Bodily Boundaries, and the Social Self*. Walnut Creek, CA: Left Coast Press.

Manderson, Lenore and Warren, Narelle (2016) '"Just one thing after another": recursive cascades and chronic conditions', *Medical Anthropology Quarterly* 30:4, 479–97.

Mapelli, Vittorio (2012) *Il sistema sanitario italiano*. Bologna: Il Mulino.

Marchesi, Simone (1999) 'Accumulazione e sviluppo: il movimento della narrazione in "Caro diario"', *Annali d'Italianistica* 17, 77–93.

Marcus, George E. (1995) 'Ethnography in/of the world system: the emergence of multi-sited ethnography', *Annual Review of Anthropology* 24, 95–117.

Marcus, George E. and Saka, Erkan (2006) 'Assemblage', *Theory, Culture & Society* 23:2–3, 101–6.

Marenzi, Anna, Rizzi, Dino and Zanette, Michele (2021) 'Incentives for voluntary health insurance in a national health system: evidence from Italy', *Health Policy* 125:6, 685–92.

Martin, Daryl, Nettleton, Sarah and Buse, Christina (2019) 'Affecting care: Maggie's Centres and the orchestration of architectural atmospheres', *Social Science & Medicine* 240: 112563.

Martin, Elise, Porteau, Lionel, Di Palma, Mario and Delaloge, Suzette (2017) 'New oral targeted therapies for metastatic breast cancer disrupt the traditional patients' management: a healthcare providers' view', *European Journal of Cancer Care* 26:6, e12624.

Maruani, Margaret (2018) 'An Overview of the Major Issues', in Jane Jenson, Jacqueline Laufer and Margaret Maruani (eds), *The Gendering of Inequalities: Women, Men and Work*. London: Routledge, 17–23.

Mathews, Holly F., Burke, Nancy J. and Kampriani, Eirini (eds) (2015) *Anthropologies of Cancer in Transnational Worlds*. New York: Routledge.

McCann, Hannah (2018) 'Beyond the visible: rethinking femininity through the femme assemblage', *European Journal of Women's Studies* 25:3, 278–92.

McPherson, Susan and Beresford, Peter (2019) 'Semantics of patient choice: how the UK national guideline for depression silences patients', *Disability & Society* 34:3, 491–7.

Meidani, Anastasia (ed.) (2020) *Masculinités et féminités face au cancer: Expériences cancéreuses et interactions soignantes*. Toulouse: Érès.

Meidani, Anastasia and Alessandrin, Arnaud (2017) 'Cancers et transidentités: une nouvelle "population à risques"?', *Sciences Sociales & Santé* 35:1, 41–63.

Ménard, Sylvie, Balsari, Andrea, Casalini, Patrizia, Tagliabue, Elda, Bufalino, Rosaria and Cascinelli, Natale (2002) 'HER-2-positive breast carcinomas as a particular subset with peculiar clinical behaviors', *Clinical Cancer Research* 8:2, 520–5.

Merrild, Camilla Hoffmann (2023) 'Cancer, Inequality, and the Expectations of Samesness', in Rikke Sand Andersen and Marie Louise Tørring (eds), *Cancer Entangled: Anticipation, Acceleration, and the Danish State*. New Brunswick, NJ: Rutgers University Press, 78–95.

Mitchell, David T. and Snyder, Sharon L. (2016) 'The matter of disability', *Bioethical Inquiry* 13:4, 487–92.

Mol, Annemarie (2008) *The Logic of Care: Health and the Problem of Patient Choice*. London: Routledge.

Molina, Rose Leonard and Palazuelos, Daniel (2014) 'Navigating and circumventing a fragmented health system: the patient's pathway in the Sierra Madre region of Chiapas, Mexico', *Medical Anthropology Quarterly* 28:1, 23–43.

Monbiot, George (2018) 'Through my cancer, I have found the key to a good life', *The Guardian*, 8 May, www.theguardian.com/commentisfree/2018/may/08/my-prostate-cancer-surgery-key-to-good-life (accessed 28 July 2023).

Montini, Theresa and Ruzek, Sheryl (1989) 'Overturning orthodoxy: the emergence of breast cancer treatment policy', *Research in the Sociology of Health Care* 8, 3–32.

Moretti, Nanni (1993) *Caro Diario*. Sacher Film.

Moriconi, Tiziana (2022) 'Tumore al seno, a rischio il diritto delle donne alla ricostruzione migliore', *La Repubblica*, 15 September, www.repubblica.it/salute/dossier/saluteseno/2022/09/15/news/tumore_al_seno_a_rischio_il_diritto_delle_donne_alla_ricostruzione_migliore-365813725/ (accessed 28 July 2023).

Moscatelli, Silvia, Golfieri, Francesca, Tomasetto, Carlo and Bigler, Rebecca S. (2021) 'Women and #MeToo in Italy: internalized sexualization is associated with tolerance of sexual harassment and negative views of the #MeToo movement', *Current Psychology* 40:12, 6199–211.

Mosconi, Paola and Kodraliu, Gentiana (1999) 'Italian forum of Europa Donna: a survey of breast cancer associations', *Health Expectations* 2:1, 44–50.

Mulvey, Laura (1975) 'Visual pleasure and narrative cinema', *Screen* 16:3, 6–18.

NICE (National Institute for Health and Care Excellence) (2018) 'Early and locally advanced breast cancer: diagnosis and management', www.nice.org.uk/guidance/ng101 (accessed 7 July 2023).

Nédélec, Élise (2018) 'Chronicité(s) et cancers gynécologiques: enjeux thérapeutiques et relationnels à Abidjan', *émulations* 27, 33–45.

Nielsen, Emilia (2019) *Disrupting Breast Cancer Narratives: Stories of Rage and Repair*. Toronto: University of Toronto Press.

O'Brien, Ruth (2005) *Bodies in Revolt: Gender, Disability, and a Workplace Ethic of Care*. New York: Routledge.

O'Halloran, Julie, Miller, Graeme C. and Britt, Helena (2004) 'defining chronic conditions for primary care with ICPC-2', *Family Practice* 21:4, 381–6.

Omrane, Dorsaf and Mignot, Pierre (2018) 'Préventions des cancers du sein: ce que la controverse fait à l'action publique', *Les Enjeux de l'information et de la communication*, 18:3, 41–55.

Ong, Aihwa (2016) *Fungible Life: Experiment in the Asian City of Life*. Durham, NC: Duke University Press.

Pantziarka, Pan, Verbaanderd, Ciska, Huys, Isabelle, Bouche, Gauthier and Meheus, Lydie (2021) 'Repurposing drugs in oncology: from candidate selection to clinical adoption', *Seminars in Cancer Biology* 68, 186–91.

Parker, Rhian (2010) *Women, Doctors and Cosmetic Surgery: Negotiating the Normal Body*. Basingstoke: Palgrave Macmillan.

Patel, Kashyap B., Arantes, Luiz H. Jr., Tang, Wing Yu and Fung, Selwyn (2018) 'The role of biosimilars in value-based oncology care', *Cancer Management and Research* 10, 4591–602.

Paton, Calon (2022) *NHS Reform and Health Politics in the UK: Revolution, Counter-Revolution and Covid Crisis*. Cham: Palgrave Macmillan.

Peters, Vera (1975) 'Cutting the "Gordian knot" in early breast cancer', *Annals of the Royal College of Physicians and Surgeons of Canada* 8, 186–92.

Petersen, Jennifer and Matuschka (2004) 'Interview with Matuschka: breast cancer, art, sexuality and activism', *International Journal of Qualitative Studies in Education* 17:4, 493–516.

Phillimore, Jenny, Bradby, Hannah, Knecht, Michi, Padilla, Beatriz and Pemberton, Simon (2019) 'Bricolage as conceptual tool for understanding access to healthcare in superdiverse populations', *Social Theory & Health* 17:2, 231–52.

Philip, Thierry, Kasparian, Christelle, Fagnani, Francis, Moatti, Jean-Paul and Meunier, Anne (2005) 'Le dépistage du cancer du sein en France: bilan et limites', *Bulletin de l'Académie Nationale de Médecine* 189:2, 321–39.

Pian, Anaïk (2015) 'Care and migration experiences among foreign female cancer patients in France: neither medical tourism nor therapeutic immigration', *Journal of Intercultural Studies* 36:6, 641–57.

Pica, Federico and Villani, Salvatore (2010) 'Questioni concernenti la nozione di *costo standard*: la mobilità dei pazienti e le mode sanitarie', *Rivista economica del Mezzogiorno* 23:3, 397–421.

Pop, Cristina A. (2022) *The Cancer Within: Reproduction, Cultural Transformation, and Health Care in Romania*. New Brunswick, NJ: Rutgers University Press.

Porroche-Escudero, Ana (2014) 'Perilous equations? Empowerment and the pedagogy of fear in breast cancer awareness campaigns', *Women's Studies International Forum* 47:A, 77–92.

Price-Robertson, Rhys and Duff, Cameron (2014) 'Family assemblages', *Social & Cultural Geography* 20:8, 1031–49.

Pritlove, Cheryl, Safai, Parissa, Angus, Jan E., Armstrong, Pat, Jones, Jennifer M. and Parsons, Janet (2019) '"It's hard work": a feminist political economy approach to reconceptualizing "work" in the cancer context', *Qualitative Health Research* 29:5, 758–73.

Quotidiano Sanità (2022) 'Tumore al seno triplo negativo: terapie mirate e l'impegno delle associazioni'. *Quotidiano Sanità*, 8 November, www.quotidianosanita.it/scienza-e-farmaci/articolo.php?articolo_id=108727 (accessed 28 July 2023).

Rabinow, Paul (1996) 'Artificiality and enlightenment: from sociobiology to biosociality', in idem, *Essays on the Anthropology of Reason*. Princeton, NJ: Princeton University Press, 91–111.

Raza, Azra (2019) *The First Cell and the Human Costs of Pursuing Cancer to the Last*. New York: Basic Books.

Roberts, Elizabeth F.S. and Scheper-Hughes, Nina (2011) 'Introduction: medical migrations', *Body & Society* 17:2–3, 1–30.

Roderick, Peter and Pollock, Allyson M. (2022) 'Dismantling the National Health Service in England', *International Journal of Health Services* 52:4, 470–9.

Rogers, Emily Lim (2022) 'Recursive debility: symptoms, patient activism, and the incomplete medicalization of ME/CFS', *Medical Anthropology Quarterly* 36:3, 412–28.

Rolland, Anne-Lise, Porro, Bertrand, Kab, Sofiane, Ribet, Céline, Roquelaure, Yves and Bertin, Mélanie (2023) 'Impact of breast cancer care pathways and related symptoms on the return-to-work process: results from a population-based French cohort study (CONSTANCES)', *Breast Cancer Research* 25, 30.

Ross, Emily, Swallow, Julia, Kerr, Anne, Chekar, Choon Key and Cunningham-Burley, Sarah (2021) 'Diagnostic layering: Patient accounts of breast cancer classification in the molecular era', *Social Science & Medicine* 278, 113965.

Ryan, Andrew (2011) 'Looking at breast cancer with an unflinching eye', *Globe and Mail*, 17 October, www.theglobeandmail.com/arts/television/looking-at-breast-cancer-with-an-unflinching-eye/article4199500/ (accessed 28 July 2023).

Sakorafas, George H. and Tsiotou, Adelais G.H. (2000) 'Ductal carcinoma in situ (DCIS) of the breast: evolving perspectives', *Cancer Treatment Reviews* 26:2, 103–25.

Saldivar, Ramón (1979) 'A dialectic of difference: towards a theory of the Chicano novel', *Melus* 6:3, 73–92.

Sanchez Taylor, Jacqueline (2012) 'Fake breasts and power: gender, class and cosmetic surgery', *Women's Studies International Forum* 35:6, 458–66.

Sarradon-Eck, Aline and Pellegrini, Isabelle (2012) 'Le traitement adjuvant du cancer du sein par tamoxifène: Entre risques et bénéfices thérapeutiques', *Science Sociales & Santé* 30:1, 47–71.

Sarti, Simone, Terraneo, Marco and Tognetti Bordogna, Mara (2017) 'Poverty and private health expenditures in Italian households during the recent crisis', *Health Policy* 121:3, 307–14.

Sassen, Saskia and Ong, Aihwa (2014) 'The Carpenter and the Bricoleur', in Michele Acuto and Simon Curties (eds), *Reassembling International Theory: Assemblage Thinking and International Relations*. Basingstoke: Palgrave Macmillan, 17–24.

Saxonberg, Steven (2013) 'From defamilialization to degenderization: toward a new welfare typology', *Social Policy & Administration* 47:1, 26–49.

Saywell, Cherise, Henderson, Lesley and Beattie, Liza (2000) 'Sexualized Illness: The Newsworthy Body in Media Representations of Breast Cancer', in Laura K. Potts (ed), *Ideologies of Breast Cancer: Feminist Perspectives*. Basingstoke: Macmillan, 37–62.

Schiebinger, Londa (1993) *Nature's Body. Gender in the Making of Modern Science*. New Brunswick, NJ: Rutgers University Press.

Schirrmacher, Volker (2019) 'From chemotherapy to biological therapy: a review of novel concepts to reduce the side effects of systemic cancer treatment (Review)', *International Journal of Oncology* 54:2, 407–19.

Schoier, Gabriella and de Luca, Patrizia (2017) 'Cause-related Marketing: A Qualitative and Quantitative Analysis on Pinkwashing', in Francesco Palumbo, Angela Montanari and Maurizio Vichi (eds), *Data Science: Studies in Classification, Data Analysis, and Knowledge Organization*. Cham: Springer, 321–32.

Seeman, Don (2004) 'Otherwise than meaning: on the generosity of ritual', *Social Analysis* 48:2, 55–72.

Selleck, Laurie Gillmore (2010) 'Pretty in pink: the Susan G. Komen Network and the branding of the breast cancer cause', *Nordic Journal of English Studies* 9:3, 119–38.
Shildrick, Margrit (2013) 'Re-imagining embodiment: prostheses, supplements and boundaries', *Somatechnics* 3:2, 270–86.
Shildrick, Margrit (2015) '"Why should our bodies end at the skin?": embodiment, boundaries, and somatechnics', *Hypatia* 30:1, 13–29.
Sifer-Rivière, Lynda (2012) 'Entre désordre et ordre: la fabrique des réseaux régionaux de cancérologie (1990–2010)', PhD dissertation, Paris: École des Hautes Études en Sciences Sociales.
Silverstein, Melvin J., Savalia, Nirav, Khan, Sadia and Ryan, Jessica (2015) 'Extreme oncoplasty: breast conservation for patients who need mastectomy', *The Breast Journal* 21:1, 52–9.
Singer, Merrill (2009) *Introduction to Syndemics: A Critical Systems Approach to Public and Community Health.* San Francisco, CA: Jossey-Bass.
Singer, Merrill and Baer, Hans A. (1995) *Critical Medical Anthropology.* Amityville, NY: Baywood.
Skeide, Annekatrin (2021) 'Experiences as actors: labor pains in childbirth care in Germany', *Medical Anthropology* 40:5, 446–57.
Skelly, Julia (2007) 'Mas(k/t)ectomies: losing a breast (and hair) in Hannah Wilke's body art', *thirdspace* 7:1, 3–16.
Skowronski, Magdalena, Risør, Mette Bech, Andersen, Rikke Sand and Foss, Nina (2019) 'The cancer may come back: experiencing and managing worries of relapse in a North Norwegian village after treatment', *Anthropology & Medicine* 26:3, 296–310.
Sledge, Piper (2021) *Bodies Unbound: Gender-specific Cancer and Biolegitimacy*, New Brunswick, NJ: Rutgers University Press.
Snow, Stephanie (2018) 'The NHS at 70: the story of our lives', *The Lancet* 392(10141), 22–3.
Sobo, Elisa J. (2009) 'Medical travel: what it means, why it matters', *Medical Anthropology* 28:4, 326–35.
Sobo, Elisa J., Elizabeth Herlihy and Bicker, Mary (2011) 'Selling medical travel to US patient-consumers: the cultural appeal of website marketing messages', *Anthropology & Medicine* 18:1, 119–36.
Sontag, Susan (1978) *Illness as Metaphor.* New York: Farrar, Straus & Giroux.
Steffen, Monika (2010) 'The French health care system: liberal universalism', *Journal of Health Politics, Policy and Law* 35:3, 353–87.
Sturdy, Steve (2017) 'Personalised medicine and the economy of biotechnological promise', *The New Bioethics* 23:1, 30–7.
Sulik, Gayle A. (2007) 'The balancing act: care work for the self and coping with breast cancer', *Gender & Society* 21:6, 857–77.

Sulik, Gayle (2011) *Pink Ribbon Blues. How Breast Cancer Culture Undermines Women's Health*. Oxford: Oxford University Press.

Sulik, Gayle (2014) '#Rethinkpink: moving beyond breast cancer awareness, SWS Distinguished Feminist Lecture', *Gender & Society* 28:5, 655–78.

Sundquist, Marie, Brudin, Lars and Tejler, Göran (2017) 'Improved survival in metastatic breast cancer 1985–2016', *The Breast* 31, 46–50.

SVIMEZ (2014) *Rapporto SVIMEZ sull'economia del Mezzogiorno*. Bologna: Il Mulino.

Taylor-Brown, Jill, Kilpatrick, Marilyn, Maunsell, Elizabeth and Dorval, Michel (2000) 'Partner abandonment of women with breast cancer: myth or reality?', *Cancer Practice* 8:4, 160–4.

Tetteh, Dinah A. (2018) *Communication Studies and Feminist Perspectives on Ovarian Cancer*. Lanham, MD: Lexington Books.

Timmermann, Carsten (2019) *Moonshots at Cancer: The Roche Story*. Basel: Editions Roche.

Tlili, Anwar (2008) 'The organisational identity of science centres', *Culture and Organization* 14:4, 309–23.

Toon, Elizabeth (2007) '"Cancer as the general population knows it": knowledge, fear, and lay education in 1950s Britain', *Bulletin of the History of Medicine* 81:1, 116–38.

Toon, Elizabeth (2012) 'Measured Responses: British Clinical Researchers and Therapies for Advanced Breast Cancer in the 1960s and 1970s', in Carsten Timmermann and Elizabeth Toon (eds), *Cancer Patients, Cancer Pathways: Historical and Sociological Perspectives*. Basingstoke: Palgrave Macmillan, 130–60.

Torjesen, Ingrid (2014) 'Analysis shows "postcode lottery" in access to GPs in England', *BMJ* 348, g3688.

Tørring, Marie Louise (2023) 'The Waiting Time Paradox: Intensifying Public Discourses on the Vital Character of Cancer Waiting Times', in Rikke Sand Andersen and Marie Louise Tørring (eds), *Cancer Entangled: Anticipation, Acceleration, and the Danish State*. New Brunswick, NJ: Rutgers University Press, 23–41.

Toth, Federico (2014a) *La sanità in Italia*. Bologna: Il Mulino.

Toth, Federico (2014b) 'How health care regionalisation in Italy is widening the north–south gap', *Health Economics, Policy and Law* 9:3, 231–49.

Toth, Federico (2016) 'The Italian NHS, the public/private sector mix and the disparities in access to healthcare', *Global Social Welfare* 3:3, 171–8.

Trusson, Diane, Pilnick, Alison and Roy, Srila (2016) 'A new normal? Women's experiences of biographical disruption and liminality following treatment for early stage breast cancer', *Social Science & Medicine* 151, 121–9.

References

Turner, Victor W. (1986) 'Dewey, Dilthey, and Drama: An Essay in the Anthropology of Experience', in Victor W. Turner and Edward M. Bruner (eds), *The Anthropology of Experience*. Urbana, IL: University of Chicago Press, 33–42.

Tursz, Thomas (2004) 'Le Cancer en France à l'aube du XXIe siècle', *Officiel santé*, September/October, 29–30.

Valent, Francesca, Sammartano, Francesca, Degano, Simonetta, Dellach, Carla, Franzo, Antonella, Gerin, Daniela, Gnesutta, Daniela et al. (2020) 'Reasons for non-participation in public oncological screening programs in the Italian region Friuli Venezia Giulia', *Public Health* 181, 80–5.

Valtorta, Roberta Rosa, Sacino, Alessandra, Baldissarri, Cristina and Volpato, Chiara (2016) 'L'eterno femminino. Stereotipi di genere e sessualizzazione nella pubblicità televisiva', *Psicologia sociale* 11:2, 159–88.

van Maarschalkerweerd, Pomme E.A., Schaapveld, Michael, Paalman, Carmen H., Aaronson, Neil K. and Duijts, Saskia F.A. (2020) 'Changes in employment status, barriers to, and facilitators of (return to) work in breast cancer survivors 5–10 years after diagnosis', *Disability and Rehabilitation* 42:21, 3052–8.

Veronesi, Umberto (2012) *Il primo giorno senza cancro: Le battaglie che abbiamo vinto e quelle che vinceremo*. Milan: Piemme.

Veronesi, Umberto, Saccozzi, Roberto, Del Vecchio, Marcella, Banfi, Alberto, Clemente, Claudio, De Lena, Mario, Gallus, Giuseppe et al. (1981) 'Comparing radical mastectomy with quadrantectomy, axillary dissection, and radiotherapy in patients with small cancers of the breast', *The New England Journal of Medicine* 305:1, 6–11.

Viesti, Gianfranco (2001) 'Un Mezzogiorno diverso', *Il Mulino* 4, 700–10.

Vigh, Henrik (2009) 'Motion squared: a second look at the concept of social navigation', *Anthropological Theory* 9:4, 419–38.

Vindrola-Padros, Cecilia (2012) 'The everyday lives of children with cancer in Argentina: going beyond the disease and treatment.' *Children & Society* 26:6, 430–42.

Vindrola-Padros, Cecilia and Brage, Eugenia (2016) 'Child Medical Travel in Argentina: Narratives of Family Separation and Moving Away from Home', in Christina R. Engler, Robin Kearns and Karen Witten (eds), *Children's Health and Wellbeing in Urban Environments*. London: Routledge, 128–44.

Vindrola-Padros, Cecilia and Johnson, Ginger A. (2017) 'Children Seeking Health Care: International Perspectives on Children's Use of Mobility to Obtain Health Services', in Caitriona Ní Laoire and Allen White (eds), *Movement, Mobilities, and Journeys*. Singapore: Springer, 289–306.

Viney, William, Day, Sophie, Bruton, Jane, Gleason, Kelly, Ion, Charlotte, Nazir, Saima and Ward, Helen (2022) 'Personalising clinical pathways in a London breast cancer service', *Sociology of Health & Illness* 44:3, 624–40.

Walker, Christine (2001) 'Recognising the changing boundaries of illness in defining terms of chronic illness: a prelude to understanding the changing needs of people with chronic illness', *Australian Health Review* 24:2, 207–14.

Webster, Charles (2002) *The National Health Service: A Political History*. Oxford: Oxford University Press.

Weeks, Kathi (2023) 'Abolition of the family: the most infamous feminist proposal', *Feminist Theory* 24:3, 433–53.

Wegenstein, Bernadette (2016) *The Good Breast*. Icarus Films.

Wegenstein, Bernadette (2022) '"Not a boob job": Nouvelles perspectives sur la reconstruction post-mastectomie', in Corinne Fortier (ed.), *Le corps de l'identité: Transformations corporelles, genre et chirurgies sexuelles*. Paris: Karthala, 215–27.

Werner, Anne, Isaksen, Lise Widding and Malterud, Kirsti (2004) '"I am not the kind of woman who complains of everything": illness stories on self and shame in women with chronic pain', *Social Science & Medicine* 59:5, 1035–45.

Whittaker, Andrea, Manderson, Lenore and Cartwright, Elizabeth (2010) 'Patients without borders: understanding medical travel', *Medical Anthropology* 29:4, 336–43.

Willen, Sarah S. and Seeman, Don (2012) 'Introduction: experience and inquiétude', *Ethos* 40:1, 1–23.

Williams, Courtney P., Pisu, Maria, Azuero, Andres, Kenzik, Kelly M., Nipp, Ryan D., Aswani, Monica S., Mennemeyer, Stephen T. et al. (2020) 'Health insurance literacy and financial hardship in women living with metastatic breast cancer', *JCO Oncology Practice* 16:6, e529–37.

Wolfgram, Matthew (2016) 'Science talk and scientific reference', *Annual Review of Anthropology* 45, 33–44.

Wright, Anthony Gerard (2023) '"Not like this": embodying Blackness and childhood cancer in the United States', *Medical Anthropology* 42:3, 236–49.

Youlden, Danny R., Cramb, Susanna M., Dunn, Nathan A.M., Muller, Jennifer M., Pyke, Christopher M. and Baade, Peter D. (2012) 'The descriptive epidemiology of female breast cancer: an international comparison of screening, incidence, survival and mortality', *Cancer Epidemiology* 36:3, 237–48.

Index

activism 14, 17, 52, 55, 57, 60, 62, 159, 164, 173
advocacy 58–9
advocacy groups 58–9
aesthetics and aestheticisation 4, 16, 99–103, 111–15, 121, 124n12
Agenzia Italiana del Farmaco/ Italian Medicines Agency 41
Andersen, Rikke Sand 17–18
anxiety 125
Arteaga Pérez, Ignacia 170n1
assemblages 26n5, 26n6, 147, 170, 182
   articulations of 7–10
   biographical 8, 10, 23, 24, 53, 68–9, 122, 135, 146, 147, 173, 174
   conceptualisation 5–7, 73, 171–4
   cultural-political 8, 10, 174
   disease–society 180–2
   levels 7–8
   medical-bodily 7–9, 23–4, 73, 98, 146, 171–3
   organisational 8, 28–9
   relational 8, 10, 25, 149, 168, 181
   strategic 171
   time-limited 6
associations and support groups 57–63, 69, 159, 173
Associazione italiana di oncologia medica (Italian Association of Medical Oncology) 84–5
asymmetrical bodies 59–60, 111, 116–20, 121–2, 151, 172
Australia 124n15
awareness raising 14, 56–7

Banerjee, Dwaipayan 66
Bartky, Sandra Lee 150
beauty and beauty standards 97, 106, 109, 119, 121, 122, 150
Belgium 70–1n5
Bell, Kirsten 13, 62, 64
Berlant, Lauren 65–6
bilateral mastectomy 124n14
biographic disruption 126
biographical assemblages 10, 23, 24, 53, 68–9, 122, 135, 146, 147, 173, 174
biographical containment 66–7
biomedical language 180
biomedical uncertainty 127, 156–7
biomedicalisation 12
biomedicine 9, 16, 17, 23–4, 73, 171–3, 179
biopsy 128–30
biosimilar medicines 41
biosociality 169
bodily integrity 98
body, public presentation of 24
body alterations 97–8
   aesthetics and aestheticisation 99–103
Böhm, Katharina 37
Botswana 179
BRCA 1 and 2 mutations 12, 77–8

Breast Cancer Action 54, 54–5, 87
Breast Cancer Awareness Month 51–2, 54, 55, 58
Breast Cancer Now 57, 103–4
breast lumps, ambiguity of 128
breast reconstruction 20, 24, 38, 47, 59, 98, 120, 132, 172, 175–6
  aesthetics and aestheticisation 100–3, 115–16, 121, 124n12
  benefits 101–2
  conservative 108–9
  contralateral symmetrisation 104, 106–10
  definitions 101
  financial considerations 104–5, 108
  France 100–2, 105
  importance of 110–12
  institutional context 103–6
  Italy 104–5, 123n6
  negative experiences 106–10
  negotiating 106–12, 116
  obstacles faced 105–6
  partners and 150–1
  post-reconstruction body experiences 112–16
  practical purposes 121–2
  rejection of 116–20, 122
  and self-image 112
  surgeon–patient relationship 107–8
  and survival time 101
  United Kingdom 103–4, 120–1, 123n6
  waiting times 105
breast surgery 8
breast-cancer-ization 13, 182
Brenner, Barbara 54–5, 87, 137
Brexit 40
bricolage-assemblages 6, 8, 9–10, 23, 24, 29, 47–8, 49, 146, 174
Brinker, Nancy 53
British Medical Association 31
Buchanan, Mary 56
budgetary limitations 29
Buy My Cancer project 72, 94

cancer
  contemporary construction of 65–6
  refusal to mention 1–2
Cancer Drugs Fund (CDF) 40
cancer knowledge, gaps in 9
cancer prevention conferences, communication strategies 62
cancer progression, linear model 74, 75, 77
cancer regimes 11–12
Cancer Research UK 56
cancer schemata 11
cancer survivorship, breast cancer as a social paradigm for 13–14
capitalisation 66
care, individualisation of 63
care work 155
cases diagnosed, EU 2
cause-related marketing 54–5
Centres de lutte contre le cancer (CLCC – Centres for the fight against cancer) 38–9
Centres Hospitaliers Universitaires (CHU – University Hospital Centres) 38–9
cervical cancer 26n8
chemotherapy 8, 11, 77, 84–5, 95n4, 97, 140–1, 155–6, 158, 159–60
Chenhall, Richard D. 5
childcare 156, 160
children 155–8, 160
chronicity 74, 88–9, 96n6, 96n8
Clinical Commissioning Groups (CCG) 30
clinical trials 50n8
Collier, Stephen J. 172
communication strategies, cancer prevention conferences 62
Community Care Act, 1990 30
comparative stance 18–19

conservative surgery 99–100
containment strategies 66–7
contralateral symmetrisation 104
control
   maintaining 131–5
   retaining 125
coping strategies 68
   containment 66–7
   refusal to mention 1–2
cosmetic surgery 28, 121, 123n9
   see also breast reconstruction
couples, post-diagnosis 149, 150–4, 169
couples therapy 151
COVID-19 pandemic 49, 105, 179
Crompvoets, Samantha 112
cultural context 5
cultural discourses 7, 9
cultural-political assemblages 8, 10, 174

deaths 2
Del Vecchio Good, Mary-Jo 72
Deleuze, Gilles 5–6, 9, 22, 26n5
Denmark 18
diagnosis 2, 11, 13
   and emotional preparation 130
   in situ cancers 76–7
   metastatic breast cancer 141
   shock 24, 65, 67
   and uncertainty 127–31, 145–6
diagnosis-treatment pathways 45–7, 48
diagnostic pathways 128–31
diagnostic technologies 128
disease 4
disease–society assemblages 180–2
diversity 21
divorce and separations 150–2
doctor/patient alliances 59
drug prices 39–41, 91–2, 179, 182n1
drug therapies 8
drugs, life cycle management 96n7
ductal carcinoma *in situ* 77
Duff, Cameron 155

early retirement 163–4
early-stage breast cancer 74, 78, 82, 85–6, 93, 126, 145, 178
economy of hope 72–3, 94
Eisenstein, Zillah 2
EMA 41
embodied transformations 15–16
Engelberg, Miriam 85
Ernaux, Annie 148, 168–9
Esserman, Laura J. 77
Estée Lauder 51–2, 70n1
ethnography 3, 4–5, 17
Europa Donna 56, 87
European Institute of Oncology 36
European Union, cases diagnosed 2
experiences 3–5, 25, 182
   and gender 175–7
   individuality of 147
   sharing 60–1
external prosthesis 118–19

family relationships, post-diagnosis 25, 149, 154–9, 169, 170n1
fashion industry, discrimination 120
fashion-beauty complex 150
femininity 15–16, 175–6, 177
Ferzacca, Steve 137
fieldwork 19–22
financial considerations, breast reconstruction 104–5
financial stratification 91–2
financial uncertainty 156–7
Fisher, Bernard 99
Fitts, Karen 115–16
Fluorouracil 95n2
Forrest, Patrick 75
Foucault, Michel 26n6
France 2, 17, 19, 21, 55
   associative landscape 58–60, 61
   breast reconstruction 100–2, 105
   cancer services available 38–9
   childcare 156
   drug prices 39, 40

funding 84
healthcare system 23, 28, 37–9, 48–9, 177–80
hormone therapy 137
patient mobility 21, 43, 44, 45, 49, 143
screening programme 75
Vivre comme avant 55–6
friendships, post-diagnosis 149, 159–62, 169
funeral planning 157

Gagnon, Marilou 141
Garrido, Ignacio 103
Geertz, Clifford 4
gender
 and illness 175–7
 norms 25n1, 175–6
 prism of 15–17
 roles 149
genetics 12
Germany 37
global financial crisis, 2008 34
Global South 17, 28, 180
Guardian 63–4
Guattari, Félix 5–6, 9, 22, 26n5

Hadji, Peyton 137
hair loss 97, 158
Haley, Charlotte 70n1
Halsted, William 99
Hamarat, Natasia 70–1n5
Haraway, Donna 98, 171
Health and Social Care Act, 2012 50n1
health expenditures, cuts 63
health insurance 34, 37–8, 48, 178–9
healthcare systems
 budgetary limitations 29
 comparison 177–80
 cost-benefit analysis 178
 diagnosis-treatment pathways 45–7, 48
 ethnographic engagement with 17

France 28, 37–9, 48–9, 177–80
improvisation 179, 180
Italy 28, 33–7, 48, 177–80
navigating 9–10, 27, 41–8, 49
patient mobility 42–5, 49
privatisation 18, 23, 28, 30–2, 177, 179
transformations of 18
United Kingdom 28, 29–33, 49, 177–80
universal 28, 29, 33, 49, 177–80, 178
USA 28, 48, 177–8
Hedgecoe, Adam 95n3
Herceptin 95–6n5
 see also trastuzumab
HIV/AIDS 89
Holmes, Dave 141
hormonal therapies 8, 78, 79–82, 84–5, 97, 134, 136–40
hormone-responsive tumours 80, 88
hormones, role of 79–80
Hortobagyi, Gabriel N. 136
Hunleth, Jean 42, 50n6

illness 4, 65–7
illness narratives 5, 20, 126–7
India 66
information seeking 132–5, 146
innovative treatments, search for 47
international discourse 23
internet, the 132–3
interviews 20–2
isolation 58
Italy 2, 17, 19, 21, 23, 55, 75
 accreditamento (accreditation system) 33–4
 associative landscape 58, 60
 breast reconstruction 104–5, 123n6
 Catholicism 67
 childcare 156
 containment strategies 66–7
 drug prices 39, 40–1

five-year cancer plan 36
health insurance 34
healthcare system 28, 33–7, 48, 177–80
hormone therapy 137
intramoenia 33–4
north–south divide 19, 34–7, 44–5, 104–5
patient mobility 21, 23, 35–6, 43, 44–5, 49, 143
practices of silence 25–6n3
private sector providers 33–4
public healthcare expenditure 34
Titolo Quinto reform 35
universality 33

Jain, S. Lochlann 177–8
Jay, David 51, 69
Jordan, Craig 80, 81

Kadcyla 91, 96n10
Keating, Peter 80
Kellaway, Kate 64
Klawiter, Maren 11–12
Kleinman, Arthur 3–4, 5
knowledge management 132–5
knowledge sharing 60–1
Kolehmainen, Marjo 151
Kushner, Rose 100

labour pain 4
Lahti, Annukka 151
language, biomedical 180
League against Cancer 39
Livingston, Julie 179
Lorde, Audre 100, 125, 145–6
Löwy, Ilana 10–11, 74, 77, 92, 127
lymphoma 161–2

McCann, Hannah 176
Macmillan Cancer Support 56
magical thinking 1
magnetic resonance imaging (MRI) 129
male breast cancer 15, 25n1

male gaze 114
Marchesi, Simone 48
Marcus, George E. 6
Marie, Marc 148, 168–9
Marie Curie charity 56
marital relations, post-diagnosis 149, 150–4, 169
Martin, Daryl 83–4
mastectomised bodies 69
mastectomy 76–7, 99–100, 102–3
 bilateral 77–8, 124n14
 radical 99
medical innovation 23
medical leave 164
medical professionals, mobility 43
medical tourists 42
medical-bodily assemblages 7–9, 23–4, 73, 98, 146, 171–3
medicalisation 12
Medicines and Healthcare products Regulatory Agency 40
memory 157
memory boxes 157
menopause, early 167
Merrild, Camilla Hoffmann 18
metastatic breast cancer 12, 14, 20, 28, 63, 96n8, 96n9, 126, 146–7, 160–1
 associative landscape 61–2
 chronicisation 85–9, 142, 145
 diagnosis 141–5
 experimental treatments 178–9
 financial impact 143–4
 living with 142, 181–2
 pain management 142
 survival time 141–2
 treatments 82–3, 92–4
 uncertainty 126, 141–5
methodology 19–22
Milan 36, 56
Mitchell, David T. 113
Mol, Annemarie 43
Monbiot, George 64
moral growth 68, 145, 168, 173–4
Mulvey, Laura 114

National Health Service (NHS) 21, 29–33, 49, 177–80
  creation 29–30
  equality in access 30
  funding 31
  GPs 30
  Integrated Care System 31
  internal mobility 30, 32
  privatisation 30–2
  referral system 32
National Institute for Health and Care Excellence (NICE) 32, 40, 91–2, 103, 137
NED (No Evidence of Disease) 78, 136
neoadjuvant therapy 82
neoliberal ideology 51, 66, 68, 156
New York Times Magazine 51

oesophageal reconstruction 113
oncological drugs, cost 39–41
oncoplasty 102–3
Ong, Aihwa 172
online activism 60, 62
optimist rhetoric, negotiating 63–9, 70
organisational assemblages 8, 28–9
ovarian cancer 26n7

pain management 142
Pancreatic Cancer Action 13
patient mobility 23, 42–5
  France 21, 43, 44, 45, 49, 143
  Italy 21, 35–6, 43, 44–5, 49, 143
  UK 21, 43–4, 45, 49
personalisation regime 12
personalised treatments 12, 78, 78–85, 94, 179
  experience of 89–93
Peters, Vera 99
pharmaceutical landscape 73
phenomenological perspectives 3
pink ribbon discourse 10, 13, 19, 23, 51–2, 53–7, 63–4, 69, 70n1, 173

pink-washing 54, 55, 63–4, 70n2
Poland 72
Pollock, Allyson M. 31, 49
Pop, Cristina A. 26n8
post-cancer care 63
post-cancer enhancement rhetoric 64–6, 69
post-cancer life 64–9, 69
post-diagnosis equilibrium 181
post-diagnosis life 148–59, 168–70
  couples 149, 150–4, 169
  family relationships 149, 154–9, 168–9, 170n1
  friendships 149, 159–62, 169
  work and working life 149, 162–8, 169
post-mastectomy bodies 98
  aesthetics and aestheticisation 99–103
  asymmetrical 59–60, 111, 116–20, 121–2, 151, 172
  see also breast reconstruction
post-reconstruction body experiences 112–16
Price-Robertson, Rhys 155
Prieto, Francisca 19
privatisation 18, 23, 28, 30–2, 177, 179
professional lives and identities 162–8
psychoanalytical perspectives 3
psycho-oncology 64

quality of life 85, 90, 145

radical mastectomy 99
radiotherapy 8, 11, 77
Raza, Azra 75
rebirth experience 64–6, 68
recomposition 126
referral systems 32
relapse
  fear of 180
  probabilistic estimates 10
  risk 8, 24, 136–7

relational assemblages 8, 10, 25, 149, 168, 181
religion 67
renewal, discourses of 64–6, 69
risk 1, 2
  relapse 8, 24
  reduction 137, 146
Ristovski-Slijepcevic, Svetlana 62
ritual 4
Roderick, Peter 31, 49
Romania 26n8

Saka, Erkan 6
SCAR (Surviving Cancer: Absolute Reality) Project 51, 69
Schiebinger, Londa 15
screening 2, 10–12, 39, 43–4, 74–6, 100, 128
Seeman, Don 3, 5
self-care 155
self-image 112
self-improvement 62–3, 167–8, 173–4
self-worth 115
Senior, Kate 5
separations and divorce 151–2
service distribution 32
sexualisation 15
silence, practices of 25–6n3
Skeide, Annekatrin 4
Skelly, Julia 122
Snow, Stephanie 30
Snyder, Sharon L. 113
social attention 2
social gaze 114
social insurance 28, 30, 37, 177, 178
social life, post-diagnosis 159–62
social norms, presentations of 4
social roles 168–9, 174, 176
social scripts 13–14
sociality 25
Sontag, Susan 53, 127
sources 22
states of being 6

Steinmetz, Emily 42, 50n6
strategic assemblages 171
Sulik, Gayle A. 176
surgery 11, 16, 20, 24, 75–6, 99–100
surgical radicalism 78
survival rates 13
survival time 73, 87, 93–5, 101, 136, 141, 141–2
Susan G. Komen Foundation 53–4, 55, 173

tamoxifen 79–81, 95n2, 137, 138, 139, 141
targeted therapies 79–84, 80–2, 93–4
techno-body, the 73
therapeutic pathways 172
therapeutic script 11
Timmermann, Carsten 81, 89, 95n2
Tóibín, Colm 71n7
Toon, Elizabeth 70n4, 96n8
Tørring, Marie Louise 17–18
trastuzumab 81–2, 83, 91, 178
  see also Herceptin
treatments 11, 73–8, 93–5, 125–6, 181
  cost 23, 28
  cost-benefit analysis 178
  elective component 47
  experience of personalised 89–93
  experimental 178–9
  gaps in 23
  linear model 92
  metastatic breast cancer 83, 92–3
  mosaic of 78
  negotiating 135–41, 174
  personalised 12, 78, 78–85, 89–93, 94
  search for innovative 47
  side effects 138–41, 146, 158, 159–60, 165, 167, 173
  standardisation 8–9, 47–8

understanding 133
and working life 162–8
triple-negative breast cancer 84–5, 88
Trusson, Diane 64
tumorectomy 76
Turner, Victor W. 4

uncertainty 90–1, 125–7, 145–7
  biomedical 127, 156–7
  containing 131–5
  diagnosis and 127–31, 145–6
  financial 156
  metastatic breast cancer 126, 141–5
United Kingdom 2, 17, 19, 21
  associative landscape 58, 60, 61, 61–2, 63
  breast reconstruction 103–4, 120–1, 123n6
  childcare 156
  drug prices 39–40
  GPs 30
  healthcare system 23, 28, 29–33, 49, 177–80
  hormone therapy 137
  patient mobility 21, 43–4, 45, 49
  screening programme 75
  unequal distribution of services 32–3
United States of America 17, 25
  healthcare system 28, 48, 177–8
  pink ribbon discourse 23
unpredictability 90

Veronesi, Umberto 36, 56, 99–100
Viney, William 46
Vivre comme avant 55–6

War on Cancer 72–3, 94
Wegenstein, Bernadette 123n3
Western Europe, breast cancer in 17–19
Wilke, Hannah 97, 122
Willen, Sarah S. 3, 5
womanhood, breast cancer as attack on 150
work and working life, post-diagnosis 25, 149, 162–8, 169

EU authorised representative for GPSR:
Easy Access System Europe, Mustamäe tee 50,
10621 Tallinn, Estonia
gpsr.requests@easproject.com